Music and the Child

Natalie Sarrazin, PhD

Open SUNY Textbooks

2016

This publication was made possible by a SUNY Innovative Instruction Technology Grant (IITG). IITG is a competitive grants program open to SUNY faculty and support staff across all disciplines. IITG encourages development of innovations that meet the Power of SUNY's transformative vision.
Published by Open SUNY Textbooks, Milne Library (IITG PI)
State University of New York at Geneseo,
Geneseo, NY 14454

About the Book

Children are inherently musical. They respond to music and learn through music. Music expresses children's identity and heritage, teaches them to belong to a culture, and develops their cognitive well-being and inner self worth. As professional instructors, childcare workers, or students looking forward to a career working with children, we should continuously search for ways to tap into children's natural reservoir of enthusiasm for singing, moving and experimenting with instruments. But how, you might ask? What music is appropriate for the children I'm working with? How can music help inspire a well-rounded child? How do I reach and teach children *musically*? Most importantly perhaps, how can I incorporate music into a curriculum that marginalizes the arts?

This book explores a holistic, artistic, and integrated approach to understanding the developmental connections between music and children. This book guides professionals to work through music, harnessing the processes that underlie music learning, and outlining developmentally appropriate methods to understand the role of music in children's lives through play, games, creativity, and movement. Additionally, the book explores ways of applying music-making to benefit the whole child, i.e., socially, emotionally, physically, cognitively, and linguistically.

About the Author

Natalie Sarrazin, PhD, is Associate Professor of Music at the College at Brockport, SUNY. She holds a PhD in ethnomusicology from the University of Maryland, College Park and a master's degree from Peabody Conservatory at Johns Hopkins University in music education. Natalie is the author of books and articles on both Hindi film music and music education. She teaches in the Department of Theatre and Music Studies and Arts for Children programs at the College at Brockport, and is a former co-director of the Hunter Institute on Young Children.

Reviewer's Notes

Natalie Sarrazin's *Music and the Child* is a well-written, thoughtful, comprehensive, up-to-date textbook. The author's audience is primarily general classroom teachers, who will want to include music into their general curriculum. Assuming that the reader has had a life-long interaction with music in the world, Sarrazin does not take for granted that the reader is well-versed in musical concept, symbolic notation, song literature, and elementary instrumental and vocal pedagogy. Her early chapters are an examination of all of these areas, and while all the information is very valuable, may choose to spend less time focusing on one or more areas in which s/he might have some knowledge of. It is important to note that although the readers may not be music educators, Sarrazin does not dumb-down any of her material. Throughout the entire text, consciously or not, the author conveys a respect for the reader's intelligence, as well as for the subject matter. The activities are excellent. The reviewer enjoyed doing many of the activities himself, watching the videos, and singing the songs. The links are easy to access, and highly suited for the text. The bibliographies are current and include some of the seminal research in the field of music education, learning theories, assessment, ethnomusicology, and inclusion. I strongly recommend this textbook.

About Open SUNY Textbooks

Open SUNY Textbooks is an open access textbook publishing initiative established by State University of New York libraries and supported by SUNY Innovative Instruction Technology Grants. This initiative publishes high-quality, cost-effective course resources by engaging faculty as authors and peer-reviewers, and libraries as publishing service and infrastructure.

The pilot launched in 2012, providing an editorial framework and service to authors, students and faculty, and establishing a community of practice among libraries.

Participating libraries in the 2012-2013 pilot include SUNY Geneseo, College at Brockport, College of Environmental Science and Forestry, SUNY Fredonia, Upstate Medical University, and University at Buffalo, with support from other SUNY libraries and SUNY Press. The 2013-2014 pilot will add more titles in 2015-16. More information can be found at http://textbooks.opensuny.org.

Contents

Songs

Chapter 1

Perspectives and Approaches

Chapter Summary: Children are inherently musical. They respond to music and learn through music. Music expresses children's identity and heritage, teaches them to belong to a culture, and develops their cognitive well-being and inner self-worth. As professional instructors, childcare workers, or students looking forward to a career working with children, we must continuously search for ways to tap into children's natural reservoirs of enthusiasm for singing, moving, and experimenting with instruments. But how, you might ask? What music is appropriate for the children I'm working with? How can music help inspire a well-rounded child? How do I reach and teach children musically? Most importantly, perhaps, how can I incorporate music into a curriculum that marginalizes the arts?

Over the past several decades, educators, world leaders, and theorists have produced a slurry of manifestos, visions and statements on what education should look like in the 21st century. Organizations such as Partnership for 21st century Learning (http://www.p21.org/) and The Center for Public Education (CPE) suggest ways to teach such skills to prepare students for the challenges ahead (see the CPE's executive summary on the topic). The results favor integrative and holistic approaches that support the ideals of what a skilled 21st century student should know.

In this book, we will explore a holistic, artistic, integrated, and forward-thinking 21st-century approach to understanding the developmental connections between music and children. Rather than teaching children about music, this book will guide professionals to work through music, harnessing the processes that underlie music learning, and outlining developmentally appropriate methods to understand the role of music in children's lives through play, games, creativity, and movement. Additionally, in this book we will explore ways of applying music-making to benefit the whole child, i.e., socially, emotionally, physically, cognitively, and linguistically.

An Arts Approach: Visions and Challenges

The life of the arts, far from being an interruption, a distraction in the life of the nation, is very close to the center of a nation's purpose—and it is the test of the quality of a nation's civilization.

—J. F. Kennedy, 1962

Kennedy's famous words, now decades old, provided the nation with legitimacy and a vision for the arts and arts education that still resonates today. There is a plethora of evidence regarding the critical role that the arts play in children's lives and learning. Organizations and researchers have produced countless studies on the arts' effectiveness and ability to engage children cognitively, emotionally, physically, and artistically: in other words, on a holistic level.

According to the National Coalition for Core Arts Standards (NCCAS), however,

> Children's access to arts education as part of their core education continues to be uneven across our nation's nearly fourteen thousand school districts. Some local education agencies currently offer a full, balanced education that includes rich and varied arts opportunities for their students. However, too many schools have succumbed to funding challenges or embraced a narrow focus on tested subjects, resulting in minimal, if any, arts experiences for the children they serve. (2013, p. 3)

One of the challenges facing teachers' use of the arts concerns a curriculum encumbered by a need to "teach to the test," both at the state and federal levels. This trend began in the 1990s with an educational reform movement that stressed teacher accountability. Measurements through testing became accepted and standardized under the No Child Left Behind Act (2001) and also under the new Common Core State Standards Initiative currently being implemented. National and state laws and a trend toward teaching and testing "core subjects" reshape social perceptions and create a permanent culture that continually marginalizes the arts in the curriculum. The result impacts teacher perceptions regarding the incorporation of the arts in their lessons as there is a sense that using the arts is somehow a diversion that will take away classroom time from what are considered more "worthy" subjects. The arts, however, can be used effectively to augment this method, motivating students and appealing to their innate artistry and humanity.

This book is intended to aid those who have little or no background in music, in order to increase their comfort in integrating music into the curriculum. The material will help guide educators in finding methods to incorporate music with other subjects in a way that is inherently beneficial to teachers and students rather than a hindrance.

A Holistic Approach

This book takes a holistic approach to the study of music, drawing from diverse fields such as music education, ethnomusicology, sociology, and cognitive sciences. The book takes into account many different perspectives on a child's development rather than approaching it by focusing on only one subject. The material in this book is inspired by an approach to holistic education, the goal of which is to lead children towards developing and inner sense of musical understanding and meaning through physical, cognitive, creative, emotional and socially developmental means.

According to the Holistic Education movement, it is essential that children learn about:
1. Themselves: including self-respect and self-esteem
2. Relationships: i.e., relationships with others through social "literacy" and emotional "literacy," understanding one's own self in relation to others
3. Resilience: overcoming difficulties, facing challenges, and learning how to ensure long-term success
4. Aesthetics: seeing the beauty around them and inspiring awe

Holistic education first addresses the question of what it is that the child needs to learn, and places the arts and aesthetics as key elements in teaching the developing child. Similarly, the holistic educator places music and the arts in a central position in a child's education, emphasizing the artistic and aesthetic experiences that only the arts can bring.

A holistic approach not only includes children's cognitive development, but their musical environment and cultural influences. In that sense, the book will address how children use music *outside* of the classroom. How do children experience music when playing or in leisure time activities? How do children think about music? How are they innately musically creative?

As an extension, the book also touches on some multicultural aspects of music, and considers the broad role of music and its importance to humanity, thus avoiding an insular and myopic **Western Cultural** view of the musical child. How do people in other cultures view music? How do children of other cultures experience music?

A 21st-Century Approach

A discussion of 21st-century skills provides an important opportunity to consider change in the current state of the curriculum, future societal needs, and the role of music and the arts. Changing economics and demographics require flexibility and adaptability. What skills will children need to obtain employment? How can children be prepared to contribute and compete in a complex society? How can educators and educational systems meet these needs?

Alarmed at the condition of American public education, various institutions such as the Kennedy Center, The Partnership for 21st-Century Skills, 21st-Century Schools and the Global Alliance for Transforming Education organized to identify particular areas of educational focus deemed crucial for future learning. Their results place a high emphasis placed on student autonomy and independent learning, problem solving, and creativity, all of which are fundamental aspects of the arts.

21st Century Skills

21st Century Skills
• Critical Thinking and Problem Solving
• Collaboration Across Networks and Leading by Influence
• Agility and Adaptability
• Initiative and Entrepreneurialism
• Effective Oral and Written Communication
• Accessing and Analyzing Information
• Curiosity and Imagination
• Child-Centered Learning

• Outcome-Based Research and Learning
• Creativity, Collaboration, Communication, Cooperation
• Experience, Knowledge, and Skills

The central components listed above continue an educational philosophy begun hundreds of years ago that stresses experiential learning, child-centered over teacher-centered learning, and process over product. It is part of what we now see as a holistic, collaborative, and integrated approach to education that emphasizes the development of social skills and inner confidence in addition to learning the subject matter.

READ MORE WHAT IS 21ST-CENTURY EDUCATION?

READ MORE ARTS INTEGRATION AND 21ST-CENTURY SKILLS

READ MORE A GLOSSARY OF 21ST CENTURY SKILLS

II. A Children's Musical World

Music at the Beginning: A Child's Musical Awareness

All children are musical—they are born musical, and are keenly aware of sounds around them. Let's begin with a journey from the perspective of the child—a very young child at the beginning of life. What does the child experience? What does he or she hear? Inside the womb, the baby hears the mother's heartbeat, the rushing sound of amniotic fluid and the mother's voice. From outside, the baby hears language and music, mostly low **sound waves** from bass instruments and loud noises. Because the visual sense is not viable at this point, the auditory senses are primary, and hearing is the most keenly developed of all of the fetal senses. Hearing develops from about 19 to 26 weeks of the pregnancy when the inner ear matures, and babies respond to voices and classical music by turning towards it and relaxing. They respond to loud noises as well by kicking, and curl up and turn away from loud rock or pop music.

Do children remember what they hear in the womb? Auditory neuroscientists say that children do remember what they hear in the womb. Children remember their mother's voice, and even melodies.

READ MORE "THE LIFE OF THE WOMB"

Music in a Child's Environment

Children are part of two overarching social categories—humankind in general, and the specific culture in which they are born. As humans, music is an innate part of our existence, as we all possess the physical mechanisms to make and process organized sound just as we do language. As music educator Edwin Gordon notes, "Music is not a language but processes for learning music and language are strikingly similar" (Gordon, 2012, p. 6). The brain is wired for music and language, a topic that will be discussed in Chapter 7.

Music making and artistic endeavors represent the heart of a culture, and are part of each culture's core identity: not only what makes us human, but also what makes each group of us unique. In the U.S., unique genres of music that are part of our cultural fabric have developed over the centuries. The melting pot that is America has yielded brand new genres such as big band, jazz, blues, rock and roll, etc. Blends of European, Caribbean, and African-American people combined in a way like that of no other culture. In America, all of the music we currently know today is derived from the musical **genres** that came before us. All children are born into that musical environment and pick up the musical repertoire and vocabulary around them.

Children's Musical Repertoires

Because societies believe that children are the key to continuing the traditions of their cultural and musical heritage, there is usually a separate category of songs that teach children their cultural and musical history.

Activity 1A

How many children's songs can you think of? What were your favorite song as a child and why were they your favorite? Did the songs have movements? Were they game songs? What does society think about children's songs? (e.g. are they important, trivial, nurtured or shunned?)

After remembering some of your favorite children's songs, you may come to understand their importance. If you ask a group of people in any age category to sing a song, more often than not, children's songs are the only songs everyone can sing in their entirety from beginning to end. Why is that? One reason is that music and identity are closely related, and groups or cohorts of people listen to particular songs targeted toward their age group produced by the market-driven music business.

Another reason is that children's songs are uniquely structured to make them easy to memorize while containing basic musical and cultural material; language and codes that we come to recognize in all of our songs. We tend to think of children's songs as simple, and in some ways, they are in terms of lyrics, structure, and music. However, there is much more to them that that.

Activity 1B

What are some of the attributes of children's songs that make them so memorable? Develop a list of characteristics that make children's songs so popular, unforgettable, and able to survive for generations. Think about the musical aspects as well as the lyrical aspects. Are there a lot of notes or very few? Is there a big range or small? Are there many words or a few? Are there big singing leaps and lots of difficult runs or none?

The body or repertoire of children's songs is extremely old. In fact, the oldest songs you probably know are children's songs! This is because children's songs often preserve the social and historical meaning of a culture and the identity of its people. Many of our most popular

American children's songs hail from centuries of ballads, hymns, popular and folk music of early New Englanders, Scottish, and English settlers inhabiting Appalachia, and African and European descendants. All of the songs are rife with musical, cultural, and historical significance.

"Twinkle, Twinkle Little Star," for example, is the product of both England and France, as an early 19th-century English poem set to an 18th-century French folk tune ("Ah, vous dirai-je, Maman"). The song also provides the music for two other very famous songs, "Baa, Baa Black Sheep" and the "A-B-C" song.

Twinkle Twinkle Little Star, Baa Baa Black Sheep, Alphabet Song

Melody: "Ah, vous dirai-je, Maman"
French folk song, 1761

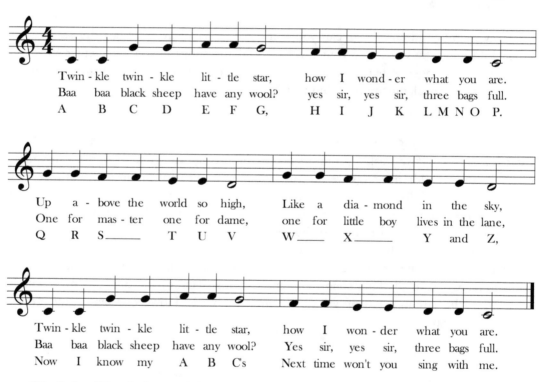

"Zudio" or "Zoodio" is an African-American children's street game song with possible roots in slavery. It is suspected that the "great big man" mentioned in the song might be the slave owner.

Here We Go Zudio

African American song

Here we go, Zu - di - o, Zu - di - o, Zu - di - o, Here we go, Zu - di - o,

all night long,   Step back Sal - ly,   Sal - ly, Sal - ly,   Step back Sal - ly,

all night long.   I looked o - ver yon - der and   what did I see?   A

great big man from Ten - ne - see.   Bet - cha five dol - lars that you

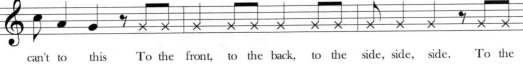

can't to   this   To the front, to the back, to the   side, side, side.   To the

front,   to the back,   to the   side, side, side.

"Mary Had a Little Lamb" was inspired by a true incident in the small town of Sterling, Massachusetts, in the 1830s, when little Mary's brother suggested that she take her pet lamb to school and chaos ensued. Below is a picture of the little schoolhouse where the incident of Mary and her lamb is believed to have taken place.

Mary Had a Little Lamb

Ma - ry had a lit - tle lamb, lit - tle lamb, lit - tle lamb.

Ma - ry had a lit - tle lamb, her fleece was white as snow.

All of these songs have musical characteristics particular to the genre from which they emerged. They have only a few notes, small vocal ranges, no fancy ornaments, and simple words. However, they also have significant social and historical meaning that helps to explain their incredible longevity in the children's song repertoire.

Dudesleeper at English Wikipedia [GFDL], CC-BY-SA-3.0 or CC BY 2.5, via Wikimedia Commons

The Redstone School, now located in Sudbury, Massachusetts, where Mary supposedly took her lamb!

To explore the idea of music as culture, let's look further at Mary and her lamb. "Mary Had a Little Lamb" is an almost 200-year-old song that remains compelling and still very popular today. Part of the song's popularity is the subject matter. It was inspired by the real-life actions of children, and did not emerge wholly from an adult's imagination. The melody is very simple, containing only four pitches and a fair amount of repetition. The meaning of this song is historically significant. The lyrics retain images of early American life: the one-room schoolhouse, the rural environment, no industrial noise and automobiles, and the prevalence of animals. A child growing up on a farm surrounded by animals would naturally befriend some of them. The idea that the child, Mary, would want to bring her favorite animal to school is more than understandable, and is akin to wanting to bring our dog or cat to school with us today. In other words, the song relives and retells the experiences of a child in another century and makes her story highly relatable to us today.

Activity 1C

THINK ABOUT IT

How much do you know about your favorite children's songs? Do some research on some older children's songs such as "Ring around the Rosie," or "London Bridge is Falling Down," and you'll be surprised!

A Child's Informal and Formal Music Experiences

> [The purpose of music in the schools]…is to prepare students for full participation in the social, economic, political, and artistic life of their homeland and the world at large. (Blacking, 1985, p. 21)

This statement, from ethnomusicologist John Blacking, highlights the holistic nature and potential impact of the educational system. Schools, however, provide formal music education, which is just one of the sources of a child's musical heritage. Often, the most important sources are informal. Children encounter music at home, in their everyday cultural environment, and while at play. All of these settings are part of a person's **enculturation**, or learning one's culture through experiences, observations, and both formal and informal settings.

At *home*, children are exposed to a family's musical heritage, which may contain music unfamiliar to those in their dominant culture. Music expresses identity, and children often take part in family celebrations that represent an ethnic or religious heritage. They are exposed to the music of their parents and siblings, friends, and relatives, casting a wide net over multiple experiences and genres.

Culturally, children are exposed to entire repertoires of music, which represent different parts of the American identity. From commercial music—pop and rock to jazz, from folk songs to national songs, religious and holiday songs, and multicultural music—children hear the rhythms, melodies, and harmonies that make up their musical environment. They unconsciously absorb **idioms** (i.e., musical styles, genres, and characteristics), which will render certain sounds familiar to them and certain sounds "foreign" and unfamiliar. Thus, the music and all of its elements that children are exposed to become as familiar as their native language.

In elementary school, or any early formal educational setting, children often learn music from a music specialist with a set music curriculum and learning goals. This has both positive and negative consequences. On the positive side, children are learning from a professional, trained to teach music to children. On the negative side, arts teachers are seen as separate "specialists," which erroneously relieves the classroom teacher of any responsibility for incorporating the arts into the daily classroom experience.

"I can't teach music; I can't sing!"

> If you can walk you can dance; if you can talk you can sing.
>
> —Zimbabwean Proverb

With restricted budgets and reductions in arts specialists in some school districts, access to the arts for many children relies *solely* on what the classroom teacher can provide. Unfortunately, many classroom teachers feel inadequately prepared to teach music, and classroom teachers' use of music varies widely according to prior exposure to music. It has been shown that teachers with "higher levels of confidence in their musical ability indicate stronger levels of beliefs about the importance of music" (Kim, 2007, p. 12). Teachers with the ability to read music notation, for example, felt more positively about including music in their classroom, and were more likely to use music in their teaching.

The truth is that we *all* know a great deal *about* music through enculturation. Everyone is familiar with certain repertoires of music (national songs, children's songs, popular songs, folk songs, and even classical pieces), and even the different elements of music (melody, harmony, rhythm, form, and **timbre**). The Zimbabwean proverb, "*If you can walk, you can dance; if you can talk, you can sing,*" is quite apropos here. By virtue of your everyday experiences with music, you know more than you think about music, and can probably easily answer the questions in Activity 1D.

Although these questions might seem to be simple, they reflect a depth of music knowledge garnered throughout a lifetime of cultural exposure to music. For example, the above questions cover music theory, analysis, repertoire, and the uses and function of music in culture. Believe it or not, your accrued, cultural knowledge, added to a little enthusiasm and singing, is more than enough to be able to incorporate music into a lesson or curriculum.

Changing Role of Music and Culture: Making vs. Listening

Most people believe that music plays a significant role in their lives. Just think about the amount of time you spend surrounded by music in your day. The role of music, however, has changed dramatically in recent years. For thousands of years, the only way to experience music was to make it. Trained musicians and amateurs made music that fulfilled a variety of functions as part of religious rituals, work, story-telling, social communication, and also entertainment (see Merriam and Gaston's functions of music in Chapter 7). Historically, music would normally be part of everyday work, worship, and leisure. Contemporary society, however, separates music making and the music makers from everyone else, who become consumers or listeners. Technology has helped to alter the balance of the musical experience, favoring music listening over music making. Children now grow up spending much of their leisure time hearing music rather than performing or making it.

Currently, almost all of the music we experience is no longer live, but pre-recorded. Technology, however, has also increased the number of opportunities we have to hear music. Recordings have made music accessible everywhere: TV, radio, CDs, Internet, video games, personal music players, etc. Music is so ubiquitous that many people don't even notice it anymore. What has not changed, however, is a child's innate *desire* to be musical, make music, and learn from it. The music room and regular classroom are some of the only places many children have to make music in their day.

Activity 1D

TEST YOUR MUSICAL KNOWLEDGE

Complete the following:

1. The _____ is the part of music that you sing.
   a. Rhythm
   b. Melody
   c. Form
   d. Tempo
2. The _____ sounds the pulse or beat, and is usually played at a low frequency.
   a. Melody
   b. Bass
   c. Harmony
   d. Timbre
3. A melody is:
   a. Supported by other instruments (accompaniment)
   b. The most dominant part of a song
   c. Where the lyrics can be found
   d. All of the above
4. The bass:
   a. Keeps the beat
   b. Maintains the song's tempo or speed
   c. Provides a foundation for the rest of the instruments and voices
   d. All of the above
5. The _____ repeats several times throughout a song, with exactly the same words and music.
   a. Refrain or chorus
   b. Verse
   c. Melody
   d. Harmony
6. "Mary Had a Little Lamb" is an example of a:
   a. National song
   b. Religious or sacred song
   c. Children's song
   d. Classical song
7. Orchestras typically play:
   a. Rock music
   b. The blues
   c. Classical music
   d. Techno
8. If you have a drum set, two electric guitars, a bass, and a synthesizer, you will most likely be playing:
   a. A classical symphony
   b. Rock 'n' roll or pop music
   c. Folk songs
   d. None of the above

Activity 1E

THINK ABOUT IT

How would you describe your relationship with music? Do you typically spend more time listening to music or making it? How much time do you spend listening to music through headphones? Listening to music with other people?

Keep track of how much music you encounter in one day. How much of it is pre-recorded? How much of it is live?

The Aesthetic and Artistic Experience

> If human beings are innately musical, and if in some societies these innate capacities are nurtured in early childhood, it has always seemed to me that we must do more in modern industrial society to place *artistic experience* and musical practice at the center of education. (Blacking, 1991, p. 55)

What if you heard of a new product that could help children focus, increase their learning potential, re-boot their cognitive functioning, and make them feel relaxed and refreshed all in a few minutes? And best of all, it's free! Would you use it?

Music is powerful, and music has the power to change people emotionally or alter the mood of room with just a few simple notes or beats. Music, as energy, has the ability to transform all those within its reach. We turn to music to feel better, relieve anxiety, overcome a difficult situation, find calm and peace, or feel empowered and fearless. Although we don't take much time in our busy day to think about it, one of the most significant uses for music is to create an **aesthetic** experience. An aesthetic response or experience concerns the nature of beauty, art, and taste. Children are capable of appreciating beauty in art, music, language, and movement. Exposure to these artistic forms develops the inner core of a child, introduces new dimensions of possibilities, and shows the brain a new way of functioning and understanding. The other good news is that it only takes a couple of minutes and a little thought to achieve this, and put some of the basic elements of music to work. Timbre, tempo, and dynamics are so powerful that a few adjustments here and there can change the entire learning atmosphere of a classroom.

For example:
- A few notes played slowly and softly on a small glockenspiel can sound like magic.
- Beating a hand drum can physically move students: the faster and louder, the more activity!
- A soft song or lullaby sung or played on a melody instrument will calm them down almost immediately.
- Children clapping, stomping, or snapping will have them focus their attention.

Activity 1F

THINK ABOUT IT

How might you go about creating an aesthetic experience (in or out of a classroom)? What if you had only a few instruments? No instruments at all? How could you accomplish an aesthetic transformation using sound?

III. The Soundscape and the Child

Before we discuss our cultural ideas of what music is, we first need to understand that music is only part of the larger category of **sound**. The sounds all around us play a significant role in our development. We spend our lives surrounded by all kinds of sounds that are unique to our environment, yet we rarely pay attention to them. As a child grows, he or she becomes **acculturated** to all of the sounds in their environment. These include not only all of the genres of music, the verbal languages, and accents, but also the mechanical, digital, human, and animal noises, and all of the **ambient** sounds around us. All of these combine to create our acoustic environment. This **soundscape**, as acoustic environmentalist R. Murray Schafer conceived it, concerns what those sounds tell us about who we are and the time in which we live.

Our soundscapes have tremendous physical and cognitive impacts on us. The soundscape affects our health, body, and learning. For example, a child's environment in a city will be vastly different than one in the country, or the soundscape of 1,000 years ago differs dramatically from a soundscape today.

As Schafer began his work on understanding the sonic environment, he realized that we don't have a very specific vocabulary to describe sounds—what we're hearing and how we're hearing it. Whereas visual vocabulary tends to be more detailed, we lack nuanced conceptual words to describe sound and our relationship to it. Schafer coined the terms *keynote*, *soundmark*, and *sound signal* to distinguish between different types of sounds, their connections to the environment, and our perception of them.

Keynote: As a musical term, keynote identifies the "key" of a piece. Although you may not always hear the key, and the melody may stray from the key, it always returns back to the key. A keynote "outlines the character of the people living there." Keynotes are often nature sounds (wind, birds, animals, water) but in urban areas can be traffic. The keynote sound for New York City might be horns of Yellow cabs and cars, for example.

Soundmark: This term is inspired by the word "landmark" and refers to the sound unique to an area. A landmark is something that is easily recognizable (e.g., the Eiffel Tower, Monument Valley, Grand Canyon, Empire State Building). Now think of a location and its sound, and imagine a recognizable sound associated for that place.

Sound signal: A foregrounded sound that we consciously hear. Sound signals compel us to pay attention to something. Some examples are warning devices, bells, whistles, horns, sirens, etc.

Shafer also makes interesting distinctions between the *sources* of sound. Some sources are made by nature, such as wind, water, and waves; some are human-made such as singing, speech, and stomping; some are made by animals, such as calls, cries, and growls; some are machine-made clanks, whistles, whirrs, and beeps. Schafer coined the term **schizophonia** to describe sound that is separated from its source, such as recorded music. Because most of the music we listen to is not live but recorded, schizophonia is a concept crucial to describe and understand a child's (and our own) relationship to sound and our environment.

Activity 1G

THINK ABOUT IT

What would life *sound* like if you lived 100 years ago? 500? 1,000? What were the loudest sounds in the environment? Softest? What types of sounds dominated the soundscape? What sounds would be keynote sounds? Soundmarks? How about music—how did people experience music in each of those time periods? Were sounds made by humans? Animals? Machines?

EXPLORE YOUR SOUNDSCAPE

I. Select a location that has an interesting soundscape. Sit silently for five minutes in that location and listen to the sounds around you. Memorize them as you experience them. How would you describe the sounds? After five minutes, write down what you heard, describing the sounds in detail. Were they loud or soft? High or low? Short or long? What was the quality (tone color or timbre) of each sound? How long did each sound last? Did it echo? Vibrate? Whirl or swoosh? Did is occur only once or did the sound repeat? What was the source of each sound? How would you categorize them? (Human made, animal, electronic, machine)? Describe any revelations or thoughts you had during your experience.

II. Would children benefit from mindfully hearing sounds in their environment? How might you adapt this experience for children to introduce them to their soundscape? Develop some activities using Schafer's ideas of soundscape, soundmark, and keynote sounds that you could use with children.

WATCH THIS <u>TED TALK: 10 THINGS YOU DIDN'T KNOW ABOUT SOUND</u>

WATCH THIS <u>"LISTEN: A PORTRAIT OF R. MURRAY SCHAFER"</u>

Resources

- Websites:
  - <u>Holistic Education, Inc., Home Page</u>
- Important Children's Music Collections
  - Erdei, P., and Komlos, K. (2004). *150 American folk songs to sing, read, and play.* New York: Boosey and Hawkes.

- Lomax, J., and Lomax, A. (1994). *American ballads and folk songs*. New York: Dover Publications.
- Jones, B. (1987). *Step it down: Games, plays, songs and stories from the Afro-American heritage*. Athens, GA: University of Georgia Press.

References

Appel, M. P. (2006). Arts integration across the curriculum. *Leadership*, Nov./Dec., 14–17.

Birth.com.au. (2013). Feeling your baby move. *From Bellies to Babies & Beyond*. http://www.birth.com.au/middle-pregnancy-sex-baby-kicking-maternity/baby-kicking-and-hiccoughs?view=full#.VQGwJSnZfdk

Blacking, John. (1985) "Versus Gradus novos ad Parnassum Musicum: Exemplum Africanum " *Becoming Human through Music: The Wesleyan Symposium on the Perspectives of Social Anthropology in the Teaching and Learning*. Middletown: Wesleyan University. Music Educators National Conference, 43-52.

Campbell, P. (1998). *Songs in their heads: Music and its meaning in children's lives*. New York: Oxford University Press.

Flake, C. L. E. (1993*). Holistic Education: Principles, Perspectives and Practices. A Book of Readings Based on "Education 2000: A Holistic Perspective."* Brandon, VT: Holistic Education Press.

Goldberg, M., and Bossenmeyer, M. (1998). Shifting the role of arts in education. *Principal, 77,* 56–58.

Gordon, E. (2012). Newborn, preschool children, and music: Undesirable consequences of thoughtless neglect. *Perspectives: Journal of the Early Childhood Music and Movement Association, 7*(3-4), 6-10.

Gullatt, D. E. (2008). Enhancing student learning through arts integration: Implications for the profession. *The High School Journal, 85,* 12–24.

Hallam, S. (2010). The power of music: Its impact on the intellectual, personal and social development of children and young people. In S. Hallam, Creech, A. (Eds.), *Music education in the 21st century in the United Kingdom: Achievements, analysis and aspirations* (pp. 2-17). London: Institute of Education.

Howard, K. (1991). John Blacking: An interview conducted and edited by Keith Howard. *Ethnomusicology 35*(1), 55–76.

Jensen, E. (2002). Teach the arts for reasons beyond the research. *The Education Digest 67*(6), 47–53.

Kim, H. K. (2007). *Early childhood preservice teachers' beliefs about music, developmentally appropriate practice, and the relationship between music and developmentally appropriate practice.* Unpublished doctoral dissertation. University of Florida, Gainesville, FL.

Mayes, C. (2007). *Understanding the whole student: Holistic multicultural education.* Washington, DC: Rowman and Littlefield.

Miller, J. (2007). *The holistic curriculum.* Toronto, Canada: University of Toronto Press.

Rabkin, N., & Redmond, R. (2006). The arts make a difference. *Educational Leadership, 63*(5): 60–64.

Ruppert, S. S. (2006). Critical evidence: How the arts benefit student achievement. Washington, DC: National Assembly of State Arts Agencies. Retrieved from http://www.nasaa-arts.org/Publications/critical-evidence.pdf

Schafer, R. M. (1993). *Our sonic environment and the soundscape: The tuning of the world.* Rochester, VT: Destiny Books.

Weinberger, N. (1998). The music in our minds. *Educational Leadership, 56*(3), 36–40.

Wagner, T. (2010). *The global achievement gap: Why even our best schools don't teach the new survival skills our children need—and what we can do about it.* Philadelphia, PA: Basic Books.

Vocabulary

acculturated: accustomed to; to assimilate the cultural traits of another group

aesthetic: how one experiences music; one's personal musical experience

ambient: of the surrounding area or environment

enculturation: learning through experiencing one's culture; the process whereby individuals learn their group's culture, through experience, observation, and instruction

genres: the different styles of music found in any given culture; a class or category of artistic endeavor having a particular form, content, or technique

idioms: musical styles, genres, and characteristics

schizophonia: R. Murray Schafer's coined term to describe sound that is separated from its source; recorded music is an example of schizophonic sound because the musicians are not performing the music live in front of you

sound: what we hear; the particular auditory effect produced by a given cause

soundscape: all the ambient sounds around us; the sounds that are part of a given environment

sound waves: the vibrations felt by people that come from musical instruments or voices; a longitudinal wave in an elastic medium, especially a wave producing an audible sensation

timbre: the tone color of each sound; each voice has a unique tone color (vibrato, nasal, resonance, vibrant, ringing, strident, high, low, breathy, piercing, rounded warm, mellow, dark, bright, heavy, or light)

Western culture: culture influenced by Europe, the Americas, and Australia; the modern culture of Western Europe and North America

Chapter 2

Music: Fundamentals and Educational Roots in the U.S.

Chapter Summary: The first half of this chapter attempts to define music as a subject and offers perspectives on music, including basic vocabulary and what you should know about music in order to incorporate it in your work with children. The second half gives a brief overview of music education and teaching in the U.S., which provides the foundation of the discipline for the book.

I. Defining Music

"Music" is one of the most difficult terms to define, partially because beliefs about music have changed dramatically over time just in Western culture alone. If we look at music in different parts of the world, we find even more variations and ideas about what music is. Definitions range from practical and theoretical (the Greeks, for example, defined music as "tones ordered horizontally as melodies and vertically as harmony") to quite philosophical (according to philosopher Jacques Attali, music is a sonoric event between noise and silence, and according to Heidegger, music is something in which truth has set itself to work). There are also the social aspects of music to consider. As musicologist Charles Seeger notes, "Music is a system of communication involving structured sounds produced by members of a community that communicate with other members" (1992, p.89). Ethnomusicologist John Blacking declares that "we can go further to say that music is sound that is humanly patterned or organized" (1973), covering all of the bases with a very broad stroke. Some theorists even believe that there can be no universal definition of music because it is so culturally specific.

Although we may find it hard to imagine, many cultures, such as those found in the countries of Africa or among some **indigenous** groups, don't have a word for music. Instead, the relationship of music and dance to everyday life is so close that the people have no need to conceptually separate the two. According to the ethnomusicologist Bruno Nettl (2001), some North American Indian languages have no word for "music" as distinct from the word "song." Flute melodies too are labeled as "songs." The Hausa people of Nigeria have an extraordinarily rich vocabulary for discourse about music, but no single word for music. The Basongye of Zaire have a broad conception of what music is, but no corresponding term. To the Basongye, music is a purely and specifically human product. For them, when you are content, you sing, and when you are angry, you make noise (2001). The Kpelle people of Liberia have one word, "sang," to describe a movement that is danced well (Stone, 1998, p. 7). Some cultures favor certain aspects of music. Indian classical music, for example, does not contain harmony, but only the three textures of a melody, rhythm, and a drone. However, Indian musicians more than make up for a lack of harmony with complex melodies and rhythms not possible in the West due to the inclusion of harmony (chord progressions), which require less complex melodies and rhythms.

What we may hear as music in the West may not be music to others. For example, if we hear the Qur'an performed, it may sound like singing and music. We hear all of the "parts" which we think of as music—rhythm, pitch, melody, form, etc. However, the Muslim understanding of that sound is that it is really heightened speech or recitation rather than music, and belongs in a separate category. The philosophical reasoning behind this is complex: in Muslim tradition, the idea of music as entertainment is looked upon as degrading; therefore, the holy Qur'an cannot be labeled as music.

Activity 2A

LISTEN

<u>Qur'an Recitation</u>, 22nd Surah (Chapter) of the Qur'an, recited by Mishary Rashid Al-'Efasi of Kuwait.

Although the exact definition of music varies widely even in the West, music contains melody, harmony, rhythm, timbre, pitch, silence, and form or structure. What we know about music so far...
- Music is comprised of sound.
- Music is made up of both sounds and silences.
- Music is *intentionally* made art.
- Music is humanly organized sound (Bakan, 2011).

A working definition of music for our purposes might be as follows: music is an intentionally organized art form whose medium is **sound** and **silence**, with core elements of **pitch** (**melody** and **harmony**), **rhythm** (**meter, tempo,** and **articulation**), **dynamics**, and the qualities of **timbre** and **texture**.

Beyond a standard definition of music, there are behavioral and cultural aspects to consider. As Titon notes in his seminal text *Worlds of Music* (2008), we "make" music in two different ways: we make music *physically*; i.e., we bow the strings of a violin, we sing, we press down the keys of a piano, we blow air into a flute. We also make music with our minds, *mentally* constructing the ideas that we have about music and what we believe about music; i.e., when it should be performed or what music is "good" and what music is "bad." For example, the genre of classical music is perceived to have a higher social status than popular music; a rock band's lead singer is more valued than the drummer; early blues and rock was considered "evil" and negatively influential; we label some songs as children's songs and deem them inappropriate to sing after a certain age; etc.

Music, above all, works in sound and time. It is a sonic event—a communication just like speech, which requires us to listen, process, and respond. To that end, it is a part of a continuum of how we hear all sounds including noise, speech, and silence. Where are the boundaries between noise and music? Between noise and speech? How does some music, such as rap, challenge our original notions of speech and music by integrating speech as part of the music? How do some compositions such as John Cage's 4'33" challenge our ideas of artistic intention, music, and silence?

READ MORE JOHN CAGE 4'33"

WATCH THIS ANNENBERG VIDEO: EXPLORING THE WORLD OF MUSIC

Activity 2B

Imagine the audience's reaction as they experience Cage's 4'33" for the first time. How might they react after 15 seconds? 30? One minute?

Basic Music Elements

- Sound (overtone, timbre, pitch, amplitude, duration)
- Melody
- Harmony
- Rhythm
- Texture
- Structure/form
- Expression (dynamics, tempo, articulation)

In order to teach something, we need a consensus on a basic list of elements and definitions. This list comprises the basic elements of music as we understand them in Western culture.

1. Sound

Overtone: A fundamental pitch with resultant pitches sounding above it according to the overtone series. Overtones are what give each note its unique sound.

WATCH THIS THROAT-SINGING

Timbre: The *tone color* of a sound resulting from the overtones. Each voice has a unique tone color that is described using adjectives or metaphors such as "nasally," "resonant," "vibrant," "strident," "high," "low," "breathy," "piercing," "ringing," "rounded," "warm," "mellow," "dark," "bright," "heavy," "light," "vibrato."

Pitch: The frequency of the note's vibration (note names C, D, E, etc.).

Amplitude: How loud or soft a sound is.

Duration: How long or short the sound is.

2. Melody

A succession of musical notes; a series of pitches often organized into phrases.

3. Harmony

The simultaneous, vertical combination of notes, usually forming chords.

4. Rhythm

The organization of music in time. Also closely related to meter.

5. Texture

The density (thickness or thinness) of layers of sounds, melodies, and rhythms in a piece: e.g., a complex orchestral composition will have more possibilities for dense textures than a song accompanied only by guitar or piano.

Most common types of texture:
- **Monophony:** A single layer of sound; e.g.. a solo voice
- **Homophony:** A melody with an accompaniment; e.g., a lead singer and a band; a singer and a guitar or piano accompaniment; etc.
- **Polyphony:** Two or more independent voices; e.g., a round or fugue.

WATCH THIS MUSICAL TEXTURE

6. Structure or Form

The sections or movements of a piece; i.e. verse and refrain, sonata form, ABA, Rondo (ABACADA), theme, and variations.

7. Expression

Dynamics: Volume (amplitude)—how loud, soft, medium, gradually getting louder or softer (crescendo, decrescendo).

Tempo: Beats per minute; how fast, medium, or slow a piece of music is played or sung.

Articulation: The manner in which notes are played or words pronounced: e.g., long or short, stressed or unstressed such as short (*staccato*), smooth (*legato*), stressed (*marcato*), sudden emphasis (*sforzando*), slurred, etc.

What Do Children Hear? How Do They Respond to Music?

Now that we have a list of definitions, for our purposes, let's refine the definition of music, keeping in mind how *children* perceive music and music's constituent elements of sound (timbre), melody, harmony, rhythm, structure or form, expression, and texture. Children's musical encounters can be self- or peer-initiated, or teacher- or staff-initiated in a classroom or daycare setting. Regardless of the type of encounter, the basic music elements play a significant role in how children respond to music. One of the most important elements for all humans is the *timbre* of a sound. Recognizing a sound's timbre is significant to humans in that it helps us to distinguish the source of the sound, i.e. who is calling us—our parents, friends, etc. It also alerts us to possible danger. Children are able to discern the timbre of a sound from a very young age, including the vocal timbres of peers, relatives, and teachers, as well as the timbres of different instruments.

Studies show that even very young children are quite sophisticated listeners. As early as two years of age, children respond to musical style, tempo, and dynamics, and even show preference for certain musical styles (e.g., pop music over classical) beginning at age five. Metz and his peers assert that "a common competence found in young children is the enacting through movement of the music's most constant and salient features, such as dynamics, meter, and tempo" (Metz, 1989; Gorali-Turel, 1997; Chen-Hafteck, 2004). On the aggregate level, children physically respond to music's beat, and are able to move more accurately when the tempo of the music more clearly corresponds to the natural tempo of the child. As we might expect, children respond to the dynamic levels of loud and soft quite dramatically, changing their movements to match changing volume levels.

The fact that children seem to respond to the **expressive elements** of music (dynamics, tempo, etc.) should not come as a surprise. Most people respond to the same attributes of music that children do. We hear changes in tempo (fast or slow), changes in dynamics (loud or soft), we physically respond to the rhythm of the bass guitar or drums, and we listen intently to the melody, particularly if there are words. These are among the most ear-catching elements, along with rhythm and melody.

This is what we would expect. However, there are other studies whose conclusions are more vague on this subject. According to a study by Sims and Cassidy, children's music attitudes and responses do not seem to be based on specific musical characteristics and children may have very idiosyncratic responses and listening styles (1997). Mainly, children are non-discriminating, reacting positively to almost any type of music (Kim, 2007, p. 23).

Activity 2C

What type of music might children best respond to given their musical perceptions and inclinations? Is there a particular genre of music, or particular song or set of songs? How might you get them to respond actively while engaging a high level of cognitive sophistication?

Music Teaching Vocabulary

After familiarizing yourself with the basic music vocabulary list above (e.g., melody, rhythm), familiarize yourself with a *practical teaching vocabulary*: in other words, the music terms that you might use when working in music with a lesson for children that correspond to their natural perception of music. For most children, the basics are easily conveyed through concept dichotomies, such as:

- Fast or Slow (tempo)
- Loud or Soft (dynamics)
- Short or Long (articulation)
- High or Low (pitch)
- Steady or Uneven (beat)
- Happy or Sad (emotional response)

Interestingly, three pairs of these dichotomies are found in Lowell Mason's *Manual for the Boston Academy of Music* (1839).

For slightly older children, more advanced concepts can be used, such as:

- Duple (2) or Triple (3) meter
- Melodic Contour (melody going up or down)
- Rough or Smooth (timbre)
- Verse and Refrain (form)
- Major or Minor (scale)

Music Fundamentals

The emotive aspects of music are what most people respond to first. However, while an important part of music listening in our culture, simply responding subjectively to "how music makes you feel" is similar to an Olympic judge saying that she feels happy when watching a gymnast's vault. It may very well be true, but it does not help the judge to understand and evaluate all of the elements that go into the execution of the gymnast's exercise or how to judge it properly. Studies show that teachers who are familiar with music fundamentals, and especially note reading, are more comfortable incorporating music when working with children (Kim, 2007). Even just knowing how to read music changes a teacher's confidence level when it comes to singing, so it's important to have a few of the basics under your belt.

Preparation for Learning to Read Music

Formal note reading is not required in order to understand the basics of music. Younger children can learn musical concepts long before learning written notation. Applying some of the vocabulary and concepts from above will help you begin to discern some of the inner workings of music. The good news is that *any* type of music can be used for practice.

- *Melodic Direction.* Just being able to recognize whether a melody goes up or down is a big step, and an important auditory-cognitive process for children to undergo. Imagine the melody of a song such as "Row, Row, Row Your Boat." Sing the song dividing it into two phrases (phrase 1 begins with "row," phrase 2 begins with "merrily"). What is the direction of phrase 1? Phrase 2? Draw the direction of the phrase in the air with your finger as you sing.

- *Timbre.* Practice describing different timbres of music—play different types of music on Pandora, for example, and try to describe the timbres you hear, including the vocal timbre of the singer or instrumental timbres.
- *Expression.* Now practice describing the expressive qualities of a song. Are there dynamics? What type of articulation is there? Is the tempo fast, slow, medium?

Learning Notation: Pitch

It sounds simple, but notes or pitches are the building blocks of music. Just being able to read simple **notation** will help build your confidence. Learning notes on a staff certainly seems dull, but coming up with mnemonics for the notes on the staff can actually be fun. For example, most people are familiar with:

- Every Good Boy Deserves Fudge to indicate the treble clef line notes
- F A C E to indicate the treble clef space notes
- Good Boys Deserve Fudge Always for the bass clef line notes
- All Cows Eat Grass for the bass clef space notes
- But allowing children to develop their own mnemonic device for these notes can a creative way to have them own the notes themselves. How about Grizzly Bears Don't Fly Airplanes for the lines of the bass clef, or Empty Garbage Before Dad Flips or Elephants Get Big Dirty Feet for the lines of the treble clef?

Notes of the Treble Staff

Notes of the Bass Staff

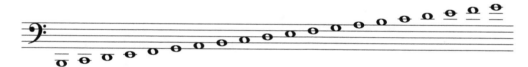

NOTE/PITCH NAME PRACTICE

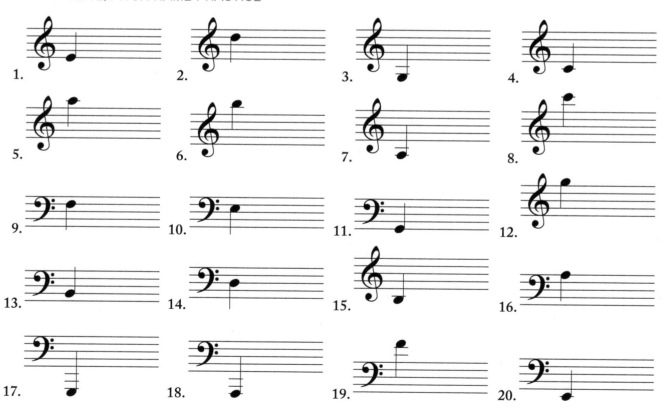

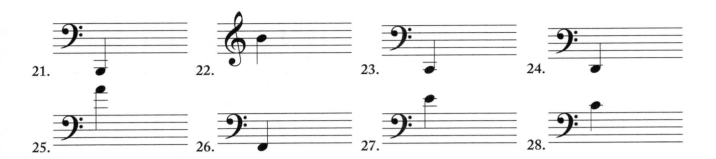

NOTE REVIEW: SPELLING WORLDS WITH NOTE NAMES

Learning Notation: Rhythm

Rhythm concerns the organization of musical elements into sounds and silences. Rhythm occurs in a melody, in the accompaniment, and uses combinations of short and long durations to create patterns and entire compositions. Rests are as important to the music as are the sounded rhythms because, just like language, rests use silence to help organize the sounds so we can better understand them.

Notes and rests

Whole note o	Whole rest ▬
Dotted half note 𝅗𝅥.	Dotted half rest ▬·
Half note 𝅗𝅥	Half rest ▬
Quarter note ♩	Quarter rest 𝄽
Eighth note ♪	Eighth rest 𝄾
Sixteenth note 𝅘𝅥𝅯	Sixteenth rest 𝄿

RHYTHM PRACTICE: LABEL EACH RHYTHM

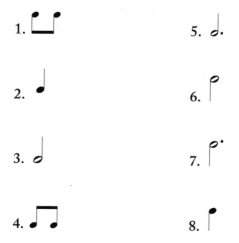

1.

2.

3.

4.

5.

6.

7.

8.

Learning Notation: Meter

Meter concerns the organization of music into strong and weak beats that are separated by measures. Having children feel the strong beats such as the **downbeat**, the first beat in a measure, is relatively easy. From there, it's a matter of counting, hearing and feeling how the strong vs. weak beats are grouped to create a meter.

Duple Meters

In **duple meter**, each measure contains groupings of two beats (or multiples of two). For example, in a 2/4 time signature, there are two beats in a measure with the quarter note receiving one beat or one count. In a 4/4 time signature, there are four beats in a measure, and the quarter note also receives one beat or count.

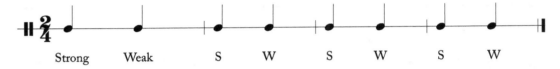

Strong   Weak   S   W   S   W   S   W

Examples of 2/4 Rhythms

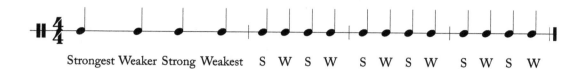

Examples of 4/4 Rhythms

Triple Meters

In **triple meter**, each measure contains three beats (or a multiple of three). For example, in a 3/4 time signature, there are three beats in a measure and the quarter note receives one beat.

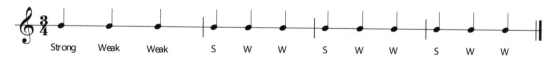

Examples of 3/4 Rhythms

Compound Meters

Both duple and triple meter are known as **simple meters**—that means that each beat can be divided into two eighth notes. The time signature 6/8 is very common for children's rhymes and songs. In 6/8, there are six beats in a measure with each eighth note receiving one beat. 6/8 is known as a **compound meter**, meaning that each of the two main beats can be divided into three parts.

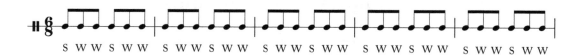

S W W S W W   S W W S W W   S W W S W W   S W W S W W   S W W S W W

Examples of 6/8 Rhythms

Learning Notation: Dynamics

Learning basic concepts such as dynamics and tempo will better equip you to involve children in more nuanced music making and listening.

The two basic dynamic indications in music are:

- **p**, for *piano*, meaning "soft"
- **f**, for *forte*, meaning "loud" or actually, *with force*, in Italian

More subtle degrees of loudness or softness are indicated by:

- **mp**, for *mezzo-piano*, meaning "moderately soft"
- **mf**, for *mezzo-forte*, meaning "moderately loud"

There are also more extreme degrees of dynamics represented by:

- **pp**, for *pianissimo* and meaning "very soft"
- **ff**, for *fortissimo* and meaning "very loud"

Terms for changing volume are:

- **Crescendo** (gradually increasing volume)

• **Decrescendo** (gradually decreasing volume)

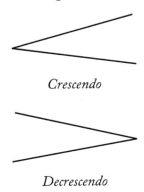

Crescendo

Decrescendo

DYNAMICS PRACTICE

Fill in the blanks below using the following terms: fortissimo, pianissimo, mezzo-forte, mezzo-piano, crescendo, decrescendo, forte, piano

1. ***p***   _____
2. ***f***   _____
3. ***ff***   _____
4. ***mp***   _____

5.   _____
6. ***mf***   _____
7. ***pp***   _____

8.   _____

Learning Notation: Tempo

Tempo is the speed of the music, or the number of beats per minute. Music's tempo is rather infectious, and children respond physically to both fast and slow speeds. The following are some terms and their beats per minute to help you gauge different tempi. The terms are in Italian, and are listed from slowest to fastest.

• *Larghissimo*: very, very slowly (19 beats per minute or less)
• *Grave*: slowly and solemnly (20–40 bpm)
• *Lento*: slowly (40–45 bpm)
• *Largo*: broadly (45–50 bpm)
• *Larghetto*: rather broadly (50–55 bpm)
• *Adagio*: slow and stately (literally, "at ease") (55–65 bpm)
• *Andante*: at a walking pace (the verb *andare* in Italian means to walk) (73–77 bpm)

- *Andantino*: slightly faster than andante (78–83 bpm)
- *Marcia moderato*: moderately, in the manner of a march (83–85 bpm)
- *Moderato*: moderately (86–97 bpm)
- *Allegretto*: moderately fast (98–109 bpm)
- *Allegro*: fast, quickly and bright (109–132 bpm)
- *Vivace*: lively and fast (132–140 bpm)
- *Allegrissimo*: very fast (150–167 bpm)
- *Presto*: extremely fast (168–177 bpm)
- *Prestissimo*: even faster than *presto* (178 bpm and above)

Terms that refer to changing tempo:

- *Ritardando*: gradually slowing down
- *Accelerando*: gradually accelerating

Activity 2D

Exploring tempo in everyday life: The average person walks at a pace between 76-108 beats per minute. Playlists can offer different tempi for different types of exercise. Find your tempo! What song fits a slow walking speed, medium, brisk, running? Stores play songs in slower tempi to encourage you to shop. Go to a supermarket or store and notice your walking speed. Is it connected to the beat of the music?

READ MORE: <u>HOW STORES USE MUSIC</u>

Scales

Scales are sets of musical notes organized by pitch. In Western culture, we predominantly use the major and minor scales. However, many children's songs use the pentatonic scales (both major and minor) as well.

The **major scale** comprises seven different pitches that are organized by using a combination of half steps (one note on the piano to the very next note) and whole steps (two half steps together). The major scale looks as follows: Whole Whole Half Whole Whole Whole Half or W W H W W W H.

A **minor scale** uses the following formula: W H W W H W W.

Pentatonic scales, found in many early American and children's songs, only use five pitches, hence the moniker "*pent*atonic." There are many types of major pentatonic scales, but one of the most popular major pentatonic scale is similar to the major scale, but without the 4th or 7th pitches (Fa or Ti). One of the common minor pentatonic scales is similar to the minor scale, but also without (Fa or Ti).

Major, minor (natural), and pentatonic scales

Major Scale (C Major)

Do   Re   Mi   Fa   Sol   La   Ti   Do'

Minor Scale (A Minor)

La,   Ti   Do   Re   Mi   Fa   Sol   La'

Major Pentatonic (C)

Do   Re   Mi   Sol   La   Do'

Minor Pentatonic (A)

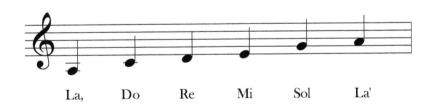

La,   Do   Re   Mi   Sol   La'

SCALE PRACTICE

Label the half steps and whole steps for the C major scale.

Practice writing your own C major scale.

Label the half steps and whole steps of the A minor scale.

Practice writing your own A minor scale.

Resources for Further Learning

There are numerous websites that cover the fundamentals of music, including the staff, notes, clefs, ledger lines, rhythm, meter, scales, chords, and chord progressions.

Music Theory

www.musictheory.net

musictheory.net is a music theory resource from basic to complex. It contains active definitions for musical terms; music lessons regarding the meanings of musical notation; and exercises designed to further understanding of musical notes, chords, and many other musical aspects. This site also includes a pop-up piano and accidental calculator specifically to help users learn and practice their developing musical skills. It also features a products page with apps people can buy to practice and use music on the go via their smartphones. The site would be appropriate for people ages 12 and up, and is extremely user friendly.

http://www.musictheoryvideos.com/

Musictheoryvideos.com was designed by Stephen Wiles in the hope to make music theory an active part of music learning. The site includes music theory lessons for students between grades 1 and 5 in the form of tables, lists, and videos to help the student better understand the many parts of music. There are videos about the importance and difference of treble and bass clefs; there is a list of music terms and what they mean, and the site even contains videos entailing the transposition of music. It would be a great resource for teachers to offer students, especially those who could benefit from some extra information outside of class. The site contains information that would take a student step by step through the basics of music theory through simple short videos, complete with British-accented narrations.

https://www.themightymaestro.com/

The Mighty Maestro website contains interactive games for children beginning with note values and pitches. Unfortunately, some of the activities require payment, but the free access games are very basic in terms of musical skill and literacy level, and very accessible.

https://www.classicsforkids.com/

Classics for Kids is an excellent website with a wealth of music information geared for children. Games, online listening, quizzes, activity sheets, information on composers, and lots of music history make this website highly valuable. The website is user friendly, bright, and cheerful, and very easy to navigate. It also contains sections for parents and teachers.

www.mymusictheory.com

Mymusictheory.com includes helpful lessons for students grades 1 through 6, as well as helpful links for teachers when it comes to teaching music theory. For the teachers, they provide music flashcards, lesson plans, music-reinforcing word searches, and many other helpful resources, all in one location. The site is broken down by grade level, with each level containing exercises and practice exams for the material learned during each lesson.

www.8notes.com

8notes.com is a large website full of music lessons for several instruments, including but not limited to piano, guitar, vocal, and percussion. Free sheet music is available for the different instruments, as well as music from different popular movies. An online metronome, guitar tuner, blank sheet music, music theory lessons, and music converters are all available at 8notes.com. This site would be helpful to those learning new instruments, as well as experienced musicians who are just looking for some new music to play.

Note Reading

- http://readsheetmusic.info/index.shtml
- https://www.teoria.com/
- https://www.classicsforkids.com/games/note_names.php

Keyboard Skills

Many classroom teachers have pianos in their rooms and don't know how to use them or underutilize them. Learning to play a basic melody on a piano or keyboard or even put a few chords to them is a great confidence builder, and the children love to sing to a piano accompaniment!

- http://www.howtoplaypiano.ca/
- http://www.pianobychords.com/

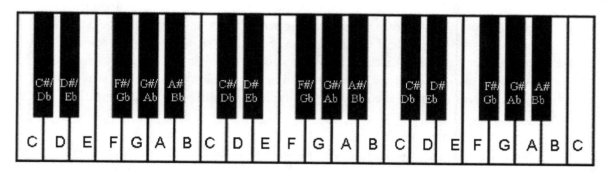

Notes on a keyboard

II. Music Education in America

> Music education does not exist isolated in the music classroom. It is influenced by trends in general education, society, culture, and politics.
>
> —Harold Abeles, *Critical Issues in Music Education*, 2010

How did music education develop into its current form? Did music specialists always teach music? What were classroom teacher's musical responsibilities? Well, to answer these questions, we need to look to the past for a moment. Initially, music and education worked hand in hand for centuries.

Early Music Teaching

18th century: Singing schools and their tune books

Before there was formal music education in the United States, there was music and education, primarily experienced through religious education. Music education in the U.S. began after the Pilgrims and Puritans arrived, when ministers realized that their congregation needed help singing and reading music. Several ministers developed **tune books** that used four notes of **solfege** (Mi, Fa, Sol, La) and **shape notes** to train people in singing the **psalms** and **hymns** required for proper church singing. By 1830, **singing schools** based on the techniques found in these books began popping up all over New England, with some people attending singing school classes every day (Keene, 1982). They were promised that they would learn to sing in a month or become music teachers themselves in three months.

Some consider the hymn music of this time to be uniquely American—borrowing styles from Ireland, England, and Europe, but using dance rhythms, loose harmonic rules, and complex vocal parts (**counterpoint**) where each voice (soprano, alto, tenor and bass) sang its own unique melody and no one had the main melody. Original American composers such as William Billings wrote hundreds of hymns in this style.

19th century

Johann H. Pestalozzi (1746–1827)

Pestalozzi was an educational reformer and Swiss philosopher born in 1746. He is known as the father of modern education. Although his philosophies are over 200 years old, you may recognize his ideas as sounding quite contemporary. He believed in a child-centered education that promoted understanding the world from the child's level, taking into account individual development and concrete, tactile experiences such as working directly with plants, minerals for science, etc. He advocated teaching poor as well as rich children, breaking down a subject to its elements, and a broad, liberal education along with teacher training. In the U.S., **normal schools** would take off by the end of the 19th century, and advocates of Pestalozzi's educational reform would put into place a system of teacher training that influences us to this day.

Lowell Mason (1792–1872) and the "Better Music" movement

Lowell Mason, considered the founder of music education in America, was a proponent of Pestalozzi's ideas, particularly the **rote method** of teaching music, where songs were experienced and repeated first and concepts were taught afterward. Mason authored the first series book based on the rote method in 1864 called *The Song Garden*.

Mason was highly critical of both the singing schools of the day and the compositional style. He was horrified at the promises that singing schools made to their students—namely that they could be qualified to teach after only a few months of lessons, and the general composition techniques used at the time. Mason felt that the music, including the work of composers such as Billings, was "rude and crude." To change this, he promoted simplified harmonies that made the melody the most prominent aspect of the music, and downgraded the importance of the other vocal parts to support the melody. He accomplished this through the establishment of shape note singing schools, which carried out his musical vision. The result was that the original hymn style became the purview of the shape note singing schools, mostly in the South, where they flourished for many years. The most famous shape-note book is called *Sacred Harp*.

Hosted at the U.S. Library of Congress (U.S Library of Congress and [1]) [Public domain], via WikiCommons

Under the title "New Britain", "Amazing Grace" appears in a 1847 publication of Southern Harmony *in shape notes*

The songs in *Sacred Harp* were religious hymns. "Amazing Grace" was one of the songs published in this book.

Amazing Grace

John Newton (1779), *Sacred Harp Songbook* (1844)

WATCH THIS <u>SHAPE NOTE SINGING</u>

WATCH THIS <u>SACRED HARP SHAPE NOTE SINGING</u>

READ MORE <u>SHAPE NOTES</u>

In 1833, Lowell Mason and others began to introduce the idea of music education in the schools. Mason, along with Thomas Hastings, went on to establish the first public school music program in Boston, beginning with the Boston Singing School, which taught children singing under his methodology. Eventually, regular classroom teachers were educated in normal schools (later called teachers' colleges), developed in the mid-19th century, where they were taught the general subjects and were expected to teach the arts as well (Brown, 1919).

The up-to-date primary school, realizing the limitations of the 3 R's curriculum, has enriched its program by adding such activities as singing, drawing, constructive occupations, story-telling, and games, and has endeavored to organize its work in terms of children rather than the subject matter (Temple, 1920, 499).

Music and the normal school

Normal schools in the 19th century grew out of a need to educate a burgeoning young American population. These schools were teacher preparation courses, usually with access to model schools where teachers in training could observe and practice teach. Music was a significant part of education. The Missouri State Normal School at Warrensburg stressed the importance of music in their catalog from 1873–74:

Vocal Music—the importance of music as one of the branches of education is fully recognized. Vocal music is taught throughout the entire course…and teachers are advised to make it a part of the course of instruction in every school with which they may be connected (Keene, 1982, p. 204).

Music and education in America: 20th century

Music supervisors, who oversaw the work of classroom teachers, received additional training in music. Music education in the early 20th century continued under the purview of the music supervisor, while classroom teachers were trained to teach music to their students. Gradually, a specialization process began to occur and music became a regular subject with its own certification, an educational tradition that continues to this day. By the 1920s, institutions in the U.S. began granting degrees in music education and, along with groups such as the Music Supervisor's Conference (later the Music Educator's National Conference and currently the National Association for Music Educators or *NAfME*), supported the use of qualified music teachers in the schools. Eventually, the arts broke into different specialties, and the separate role of music teacher as we know it was created.

Ironically, there was great concern at the time regarding these special music teachers. Because music was no longer in the hands of the classroom teachers, great effort was made to "bring music in as close a relation to the other work as is possible under the present arrangement of a special music teacher" (Goodrich, 1901, p. 133).

Contemporary Music Education

Instructional methods

The role of music in the U.S. educational system is perpetually under discussion. On one hand, many see structural problems inherent in music's connection to its history and the glaring distinction between the prevalence, importance, and function of music's role in everyday life and its embattled role in the classroom Sloboda (2001). On the other, increased advocacy is required in order to justify music's existence and terms of benefits to the child amidst the threat of constant budget cuts. Given this, it is important to remember music education's history, origin and deep roots in the American education experience.

The beginning of the 20th century was an exciting time for music education, with several significant instructional methods being developed and taking hold. In the United States, music education developed around a method of instruction, the Normal Music Course, the remnants of which are adhered to even today in music classrooms. The books used a "graded" curriculum with successively more complex songs and exercises, and combined author-composed songs in these books with folk and classical material. An online copy of the *New Normal Music Course* (1911) for fourth and fifth graders is accessible via Google Books.

In Europe and Asia, four outstanding and very different music instruction methods developed: the Kodály Method, Orff Schulwerk, Suzuki, and Dalcroze all played significant roles in furthering music education abroad and in the U.S., and were methods based on folk and classical genres (see Chapter 4 for further discussion about these methods). In contrast to the early music books for the Normal School, for which there was "a paucity of song material prompting the authors of the original course to chiefly use their own song material" (Tufts & Holt, 1911, p. 3), Kodály and Orff in particular used authentic music in their methods, and authentic music directly related to children's lives (see Chapter 4 for more on this).

Resources

Gregory, A., Worrall, L., & Sarge, A. (1996). The development of emotional responses to music in young children. *Motivation and Emotion.* December 20 (4), 341–348.

Boone, R., & Cunningham, J. (2001). Children's expression of emotional meaning in music through expressive body movement *Journal of Non-verbal Behavior.* March, 25 (1), 21–41.

- Children as young as four and five years old were able to portray emotional meaning in music through expressive movement.

Metz, E. R. (1989). Movement as a musical response among preschool children. *Journal of Research in Music Education 37,* 48–60.

- The primary result of "Movement as a Musical Response Among Preschool Children" was the generation of a substantive theory of children's movement responses to music. The author also derived implications of the seven propositions of early children education and movement responses to music.

Sims, W., & Cassidy, J. (1997). Verbal and operant responses of young children to vocal versus instrumental song performances. *Journal of Research in Music Education, 45*(2), 234–244.

- Young children's music attitudes and responses do not seem to be based on specific musical characteristics; children may have very idiosyncratic responses and listening styles.

References

Abeles, H. (2010). The historical contexts of music education. In H. Abeles & L. Custodero (Eds.), *Critical issues in music education: Contemporary theory and practice* (1–22). Oxford, UK: Oxford University Press.

Abeles, H., and Custodero, L. (2010). *Critical issues in music education: Contemporary theory and practice.* Oxford, UK: Oxford University Press.

Andress, B. (1991). From research to practice: Preschool children and their movement responses to music. *Young Children,* November, 22–27.

Atkinson, P., & Hammerley, M. (1994). Ethnography and participant observation. In N. K. Denzin & Y. S. Lincoln (Eds.), *Handbook of qualitative research* (248–261), Thousand Oaks, CA: Sage Publications.

Attali, J. (1985). *Noise: The Political Economy of Music.* Minneapolis: University of Minnesota Press.

Bakan, M. (2011). *World music: Traditions and transformations.* New York: McGraw-Hill.

Blacking, J. (1973). *How Musical is Man?* Seattle: University of Washington Press.

Boone, R. T., & Cunningham, J. G. (2001). Children's expression of emotional meaning in music through expressive body movement. *Journal of Nonverbal Behavior 5*(1), 21–41.

Bresler, L., & Stake, R. E. (1992). Qualitative research methodology in music education. In R. Colwell (Ed.), *Handbook of research on music teaching and learning* (75–90). New York: Schirmer Books.

Brown, H. A. (1919). The Normal School curriculum. *The Elementary School Journal 20*(4), 19, 276–284.

Chen-Hafteck, L. (2004). Music and movement from zero to three: A window to children's musicality. In L. A. Custodero (Ed.), *ISME Early Childhood Commission Conference—Els Móns Musicals dels Infants* (The Musical Worlds of Children), July 5–10. Escola Superior de Musica de Catalunya, Barcelona, Spain. International Society of Music Education.

Cohen, V. (1980). *The emergence of musical gestures in kindergarten children* (Unpublished doctoral dissertation). University of Illinois, Champaign, IL.

Flohr, J. W. (2005). *The musical lives of young children*. Upper Saddle River, NJ: Pearson Prentice-Hall Music Education Series.

Goodrich, H. (1901). Music. *The Elementary School Teacher and Course of Study*, 2(2), 132–33.

Graue, M. E., & Walsh, D. J. (1998). *Studying children in context: Theories, methods and ethics*. Thousand Oaks, CA: Sage Publications.

Heidegger, Martin. (2008). On the Origin of the Work of Art. In D. Farrell Krell (Ed.) *Basic Writings* (143-212). New York: Harper Collins

Holgersen, S. E., & Fink-Jensen, K. (2002). "The lived body—object and subject in research of music activities with preschool children." Paper presented at the meeting of the10th International Conference of the Early Childhood Commission of the International Society for Music Education, August 5–9, Copenhagen, Denmark.

Janesick, V. J. (1994). The dance of qualitative research design: Metaphor, methodology, and meaning. In N. K. Denzin & Y. S. Lincoln (Eds.), *Handbook of qualitative research* (209–219). Thousand Oaks, CA: Sage Publications.

Jordan-DeCarbo, J., & Nelson, J. A. (2002). Music and early childhood education. In R. Colwell & C. Richardson (Eds.), *The new handbook of research on music teaching and learning* (210–242). Oxford, UK: Oxford University Press.

Keene, J. (1982). *History of music education in the United States*. Hanover, NH: University Press of New England.

Kim, H. K. (2007). Early childhood preservice teachers' beliefs about music, developmentally appropriate practice, and the relationship between music and developmentally appropriate practice (Unpublished doctoral dissertation). University of Florida, Gainesville, FL.

Mason, L. (1839). *Manuel of the Boston Academy of Music for the instruction of vocal music in the system of Pestalozzi*. Boston, MA: Wilkins and Carter.

Mason, L. (1866). *The song garden*. Boston, MA: Oliver Ditson and Co.

Metz, E. (1989). Movement as a musical response among preschool children. *Journal of Research in Music Education 37*(1), 48–60.

Moog, H. (1976). *The musical experience of the pre-schoolchild*. (C. Clarke, Trans.). London: Schott Music. (Original work published 1968)

Moorhead, G. E., & Pond, D. (1978). Music of young children: General observations. In *Music of Young Children* (29–64). Santa Barbara, California: Pillsbury Foundation for Advancement of Music Education. (Original work published 1942)

Nettl, B. (2001). Music. In S. Sadie (Ed.), *New Grove dictionary of music and musicians* (Vol. 17, 425-37) London: Grove's Dictionaries of Music Inc.

Peery, J. C., & Peery, I. W. (1986). Effects of exposure to classical music on the musical preferences of pre-school children. *Journal of Research in Music Education 33*(1), 24–33.

Retra, J. (2005). Musical movement responses in early childhood music education practice in the Netherlands. Paper presented at the meeting of Music Educators and Researchers of Young Children (MERYC) Conference, April 4–5, at the University of Exeter.

Sims, W. L. (1987). The use of videotape in conjunction with systematic observation of children's overt, physical responses to music: A research model for early childhood music education. *ISME Yearbook 14*, 63–67.

Sims, W. L., & Nolker, D. B. (2002). Individual differences in music listening responses of kindergarten children. *Journal of Research in Music Education 50*(2), 292–300.

Singing Schools. (n.d.). Library of Congress. https://www.loc.gov/collections/music-of-nineteenth-century-ohio/articles-and-essays/singing-schools/ (accessed June 24, 2021).

Sloboda, J. (2001). Emotion, functionality and the everyday experience of music: Where does music education fit? *Music Education Research 3*(2).

Smithrim, K. (1994). Preschool children's responses to music on television. Paper presented at the International Society for Music Education Early Childhood Commission Seminar "Vital Connections: Young Children, Adults & Music," July 11–15, University of Missouri-Columbia.

Stone, R. (1998). *Africa, the Garland encyclopedia of world music*. New York: Garland Publishing, Inc..

Temple, A. (1920). The kindergarten primary unit. *The Elementary School Journal, 20/7*(20), 498–509.

Titon, J. T. (2008). *Worlds of music: An introduction to the music of the world's people.* Boston, MA: Cengage.

Tobin, J. J., Wu, D. Y. H., & Davidson, D. H. (1989). *Preschool in three cultures—Japan, China, and the United States.* New Haven and London: Yale University Press.

Tufts, J., and Holt, H. (1911). *The New Normal music course.* Need location of publisher: Silver Burdett and Co.

Vocabulary

articulation: the manner in which notes are played or words pronounced; e.g., long or short, stressed or unstressed

counterpoint: the art of combining melodies

dynamics: indicates the volume of the sound, and the changes in volume (e.g. loudness, softness, crescendo, decrescendo).

harmony: the simultaneous combination of tones, especially when blended into chords pleasing to the ear; chordal structure, as distinguished from melody and rhythm

homophony: a melody with an accompaniment; e.g., a lead singer and a band

indigenous groups: people associated with a certain area who formulate their own culture

melody: musical sounds in agreeable succession or arrangement

meter: the organization of strong and weak beats; unit of measurement in terms of number of beats in a measure

monophony: single layer or sound; e.g.; a soloist

notation: how notes are written on the page

pitch: the frequency of a note's vibration

polyphony: two or more independent voices; e.g., a round of a fugue

psalms and hymns: examples of church music

recitation: reading a text using heightened speech, similar to chanting

rhythm: the pattern of regular or irregular pulses caused in music by the occurrences of strong or weak melodic and harmonic beats

rote method: memorization technique based on repetition, especially when material is to be learned quickly

shape notes: notation style used in early singing schools in the U.S. where each note had a unique shape by which it was identified

silence: the absence of sound

solfege: a music education method to teach pitch and sight reading, assigning syllables to the notes of a scale; i.e., Do, Re, Mi, Fa, Sol, La, Ti, Do would be assigned to represent and help hear the major scale pitches

sound: vibrations travelling through air, water, gas, or other media that are picked up by the human ear drum

tempo: relative rapidity or rate of movement, usually indicated by terms such as adagio, allegro, etc., or by reference to the metronome. Also, the number of beats per minute

texture: the way in which melody, harmony, and rhythm are combined in a piece; the density, thickness, or thinness or layers of a piece

timbre: the tone color of each sound; each voice has a unique tone color (vibrato, nasal, resonance, vibrant, ringing, strident, high, low, breathy, piercing, rounded warm, mellow, dark, bright, heavy, or light)

Chapter 3

Assessment and Learning Goals

Chapter Summary: This chapter is divided into two parts. The first section addresses the role of assessment in education. The second section addresses personal assessment in relation to your professional development and career goals.

Regardless of which field you find yourself in, you will more than likely be responsible for implementing a plan of goals and assessment. In business, education, science, and so forth, most productivity is determined by an evaluation of employees or students, and funding is often allocated based on that assessment.

As mentioned in Chapter 1, education assessment for all subjects and the arts has undergone significant change over the past 30 years, from No Child Left Behind to the Common Core State Standards Initiative. In this section, we will examine various discipline and national standards for the arts, particularly music.

I. Discipline-Based Assessment: National and Common Core State Standards

Beginning in the 1990s, a "Standards and Accountability" movement resulted in states writing goals for what students should know. This movement fueled the Common Core Standards Initiative, which produced the Common Core Standards that most states have adopted as of 2014. The Common Core Standards, however, are only written for English Language Arts and Mathematics, with no further intent to include other subject areas. However, this chapter will introduce the National Core Arts Standards for Music, while the Common Core standards in ELA and Math can be used when creating integrated lesson plans as introduced in later chapters.

National Core Arts Standards: 2014

The National Coalition for Core Arts Standards (NCCAS) is the organization responsible for creating standards for music, dance, theatre, and visual art. Below is an excerpt from the "National Core Arts Standards: A Conceptual Framework for Arts Learning," which explains some of the background in their creation.

The standards movement emerged with the 1994 passage of the Goals 2000: Educate America Act. Title II of that act established a National Education Standards Improvement Council, which was charged with finding appropriate organizations to write standards. In doing so, there were three goals for the process: (1) to ensure that the standards reflect the best ideas in education, both in the United States and internationally; (2) to ensure that they reflect the best knowledge about teaching and learning; and (3) to ensure that they have been developed through a broad-based, open adoption process. The standards themselves were to define what students should "know and be able to do" to the end that "all students learn to use their minds well, so that they may be prepared for responsible citizenship, further learning, and productive employment in our nation's modern economy."

Standards for arts education are important for two fundamental reasons. First, they help define what a good education in the arts should provide: a thorough grounding in a basic body of knowledge and the skills required both to make sense and to make use of each of the arts discipline—including the intellectual tools to make qualitative judgments about artistic products and expression.

Second, when states and school districts adopt the standards, they are taking a stand for rigor, informed by a clear intent. A set of standards for arts education says, in effect, "an education in the arts means that students should know what is spelled out here, reach specified levels of attainment, and do both at defined points in their education" (NCCAS, 2014, p. 4).

The completed **National Core Arts Standards** include dance, media arts, music, theater, and visual arts. The common Core Standards in the arts addresses some of the 21st-century goals in education as well. Goals in the Core Standards focus on the 4 Cs: Creativity, Communication, Cooperation, and Collaboration. Below is a section from a College Board study entitled "The Arts and the Common Core: A Review of Connections Between the Common Core State Standards and the National Core Arts Standards Conceptual Framework" (2012), which addresses the connections between the two sets of standards.

The standards are based on assessing four areas of artistic process (creating; performing, presenting, producing; responding; and connecting), with each artistic process supported by several anchor standards. In each subject, the anchor standards are broken down further into individual goals and objectives for each grade level. These goals and objectives are used in lesson planning to focus the lesson, and to aid in effective assessment.

Anchor processes and standards as defined by the <u>National Coalition for Core Arts Standards</u>

Artistic Processes			
Creating: Conceiving and developing new artistic ideas and work.	Performing/Presenting/Producing Performing: Realizing artistic ideas and work through interpretation and presentation. Presenting: Interpreting and sharing artistic work. Producing: Realizing and presenting artistic ideas and work.	Responding Understanding and evaluating how the arts convey meaning.	Connecting Relating artistic ideas and work with personal meaning and external context.
Anchor Standards			
Students will: 1. Generate and conceptualize artistic ideas and work. 2. Organize and develop artistic ideas and work. 3. Evaluate and refine a complete artistic work.	Students will: 4. Analyze, interpret, and select artistic work for presentation. 5. Develop and refine artistic work for presentation. 6. Convey meaning through the presentation of artistic work.	Students will: 7. Perceive and analyze artistic work. 8. Interpret intent and meaning in artistic work. 9. Apply criteria to evaluate artistic work.	Students will: 10. Synthesize and relate knowledge and personal experiences to make art. 11. Relate artistic ideas and works with societal, cultural, and historical context to deepen understanding.

<u>The National Core Standards for music takes the details from each of these anchor areas and breaks them down into specific, individual standards for use by each grade level.</u>

1994 National Standards for Arts Education

Because the Common Core Standards in the arts or music are quite new, in many organizations the National Standards in Music from 1994 are still in use

1994 National Standards in Music Education content and
achievement standards for grades K-4 (NAfME, 1994).

Standards in the Arts: Music, Grades K-4	
Content Standard 1	**Singing, alone and with others, a varied repertoire of music**
Achievement Standard 1	• Students sing independently, on pitch and in rhythm, with appropriate *timbre*, diction, and posture, and maintain a steady tempo • Students sing expressively, with appropriate dynamics, phrasing, and interpretation • Students sing from memory a varied repertoire of songs representing genres and styles from diverse cultures • Students sing ostinatos, partner songs, and rounds • Students sing in groups, blending vocal timbres, matching dynamic levels, and responding to the cues of a conductor
Content Standard 2	**Performing on instruments, alone and with others, a varied repertoire of music**
Achievement Standard 2	• Students perform on pitch, in rhythm, with appropriate dynamics and timbre, and maintain a steady tempo • Students perform easy rhythmic, melodic, and chordal patterns accurately and independently on rhythmic, melodic, and harmonic classroom instruments • Students perform expressively a varied repertoire of music representing diverse genres and styles • Students echo short rhythms and melodic patterns • Students perform in groups, blending instrumental timbres, matching dynamic levels, and responding to the cues of a conductor • Students perform independent instrumental parts (e.g., simple rhythmic or melodic ostinatos, contrasting rhythmic lines, harmonic progressions, and chords) while other students sing or play contrasting parts
Content Standard 3	**Improvising melodies, variations, and accompaniments**
Achievement Standard 3	• Students improvise "answers" in the same style to given rhythmic and melodic phrases • Students improvise simple rhythmic and melodic ostinato accompaniments • Students improvise simple rhythmic variations and simple melodic embellishments on familiar melodies • Students improvise short songs and instrumental pieces, using a variety of sound sources, including traditional sounds (e.g., voices, instruments), nontraditional sounds available in the classroom (e.g., paper tearing, pencil tapping), body sounds (e.g., hands clapping, fingers snapping), and sounds produced by electronic means (e.g., personal computers and basic MIDI devices, including keyboards, sequencers, synthesizers, and drum machines)

Content Standard 4	Composing and arranging music within specified guidelines
Achievement Standard 4	• Students create and arrange music to accompany readings or dramatizations • Students create and arrange short songs and instrumental pieces within specified guidelines (e.g., a particular style, form, instrumentation, or compositional technique) • Students use a variety of sound sources when composing
Content Standard 5	**Reading and notating music**
Achievement Standard 5	• Students read whole, half, dotted half, quarter, and eighth notes and rests in 2/4, 3/4, and 4/4 meter signatures • Students use a system (i.e., syllables, numbers, or letters) to read simple pitch notation in the treble clef in major keys • Students identify symbols and traditional terms referring to dynamics, tempo, and articulation and interpret them correctly when performing • Students use standard symbols to notate meter, rhythm, pitch, and dynamics in simple patterns presented by the teacher
Content Standard 6	**Listening to, analyzing, and describing music**
Achievement Standard 6	• Students identify simple music forms when presented aurally • Students demonstrate perceptual skills by moving, by answering questions about, and by describing aural examples of music of various styles representing diverse cultures • Students use appropriate terminology in explaining music, music notation, music instruments and voices, and music performances • Students identify the sounds of a variety of instruments, including many orchestra and band instruments, and instruments from various cultures, as well as children's voices and male and female adult voices • Students respond through purposeful movement (e.g., swaying, skipping, dramatic play) to selected prominent music characteristics or to specific music events (e.g., meter changes, dynamic changes, same/different sections) while listening to music
Content Standard 7	**Evaluating music and music performances**
Achievement Standard 7	• Students devise criteria for evaluating performances and compositions • Students explain, using appropriate music terminology, their personal preferences for specific musical works and styles

Content Standard 8	Understanding relationships between music, the other arts, and disciplines outside the arts
Achievement Standard 8	• Students identify similarities and differences in the meanings of common terms (e.g., form, line, contrast) used in the various arts • Students identify ways in which the principles and subject matter of other disciplines taught in the school are interrelated with those of music (e.g., foreign languages: singing songs in various languages; language arts: using the expressive elements of music in interpretive readings; mathematics: mathematical basis of values of notes, rests, and time signatures; science: vibration of strings, drum heads, or air columns generating sounds used in music; geography: songs associated with various countries or regions)
Content Standard 9	**Understanding music in relation to history and culture**
Achievement Standard 9	• Students identify by genre or style aural examples of music from various historical periods and cultures • Students describe in simple terms how elements of music are used in music examples from various cultures of the world • Students identify various uses of music in their daily experiences and describe characteristics that make certain music suitable for each use • Students identify and describe roles of musicians (e.g., orchestra conductor, folksinger, church organist) in various music settings and cultures • Students demonstrate audience behavior appropriate for the context and style of music performed

For a summary of the 1994 K–12 standards in dance, music, theater, and visual arts, see The Kennedy Center's easy to navigate overview.

1994 National Music Standards for early childhood education (NAfME, 1994).

Pre-K Standards for Music Educators
Infants
The National Music Education Pre-K Standards are intended for ages two to four. However, guidelines are given below for infant and toddler music experiences. These guidelines include: 1. Singing and chanting to them, using songs and rhymes representing a variety of meters and tonalities 2. Imitating the sounds infants make 3. Exposing them to a wide variety of vocal, body, instrumental, and environmental sounds 4. Providing exposure to selected live and recorded music 5. Rocking, patting, touching, and moving with children to the beat, rhythm patterns, and melodic direction of the music they hear 6. Providing safe toys that make musical sounds the children can control 7. Talking about music and its relationship to expression and feeling

Toddlers (Two- to three- year olds)

By age four, children should be prepared to learn music at the kindergarten level when they enter school. Guidelines for musical experiences for two-, three-, and four-year-olds are:

1. Two-, three-, and four-year-olds need an environment that includes a variety of sound sources, selected recorded music, and opportunities for free improvised singing and the building of a repertoire of songs
2. An exploratory approach, using a wide variety of appropriate materials, provides a rich base from which conceptual understanding can evolve in later years
3. A variety of individual musical experiences is important at this age, with little emphasis on activities that require children to perform together as a unit

Pre-school (Four-year-olds)

1. Content Standard: Singing and Playing Instruments
   a. Use their voices expressively as they speak, chant, and sing
   b. Sing a variety of simple songs in various keys, meters, and genres alone and with a group, becoming increasingly accurate in rhythm and pitch
   c. Experiment with a variety of instruments and other sound sources
   d. Play simple melodies and accompaniments on instruments
2. Content Standard: Creating Music Achievement Standards:
   a. Improvise songs to accompany their play activities
   b. Improvise instrumental accompaniments to songs, recorded selections, stories, and poems
   c. Create short pieces of music, using voices, instruments, and other sound sources
   d. Invent and use original graphic or symbolic systems to represent vocal and instrumental sounds and musical ideas
3. Content Standard: Responding to Music Achievement Standards:
   a. Identify the sources of a wide variety of sounds
   b. Respond through movement to music of various tempos, meters, dynamics, modes, genres, and styles to express what they hear and feel in works of music
   c. Participate freely in music activities
4. Content Standard: Understanding Music Achievement Standards:
   a. Use their own vocabulary and standard music vocabulary to describe voices, instruments, music notation, and music of various genres, styles, and periods from diverse cultures
   b. Sing, play instruments, move, or verbalize to demonstrate awareness of the elements of music and changes in their usage
   c. Demonstrate an awareness of music as a part of daily life

Complete National Arts Standards are available on the National Association for Music Educators website, as well as a comparison between the 1994 standards and the most recent revision.

State Policy in Education Database

Because information on state policy in education changes continuously, the Arts Education Partnership has made available a searchable state policy database. This site allows you to track any changes regarding teaching and learning in the arts.

Professional and Standards Organizations

- Arts Education Partnership. www.aep-arts.org
- Common Core State Standards. (2010). National Governors Association Center for Best Practices, Council of Chief State School Officers, Washington, D.C.
- Kennedy Center ArtsEdge. https://www.kennedy-center.org/education/resources-for-educators/classroom-resources/
- National Art Education Association (NAEA). www.artseducators.org
- National Association for Music Education (NAfME). www.nafme.org
- National Coalition for Core Arts Standards. (NCCAS). https://www.nationalartsstandards.org/
- The State Education Agency Directors of Arts Education (SEADAE). www.seadae.org

II. Personal Assessment

As you begin to develop the professional goals for yourself and your career, it is crucial to be able to assess these goals in relation to who you are, the people you work with, and the students you teach. Knowing who you are and being able to assess your abilities, strengths, and weaknesses is critical to your success in any field. As you learn to master the core material for your career, you might also be ready to find your moorings in terms of your professional self. This will require the maturity to self-assess and thoughtfully apply criticism towards self-enhancement and development as a professional in your field. Below are some materials to help you create a vision of your "professional" self that will serve you throughout your career and lifetime.

What Is a Professional?

Right now, you are a "professional student," so as you read the material below, apply the criteria to your behavior and professional as a student.

- Are you the best student you can be?
- Do you approach your assignments and classes in earnest and with a commitment towards learning?
- Are you able to apply the material you're learning towards your development as a person?
- Are you developing excellent work habits?

Below, you'll find a definition of what a professional is, as well as a chart explaining the top 10 dimensions of what it means to be professional, and a professional assessment rubric to determine where you fall on the spectrum of "professionalism."

Professionals follow through on each commitment and organizational role in a way that exceeds the expectations of others. Professionals are positive, action oriented, opened minded, poised, adaptable, respectful, self-regulated, empathic, organized, prepared, and collaborative. Professionals perform effectively in teams and communicate effectively to individuals and groups through various means. They have special expertise and contribute to a range of challenging disciplinary areas. Life-long learning and self-growth are valued, practiced, and mentored in others. They take care with appearance, language, and productive behaviors to create an image of success. Professionals encourage and support environments that produce trust by demonstrating integrity through ethical and inclusive decision-making.

Dimensions of a Professional

© 2013 Daniel Apple, Sheri Treadwell, Natalie Sarrazin

Professionals Are:	
Accountable	Professionals take full responsibility before, during, and after each effort or decision; share credit for positive results with others; and readily accept consequences when things don't go as expected.
Reliable	Professionals can be counted on doing what they say within the allocated time and committed resources; they are ready to help others when needed.
Self-assessors	Professionals set criteria for each performance; make key observations; reflect and analyze on these observations, behaviors, and actions; and consistently make improvements without being prompted by others.
Self-aware	Professionals understand the implications of their behaviors and actions on others and adapt appropriately for each changing situation.
Self-motivators	Professionals are energetic, passionate, and invested in living their daily values.
Risk-takers	Professionals achieve success by taking risks that others may consider to be unpopular, and are willing to deal with temporary failure and resistance so long as it is in the best interest of the project or activity.
Experts	Professionals actively advance disciplinary and interdisciplinary knowledge with every learning opportunity to remain current on relevant innovations, methodologies, and practices in their own and related areas of expertise.
Communicators	Professionals effectively express informally and formally through a range of modes and refined interpersonal skills their expertise, expectations, and means to both large groups and individuals.
Ethical	Professionals place a high and consistent focus on aligning decisions and actions with quality individual, disciplinary, and organizational values.
Presentable	Professionals represent themselves in a manner that is above reproach at all times in their appropriate dress, language, and behaviors.

Taking Stock: A Professional Self-Assessment Rubric

Even though you may not have officially begun your "professional" career, you are, in a sense, practicing the behaviors that you will perform in your jobs right now. How you organize your time, how you present yourself, and most importantly the type of attitudes you have towards your responsibilities as students, are all harbingers of how you will comport yourself in your future career.

Although you may still be a student, you can begin to develop the personal goals that you will need to succeed. Being honest with yourself is the best policy when assessing. As you read through the section below, try to imagine your behaviors in different circumstances (e.g., behavior as a student alone or in a group, or as a colleague or worker) to see where you are excelling or where you need to apply yourself. Remember, self-assessment is only for your benefit to develop and grow as a person, and is not punitive.

Take a moment to read the rubric below and see where you fit in. Now is the time to grow and develop, so keep in mind where you are, where you want to be, and how you might get there.

Professional Self-Assessment Rubric.

A. Polished Professionals	• Take full public responsibility of all actions and decisions and follow through in everything on time and above expectations. • Use every performance to produce opportunities for increasing future performances, thus seeing what must be accomplished in every new situation. • Are very passionate in all that they do and step out in front to do what must be done to accomplish every task with quality. • Have extensive interdisciplinary expertise and can help others understand and make connections through formal and informal communications. • Constantly make the "right" difficult decisions and represent themselves and their organizations as the leaders they are.
B. Professionals	• Tackle tough assignments with full responsibility and bring in results that meet the expectations of the immediate stakeholders. • Frequently use self-assessment as a means to improve future performance and to increase their effectiveness with those around them. • Have aligned their careers with their values. • Take risks in their domain that others fear making. • Have extensive disciplinary knowledge and some interdisciplinary understanding. • Communicate effectively within their discipline. • Can be trusted to do what is right in almost all situations and consistently represent themselves and their organization in a positive way.
C. Inconsistent Professionals	• Will accept responsibility on those things they choose and decisions they owned and will meet common expectations consistently. • Self-assess on their very important efforts and know what to do during the routine enterprises, but struggle in new situations. • Do extremely well in what they enjoy doing and take risks in areas, but do not seem to like taking risks themselves. • Have pockets of strong expertise and can communicate in areas of their expertise when focused. • Consistently do what is right in common situations and know how to behave and dress in normal situations.

D. Pre-Professionals	• Are willing to take responsibilities with moderate consequences and will do their best to please the key stakeholder. • Will try to assess themselves when requested and take in things that others point out as important in their surroundings. • Occasionally find things that excite and motivate them and will take risks when others in power support them. • Will work to become knowledgeable in areas of their current job responsibility and put efforts in trying to communicate effectively.
E. Unprofessional People	• Constantly shift responsibility to others and often find extensive justification for why they couldn't deliver what's been asked for. • On rare occasions see the need for reflection and are often overwhelmed by the current changing context. • Need to be prompted with monitoring on a daily basis and take risks that are small and calculated. • Have a small set of trained knowledge and constantly need to have things explained again and their communications verified. • Are constantly challenged to do what is right and not convenient and come across as questionable in behaviors and dress.

Activity 3A

TRY THIS

Go through the Professional Assessment Rubric in a group. Discuss what types of behaviors fall under each of the five categories. What does an unprofessional person do? A Pre-Professional person? An Inconsistent Professional? Give specific examples.

Now assess yourself as a "student." Go through the Professional Assessment Rubric, and honestly appraise yourself in terms of how you behave currently as a student in your classes. Where do you fit in? Do you see yourself near the top of the list or towards the bottom? What behaviors do you engage in? What skills and attitudes do you need to work on?

References

National Association for Music Educators. (1994). *National Standards for Arts Education: What Every Young American Should Know and Be Able to Do in the Arts. Content and achievement standards for dance, music, theatre, and visual arts; grades K-12*. Reston, VA: Music Educators National Conference.

National Coalition for Core Arts Standards. (2014). Conceptual framework: National Core Arts Standards: A conceptual framework for arts learning. Retrieved from http://nccas.wikispaces.com/Conceptual+Framework

Chapter 4

Approaches to Music Education

Chapter Summary: The goal of this chapter is to introduce the reader to the most well-known music teaching methods used in music education. They are Zoltan Kodály, Emile-Jacques Dalcroze, Orff Schulwerk, Edwin Gordon, Shinseki Suzuki, and Reggio Emilia. This chapter also familiarizes the reader with each method's philosophy and principles, unique pedagogy, and practices and activities.

The material introduced in this chapter will be referenced and built upon throughout the remainder of the book.

Music Methods for Working With Children

What Is a Method?

A music education, or any other type of education method, is a teaching approach that has: 1) an identifiable underlying philosophy or set of principles; 2) a unified body of pedagogy unique to it with a body of well-defined practice; 3) goals and objectives worthy of pursuit; and 4) integrity (i.e., its reason for existence must not be commercial) (Chosky et al.).

Although these approaches are often taught in music education classes, they are highly applicable, accessible, and integrated methods appropriate for anyone interested in working with children and the arts, or *music in education* in addition to *music education*. All educators can incorporate the basic techniques used in these methods as they offer creative, arts-driven curricula through which to teach.

Method Similarities

The music methods of Jaques-Emile Dalcroze, Zoltan Kodály, Carl Orff, and S. Suzuki are time-tested and contain well-practiced and researched techniques for teaching music. All of these approaches to music learning contain fundamental similarities in that they:

- Are systematic and sequential in design;
- Utilize music with authenticity and integrity, such as folk music;
- Are based on incorporating the "mother-tongue" approach to rhythm, pitch, and timbre from the child's persepctive, innate behaviors and how interaction with their natural environment; and
- Encourage active engagement with the student.

They are also "comprehensive and holistic [in preparing] children to be artists, creators, and producers and not just consumers of music. They pair active and actual music-making with conceptual learning experiences offered in a systematic approach" (Moore).

The holistic nature of these highly integrated approaches, is still conducive today for implementation in an integrated arts program. This is due to the fact that their core identities, particularly Orff and Dalcroze, contain elements of drama, movement, sound, and music.

Orff Schulwerk

Philosophy

Since the beginning of time, children have not liked to study. They would much rather play, and if you have their interests at heart, you will let them learn while they play; they will find that what they have mastered is child's play.

—Carl Orff

Orff Schulwerk is the only approach that is not a systematic "method" per se, although it does entail fostering creative thinking through improvisational experiences. Rather than a system, Schulwerk combines **instruments, singing, movement, and speech** to develop children's innate musical abilities. There are four stages of teaching:

- Imitation
- Exploration
- Improvisation
- Composition

Orff Schulwerk is rooted in arts and subject integration. In the early 20th century, Carl Orff met gymnastics and dance educator Dorothée Gunther and established an innovative school for children based on the idea that all human beings are musical by nature. Their approach was to combine movement (gymnastics), music, and dance. Orff developed the concept of **elemental music** based on the synthesis of the arts of the Greek Muses, which combined tone, dance, poetry, image, design, and theatrical gesture. Gunther and Orff's approach was to create a comfortable environment that approximates the child's natural world of play, thus allowing children to be introduced to a range of musical skills in a relaxed and stress-free setting.

Carl Orff's definition of elemental music is based on small-scale musical patterns (e.g., ostinato, drone) familiar to the students.

What then is elemental music? Elemental music is never music alone but forms a unity with movement, dance and speech. It is music that one makes oneself, in which one takes part not as a listener, but as a participant. It is unsophisticated, employs no big forms and no big architectural structures, and it uses small sequence forms, ostinato and rondo. Elemental music is near the earth, natural, physical, within the range of everyone to learn it and experience it and suitable for the child... (1963)

Orff Schulwerk utilizes children's natural behaviors of play—experimenting, improvising—to access children's innate musicality. Schulwerk uses the native language, sounds, timbres, rhythms, melodies, and tonal material surrounding the child, particularly in its folk music repertoire. Similar to many of the other methods, the Orff Schulwerk emphasizes that children should experience first and then analyze or intellectualize about music afterwards, and encourages hands-on music-making regardless of skill level.

The Orff Instrumentarium

In early 20th century Germany, there were few instruments accessible to children. Orff began by buying recorders, which were rare at the time. Since no one knew how to play them, Dorothée Gunther created instructional books to teach recorder to children. No one knew how to play them, so Dorothée Gunther created instructional books to teach them. Carl Orff came across an African **xylophone**, and developed a way to transform the xylophone into an instrument for the children at the school to play. He then developed the metal-barred **metallophones** from the idea of the Indonesian **gamelan** orchestra and the German **glockenspiels**, which were small metal-plated instruments found in Germany. Thus the **instrumentarium** was born—the complete set of which includes bass bars, bass, alto/tenor, and soprano metallophones, xylophones and alto and soprano glockenspiels. While each instrument is limited in range to fewer than two octaves, all together, from bass bars to soprano glockenspiel, the ensemble covers six octaves, creating an entire orchestra!

Soprano Glockenspiel Range (C7–A9)

Soprano Xylophone–Soprano Metallophone–Alto Glockenspiel Range (C5–A7)

Alto Xylophone–Alto Metallophone Range (C4 [Middle C]–A6)

Bass Xylophone–Bass Metallophone (C3–A5)

Contra Bass Bar Range (C2–C3)

The Orff Instrumentarium

Patterned accompaniments

Orff believed that one of the easiest ways to encourage student participation in music while also contributing to beautiful music-making is to have them play a simple accompaniment on a xylophone. By second grade, most students will be able to keep a steady beat, with a fair number able to do so by first grade. Below are some basic accompaniment patterns on the xylophone or metallophone that students should be able to perform easily.

Bordun/Chord Bordun: An open 5th, containing the 1st and 5th degrees of the chord. The 3rd is not played. For example, a bordun in C will include the two pitches C and G; in F, the F and C; in G the G and D; in d minor the d and a, etc. A chord bordun means that the 1st and 5th degrees are played simultaneously.

Example of Bass Bordun With Introduction and Simple Pentatonic Melody

Broken Bordun: The notes of the bordun are played separately.

Moving/Broken Chord Bordun

Example of Moving Chord Bordun With "Lil' Liza Jane" Melody

Level Bordun: The bordun plays in different octaves.

Crossover Bordun: The mallets cross over to play the pattern.

Drone: A note or chord continuously sounding without change. A bordun functions as a type of drone.

Ostinato: Motif or phrase that repeats.

Orff as arts integration

One of Orff Schulwerk's major contributions is its emphasis on arts integration. Orff includes language (stories, poetry, rhythmic speech), movement (dance, improvisation), and drama as well as music.

The Orff process

The American adaptation of Orff Schulwerk utilizes four stages to organize the process of teaching music: imitation, exploration, improvisation, and composition. These four stages establish the fundamental building blocks for children to develop musical literacy. They are similar to Bloom's taxonomy, in that they begin by introducing a very basic skill set and then gradually move on to more complex activities such as composition, which is represented in the upper phases of the taxonomy.

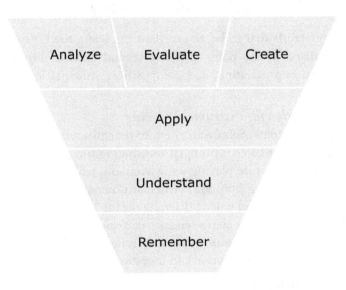

Source: Bloom's Cognitive Domain *by* user:Nesbit*, PD.*

Bloom's Taxonomy

Parallels between Orff's building blocks and Bloom's taxonomy

Orff's Building Blocks	Bloom's Taxonomy
Imitation	Remember
Exploration	Understand
Improvisation	Apply
Composition	Create, Analyze

Imitation: Echoing, responding

Imitation builds the student's repertoire of pitches, rhythms, meter, tempo, and dynamics. Students absorb the fundamental music materials for their "tool box" to be used in more complex activities in the future.

Exploration

Students begin to understand and even apply the knowledge learned through imitation. They hear the movement of pitches, the content of rhythms, the movement of meter, and explore the timbre of whatever instrument or voice with which they have access. The Orff Instrumentarium provides almost limitless possibilities for exploration.

Improvisation

After exploration and imitation, students not only understand, but also can apply some of the possible combinations of rhythms and pitches, form and dynamics, etc., within a musical framework.

Composition

Composing is a pinnacle of music-making in that the composer must also analyze the musical material s/he is working with in order to create a new piece.

Applying the Orff approach developmentally

Schulwerk understands that to be an excellent musician, the art form must be highly familiar and internalized to the point of being second nature. Through the practice of imitation, exploration, improvisation, and composition, students learn what music is by performing.

Step 1: Preparation for instrument playing

Before playing instruments, Schulwerk requires that all sounds be internalized, or practiced on and in the body. The voice is primary, and singing songs and speaking and creating poems should be mastered before playing an instrument, which is seen as an activity that extends the body. Before playing a bordun on an instrument, the musician should be able to simultaneously sing a melody and patsch (literally means "smack" in German, but refers to patting legs with an open hand) or clap a separate part such as a bordun as body percussion.

The Orff method makes use of nursery rhymes, folktales, folksongs, folkdances, and authentic, classical compositions—all music and literature of primary importance and quality.

Step 2: Body percussion

Orff also made use of body percussion—i.e. use of snap, clap, patsch, and stamping. The use of body percussion is not only a helpful stage towards externalizing rhythm before instrument playing, but when coupled with singing or rhythmic speaking, it allows practice towards the type of multitasking required to perform multiple parts, e.g., harmony, polyphony, and so forth.

Body percussion is usually written in a four-line staff, which includes (ST = stamp, P = patsch, CL = clap, and FN or SN for snap).

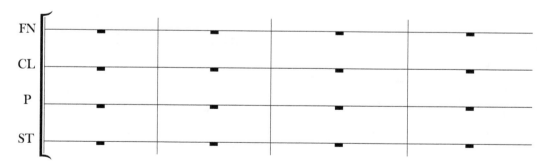

Patsching, which is done on the lap, and snapping can have markings indicating which hand should be used, right or left. For patsching or snapping, if there is no R or L indicated, both hands play simultaneously.

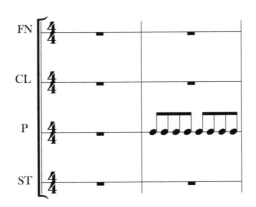

Body Percussion Examples

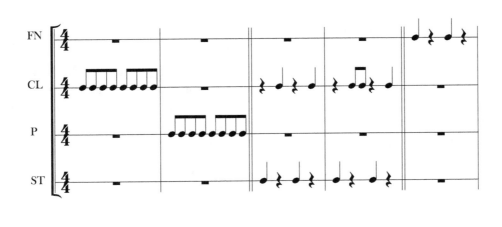

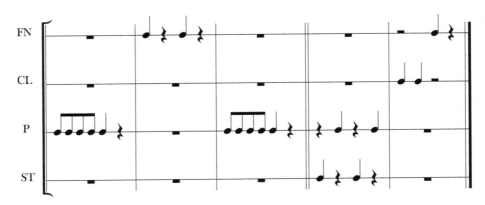

Simple Rhyme With Basic Body Percussion

One Two Three

A good way to internalize the rhythm is to by first learning the rhyme, then adding the body percussion. After that, gradually drop the lyrics one measure at a time (either from the beginning to the end or from the end to the beginning) so that children end up only performing the body percussion, as the following example shows.

One two three ≹	Johnny caught a flea ≹	Flea died Johnny cried,	"tee, hee, hee" ≹
One two three ≹	Johnny caught a flea ≹	Flea died Johnny cried,	♩ ♩ ♩ ≹
One two three ≹	Johnny caught a flea ≹	♩ ♩ ♪♪ ♩	♩ ♩ ♩ ≹
One two three ≹	♪♪ ♪♪ ♩ ≹	♩ ♩ ♪♪ ♩	♩ ♩ ♩ ≹
♩ ♩ ♩ ≹	♪♪ ♪♪ ♩ ≹	♩ ♩ ♪♪ ♩	♩ ♩ ♩ ≹

Extension: Small groups can also perform this as a round with each group starting one measure apart.

Body percussion can become increasingly challenging as well. The next step would be to say (or sing) a rhyme along with an ostinato. The "One two three" rhyme, for example, uses all four maintypes of body percussion—stamping, clapping, patsching, and snapping—but not all of the types of body percussion need to be incorporated.

Jack and Jill

English nursery rhyme, 1760s

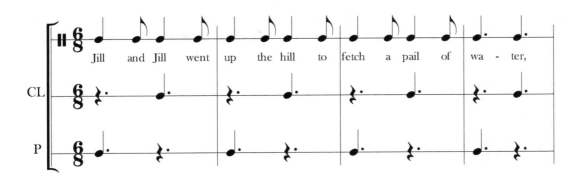

Jill and Jill went up the hill to fetch a pail of wa - ter,

CL

P

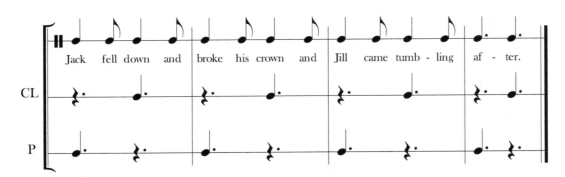

Jack fell down and broke his crown and Jill came tumb - ling af - ter.

CL

P

An even more challenging and creative way to use body percussion is to create onomatopoeia in accordance with the lyrics, mimicking or relating to the sounds presented in the rhyme. For example, in the rhyme "Banbury Cross," the patching eighth notes in measures 3 and 4 could be mimicking the hoofbeats of the horse. Also, the finger snaps in measure 5 indicate the rings-on-her-fingers line and likewise the stomps fit the bells-on-her-toes line. There is no right or wrong way to add body percussion to enhance the rhyme; it is all in the ear of the beholder!

By Stratford490 [CC BY-SA 3.0 or GFDL], via Wikimedia Commons

The Fine Lady statue at Banbury Cross, Oxfordshire

Ride a Cock Horse to Banbury Cross

English Rhyme, 1780

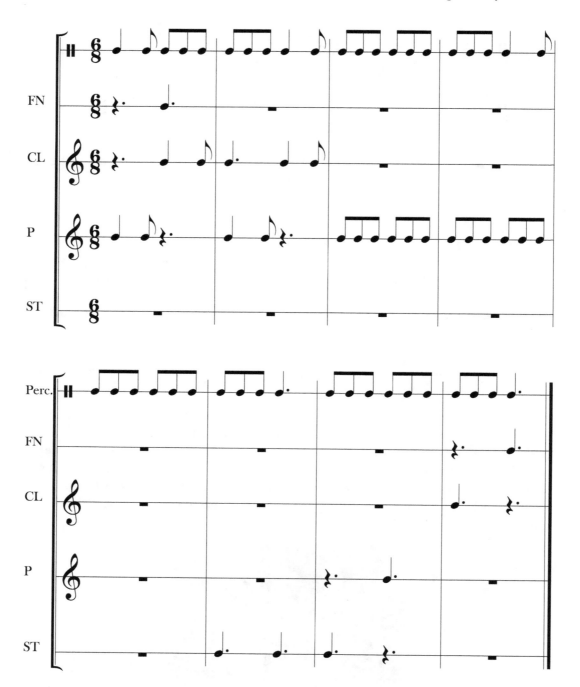

Activity 4A

TRY THIS

Select a nursery rhyme. Say it a few times as rhythmically as possible. Then create a simple body percussion accompaniment such as patsch clap, patsch clap. Now try to vary the accompaniment to highlight or mimic the lyrics in some way.

Orff Improvisation

Schulwerk's elemental music is based on both experimentation and improvisation, allowing children to explore the tones, rhythms, and timbres of music from their own abilities and creative perspectives. To this end, Orff created frameworks or pathways to help children experiment without pressure or stress.

The easiest way to experiment on the Orff instruments is to begin with the **pentatonic scale**, a scale with only five pitches. The pentatonic scale may be **major** or **minor**. For a major pentatonic scale, have children remove the F and B bars from their instrument leacing them with C, D, E, G, and A. This allows them to create beautiful music beginning and ending on C without having to worry about not sounding beautiful or making mistakes. For the minor pentatonic scale, keep the same five pitches, but begin and end on A.

Pentatonic Scales

Major Pentatonic (C Major)

Major Pentatonic (F Major)

This is an example of F Major Pentatonic in the folk song "Great Big House."

Great Big House in New Orleans

Minor Pentatonic (D minor)

This is an example of D Minor Pentatonic in the folk song "My Paddle's Keen and Bright."

My Paddle's Keen and Bright

Margaret Embers McGee (1889-1975), 1918

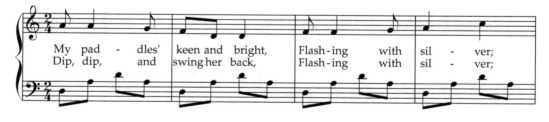

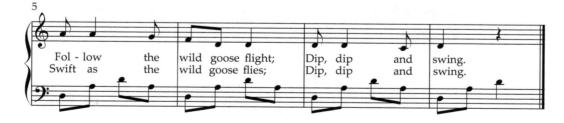

Modes

Orff also made use of modes, which are types of scales with non-musical characteristics. The Greeks used modes such as Lydian (F to F on the white keys of a piano), Dorian (D to D on the white keys), Aeolian (A to A on the white keys or the natural minor scale), and Mixolydian (G to G on the white keys).

Lydian Mode

This is an example of Lydian mode in the "Simpson's Theme Song" by Danny Elfman.

Simpson's Theme Song (excerpt)

Dorian Mode

This is an example of Dorian mode in "Scarborough Fair," an English folk song.

Scarborough Fair (excerpt)

Pars - ley, sage, rose - ma - ry and thyme.

Aeolian Mode (also known as the natural minor scale)

This is an example of Aeolian mode in the American folk song "Aeolian Lullaby."

Aeolian Lullaby

Go to sleep - y ba - by, loo loo loo loo loo,

Close your eyes and go to sleep, while I sing to you.

Mixolydian Mode

This is an example of Mixolydian mode in "Norwegian Wood" by Lennon/McCartney.

Norwegian Wood (excerpt)

These modes are easily performed on the xylophone and beautiful and interesting in their construction. In particular, they can raise a child's awareness of different moods and aesthetics, allowing them new modes through which to experiment with self-expression and also new material with which to enhance stories and narratives.

Activity 4B

TRY THIS

The easiest way to experiment with modes is to begin and end on the pitches outlined above. Try experimenting with the Dorian D-to-D scale or Mixolydian G-to-G scale.

Speech and drama

Both Orff and Kodály techniques allow children to experiment with language to feel comfortable with their own internal speech and body rhythms. Creating poems or speech pieces and adding dynamics, musical instruments/timbres, playing with form (adding a musical introduction, bordun, etc.), and then acting them out enables a child's creative process through language.

Adding music to drama

Taking a story and adding sound effects, **leitmotifs**, instruments, vocal sounds, body percussion, and actors and/or a narrator also brings literature to life. The goal of a leitmotif is to help the listener identify a main character or theme in the story. For example, characters and themes are given a short musical pattern, and every time that character or theme appears, the musical pattern is performed. Also, sound effects are added to enhance the action or bring a fuller meaning or experience. For example, if the story speaks of a bell chiming, play a bell peal on the glockenspiels for older children's response, or more minimally, hit a triangle. Excellent stories for this type of activity include folk tales or fairy tales from around the world. (See Chapter 12 on Integration for an example).

Activity 4C

TRY THIS

Use basic instruments to experiment with creating or changing the mood. For pre-school and lower elementary students, use a small instrument such as a glockenspiel to play soft, slow music to set the mood for naptime or to quiet children down for a transition to a new activity. Perform an energetic rhythm on a drum to engage children to move or prepare for a more rigorous physical transition.

QUICK PLAY TIP

The easiest way to make beautiful music on one of the Orff instruments is to remove the "F" and "B" bars and then play on the remaining notes. Anything you play will sound wonderful!

The Kodály Method

It is a long accepted truth that singing provides the best start to music education; moreover, children should learn to read music before they are provided with any instrument… Even the most talented artist can never overcome the disadvantages of an education without singing. (Kodály, 1974, p. 201, 204)

Kodály's Philosophy

The Kodály philosophy of music education supports music's role in the intellectual, emotional, physical, social, and spiritual development of every child. A central tenet of the Kodály approach is that music belongs to everyone—that an education in music is the right of every human being and cannot be left to chance.

Zoltán Kodály (1882–1967) was an ethnomusicologist and composer from Hungary. He was appalled by children's poor singing quality, and began to create teaching methods to improve it. His approach was highly sequential. He began with sight-reading and mastering basic rhythms and pitches that gradually increased step by step to become more complex, sometimes by adding only one new note or rhythmic value at a time.

Kodály was also appalled at the type of songs and repertoire children were learning in school, and began to focus on utilizing authentic folk music and composed music of excellent quality through which to teach children.

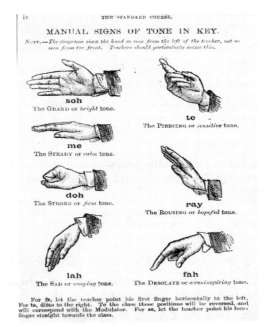

"Curwen Hand Signs" *from* *The Standard Course of Lessons and Exercises* by John Curwen. *PD-US.*

Depiction of Curwen's Solfege hand signs. This version includes the tonal tendencies and interesting titles for each tone.

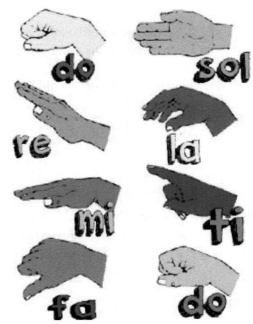

Figure 5. Kodály Hand signs adopted from Curwen

Kodály hand signs

Although he did not invent the hand signs, Kodály did make alterations based on two previously established hand sign systems—Sarah Glover's Norwich sol-fa (1845) and John Curwen's tonic sol-fa (1858). The hand signs are very much associated with the Kodály method, which uses the hand signs to help children visualize the spatial relationship between notes. This aids in proper and correct on-pitch singing as well as sight reading and ear training.

Positioning the hand signs

When using hand signs, the low Do should be placed at your waist or midsection, with the upper Do at about eye-level. The other hand signs are placed equidistantly between the two Do's.

Solfege in Kodály

Although solfege singing was around long before Kodály, he became known for it as he used it extensively in his sight-singing system exercises and throughout his method. Solfege corresponds to the notes of the major scale, using the syllables Do, Re, Mi, Fa, Sol, La, and Ti. These words are often abbreviated to D, R, M, F, S, L, T, and D.

In terms of notation, Kodály's exercises do not have to use the regular musical staff. Instead, exercises and even songs can be written out using just the D, R, and M, etc., with the rhythm notated about it.

For example, the song "Mary Had a Little Lamb" would look like this.

M R D R | M M M | R R R | M S S
M R D R | M M M M | R R M R | D

Use of the solfege is a highly effective way to teach children that music or notes are separate entities from lyrics. Teaching a song using solfege rather than the lyrics helps the listener hear patterns and intervals, and even understand phrases and form that otherwise might be obscured by lyrics.

Solfege teaching sequence

Kodály singing technique begins with the child practicing only a few pitches and mastering them before moving on to another note; e.g., beginning with only a minor 3rd interval of Sol and Mi, and gradually adding the La after the Sol and Mi are mastered. Gradually, the child will expand the number of pitches learned to include the major pentatonic scale (Do, Re, Mi, Sol, La), and minor pentatonic scale (La, Do, Re, Mi, S).

Kodály Exercise Examples

After these are mastered, the student is introduced to all of the diatonic pitches (Do, Re, Mi, Fa, Sol, La, Ti, etc.) and then the accidentals.

Repertoire

Kodály was not only a composer and musicologist, but an early ethnomusicologist. He collected dozens of folk songs from his native Hungary and used them in his method. When using the Kodály method in the U.S., American folk songs are used.

Love Somebody, Yes I Do

American folk song

On Top of Old Smoky

Appalachian courting song

The Kodály Song Web contains hundreds of American and other folk songs from around the world, as well as musical information on every song to help teachers learn and teach them.

Kodály rhythm syllables

Kodály also incorporates rhythmic syllables in his method. These syllables are based on the work of Emile-Joseph Chêvé, a French theoretician. These syllables are taught sequentially as well, and begin from basic note values (i.e., quarter notes) up to more complex combinations.

ta	I	ta-ah-ah	♩.
ti-ti	⊓	ta-ah-ah-ah	○
tri-o-la	⊓⊓	syn-co-pa	⌐I ⌐
tiri-tiri	⊓⊓	tai ti	I. ⌐
tiri-ti	⊓⊓	ti tai	⌐I.
ti-tiri	⊓⊓	tim-ri	⌐⌐
ta-ah	♩	ri-tim	⊓.

Kodály rhythm syllables

Movement in Kodály

Although he was mostly known for popularizing the solfege hand signs and rhythm syllables, Kodály recognized the value of bodily movement as well. He was inspired by Swiss educator Emile-Jacques Dalcroze's use of movement (see below), and incorporated walking, running, and clapping into his teaching strategies.

READ MORE EXPLORING KODÁLY: PHILOSOPHIES, MATERIALS AND PEDAGOGY (DR. PATTYE CESAROW)

Edwin Gordon

Edwin Gordon developed his Music Learning Theory after years of music research and studies. Music Learning Theory explores how we learn when we're learning music. Like many other researchers before him, Gordon realized we are lacking in terminology to explain all of the complex processes that go on with music learning and listening. Gordon's main concept is called **audiation,** which he defines as "hearing and comprehending in one's mind the sound of music that is not, or may never have been, physically present" (2007, p. 399).

Philosophy

According to Gordon, we are each born with music aptitude. As with other human learning potentials, there is a wide range of music aptitude levels distributed among the human population. Moreover, both music aptitude and music achievement are dependent on audiation; i.e., our music learning potentials and our music learning achievements are based on our music thinking. Most importantly, music thinking goes beyond mere imitation and leads to music comprehension (2007).

Gordon's Skill Learning Sequence is based on two main categories of learning: Discrimination and Inference. Discrimination learning occurs by rote, and occurs when a teacher teaches the basic building blocks of music—vocabulary and aural and rhythmic patterns. Inference learning occurs conceptually, where the student is able to identify, create, and improvise with musical materials already learned. The student at this point is discovering music on his or her own.

Rhythmic learning concerns understanding three basic concepts: the macrobeat, the microbeat, and melodic rhythm. Macrobeats are those we feel as main beats or longer beats such as when we're dancing. In 4/4 or 2/4 time, for example, the macrobeat is represented by quarter notes, while in 3/4 time it is represented by the dotted half.

Examples of Macrobeats

Microbeats are shorter than macrobeats and represent the equal division of the macrobeat. In 4/4 or 2/4 time, microbeats would be represented by the eighth notes, while in 3/4 time microbeats would be represented by the quarter notes.

Examples of Microbeats

Melodic rhythm refers to any rhythmic patterns in a piece. Rhythms can relate to the melody or text from a piece of music. Similar to Kodály, Gordon also used two types of solfege—tonal solfege (do, re, mi, etc.) for the pitches and rhythm solfege for rhythm (du de, du de, etc. to represent duple meter, and du da di, du da di to represent triple).

His approach begins on a holistic level, where the student experiences the whole song, piece, and so forth; applies analysis; and then re-experiences the whole again but now through the lens of having analyzed the inner workings in detail.

Similar to other sequenced learning approaches, such as Vygotsky's Zone of Proximal Development or scaffolding, Gordon's approach relies on a gradual increase in skill level difficulty as the student progresses. For example, because improvising music is far more complex than imitating basic patterns, the latter is required in order to perform the former. This "Whole-Part-Whole" process recommends first engaging in generalized activities to "experience the whole," then progressing to "Study the parts," finally returning again to the entire piece of music (Valerio, n.d.)

READ MORE THE GORDON APPROACH

Dalcroze

Emile-Jacques Dalcroze is a Swiss educator best known for eurhythmics, which incorporates rhythm, structure, and musical expression with movement. The ultimate goal is to develop total cognitive and kinesthetic awareness through sound. The music acts as a stimulus to which the body responds, after which sensation returns to the brain to form emotions, which deepens the significance of the experience.

Philosophy

The Dalcroze philosophy centers on the concept that the synthesis of the mind, body, and resulting emotions is fundamental to all meaningful learning. Plato said in his Laws: "Education has two branches, one of gymnastics, which is concerned with the body, and the other of music, which is designed for the improvement of the soul" (Pennington, 1925, p. 9). Emile-Jaques Dalcroze believed that every musician should strive to be sensitive and expressive, and to express music through purposeful movement, sound, thought, feeling, and creativity.

Mead (1994) cites four basic premises that encapsulate the Dalcroze philosophy:
1. Eurhythmics awakens the physical, aural, and visual images of music in the mind.
2. Solfege (sight singing and ear training), improvisation, and eurhythmics together work to improve expressive musicality and enhance intellectual understanding.
3. Music may be experienced through speech, gesture, and movement.
4. These can likewise be experienced in time, space, and energy. Humans learn best when learning through multiple senses. Music should be taught through the tactile, kinesthetic, aural, and visual senses.

The Dalcroze approach is based on eurhythmics, which teaches rhythm, structure, and musical expression through music. Eurhythmics begins with ear training, or solfege, to develop the inner musical ear. This differs from Kodály's use of solfege in that it is always combined with movement. Another component of the method concerns **improvisation**, which helps students sharpen their spontaneous reactions and physical responses to music.

Types of movement

Each movement involves **time, space,** and **force,** and all three should be taken into account when moving, paying close attention to the musical attributes of the movement. **Time:** Tempo (rate of speed) and duration (fast, moderate, slow)
- **Space:** Direction, distance covered, level, dimension (large, small), path (straight, twisted), and focus
- **Force:** Energy or power expended, quality of the movement, and any adjectives to describe the movement (e.g., heavy, light, sharp, energetic, gentle)

Movement that stays stationary is called **non-locomotor,** while movement that moves through space is **locomotor.**
- **Non-locomotor** (movement in place):
  - Stretch, curl, clap, snap, patsch, tap, stomp, twist, turn, conduct, sway, jump, bend, speak, stretch, swing, reach
- **Locomotor** (movement through space):
  - Walk, slide, skip, run, leap, gallop, hop, jump, slither, creep, roll, jog

Regardless of the type, movements should above all be musical. Movements should also be focused and thoughtful; i.e. preparation should occur before each movement; the movement should take into account the full length of the beat; and the movement should return back to pre-preparation status. It is essential that the movement coordinate with the beat of the music, the rhythm, and the phrasing (depending on the exercise).

Dalcroze's exercises are always sequential, beginning with the simplest and becoming more complex as students master and develop their skills. Children are introduced to key musical elements such as meter, dynamics, rhythms, tempo, duration, melody, form, phrase, and pitch.

Types of eurhythmics

There are four types of basic eurhythmic exercises:
1. Follow
2. Quick reaction
3. Interrupted canon
4. Canon

1. A **follow** exercise is a basic music-movement response exercise. Students physically respond to the sounds they hear.

Examples:

Students walk to the beat of music (piano, drum, etc.) and respond to changes of tempo (speeding up or slowing down), rhythms (walking on quarter notes, running on eighth notes, skipping on dotted rhythms), etc.

2. A **quick reaction** exercise requires students to respond to verbal signals or cues.

Examples:

Students move while the music is playing and freeze when the music stops or the teacher yells out a command. Students also can change their movements on a given signal, such as switching from a loco-motor to a non-loco-motor when they hear a drum beat or chime or when the music stops.

3. An **interrupted canon** is similar to an "echo" where students imitate or echo a beat, pattern, etc. The interrupted canon is a preparatory exercise for the canon.

Examples:

Students hear a rhythm and then echo it back on their body (lap, clap, etc.).

4. A **canon** requires students to echo back a pattern, but one measure later. While they are performing their pattern, they are simultaneously listening and memorizing the new pattern.

Examples:

The teacher claps patterns. Students respond one measure later while continually absorbing the pattern currently being performed. Pass the pattern: A more challenging version of this is to have students form two straight lines. The teacher stands in front and "passes" a pattern to the first student in one of the lines. That student then "passes" it to their partner across the aisle, who then passes it across the aisle, etc. All the while, new patterns are being formed and passed.

Dalcroze movement requires that children listen and respond simultaneously. The music mirrors the physical motions expected. For example, music for walking or marching is in duple meter and uses steady quarter notes, running music contains eighth notes, skipping music uses dotted rhythms, jumping music contains large interval leaps, and so forth.

Examples of music for Dalcroze movement exploration

READ MORE THE DALCROZE APPROACH

Reggio Emilia

Although not an approach to music teaching in and of itself, this popular educational method is worth exploring in its relation to music education. The basic approach utilizes discovery in terms of music learning, and also is synchronous with many of the 21st-century learning approaches discussed in Chapter 1.

1. The child as the creator of his/her own learning
2. The child and adult as researchers
3. The environment as the third teacher
4. Documentation as communication
5. The 100 expressive languages of children
6. The dialogue between child and adult
7. Collaborative work (Smith, 2011)

Suzuki

> I want to make good citizens. If a child hears fine music from the day of his birth and learns to play it himself, he develops sensitivity, discipline and endurance. He gets a beautiful heart.
>
> —Shin'ichi Suzuki

More than 50 years ago, Japanese violinist Shin'ichi Suzuki realized the musical implication of the fact that all children learn to speak their native language with ease. He began to apply the basic principles of language acquisition to music learning, and called his method the **mother-tongue approach.**

Suzuki understood that making good musicians requires investment in developing the whole child - from their morality to their character and ability to be good citizens. Only in this larger context can the child focus on developing their musical ability. The ideas of parent responsibility, loving encouragement, constant repetition, etc., are some of the special features of the Suzuki approach.

When a child learns language, they undergo a very extensive form of enculturation. They begin by listening and repeating, mastering the linguistic process step-by-step. They have to then memorize, build vocabulary, and are motivated by environmental, cultural and social factors, including that of love. To learn music using the Suzuki approach, the child must replicate the steps of language learning by listening to excellent recordings so that beautiful music becomes part of their natural environment. Recordings also provide inspiration, and lay the groundwork for understanding music's vocabulary and structure. Parental involvement is also key to the student's success, and parents provide daily motivation, encouragement, and support. Parents often learn the instrument along with the child, acting as musical role models, and maintaining a positive learning atmosphere for the child to succeed.

Resources

Organization of American Kodály Educators https://oake.org/default.aspx

The Dalcroze Society of America http://www.dalcrozeusa.org/

The Gordon Institute for Music Learning http://giml.org/

The American Orff-Schulwerk Association http://www.aosa.org/

The Suzuki Association of the Americas http://suzukiassociation.org/teachers/twinkler/

Alliance for Active Music Making http://www.allianceamm.org/

References

Orff

Campbell, P. S. (2008). *Musician and teacher*. New York: W.W. Norton and Company.

Goodkin, D. (2004). *Play, sing and dance: an introduction to Orff Schulwerk*. New York: Schott Music Publishers.

Gray, E. (1995). Orff-Schulwerk: Where did it come from? *The Orff Beat-Centenary Issue* XXIV (June 1995). Victorian Orff Schulwerk Association. 03 May 2009 http://www.vosa.org/aboutorff/?pageID=14

Orff, C. (1963). "Orff Schulwerk: Past and Future." Speech. Opening of the Orff Institute in Salzburg, October 25. Trans. Margaret Murray.

Orff, C., & Keetman, G. (1976). *Music for children (Vols. 1-5)* (M. Murray, Trans.). London: Schott & Co. (Original work published 1950-1954).

Shamrock, M. (1997). "Orff-Schulwerk: An integrated method. *Music Educator's Journal, 83*, 41–44.

Dalcroze

Abramson, R. M. (1980). Dalcroze-based improvisation. *Music Educators Journal, 66*(5), 62–68.

Anderson, W. T. (2012). The Dalcroze approach to music education: Theory and Application. *General Music Today, 26*(1), 27–33.

Aronoff, F. W. (1983). Dalcroze strategies for music learning in the classroom. *International Journal of Music Education, 2*, 23–25.

Bachmann, M. L. (1991). *Dalcroze today: An education through and into music* (D. Parlett, Trans.). New York: Oxford University Press.

Boyarsky, T. L. (1989). Dalcroze eurhythmics: An approach to early training of the nervous system. *Seminars in Neurology, 9*, 105–114.

Bugos, K. M. (2011). *New York State early-career teachers' selection and use of pedagogical approaches in elementary general music*. Ph.D. dissertation, University of New York at Buffalo, New York. Dissertation & Theses: 3475296.

Caldwell, T. (1992). *Dalcroze eurhythmics* [videorecording]. Chicago: GIA Publications.

Dale, M. (2000). *Eurhythmics for young children: Six lessons for fall*. Ellicott City, MD: MusiKinesis.

Driver, E. (1951). *A pathway to Dalcroze eurhythmics.* London: T. Nelson and Sons.

Findlay, E. (1971). *Rhythm and movement: Applications of Dalcroze eurhythmics.* Secaucus, NJ: Summy Birchard.

Jaques-Dalcroze, E. (1920). *The Jaques-Dalcroze method of eurhythmics: Rhythmic movement* (Vols. 1 & 2). London: Novello.

Leck, H., & Frego, R. J. D. (2005). *Creating artistry through movements.* (DVD). Milwaukee, WI: Hal Lenard. #08744511. ISBN: 0634098381.

Mead, V. H. (1994). *Dalcroze eurhythmics in today's music classroom.* New York: Schott Music Corporation.

Pennington, J. (1925). *The importance of being rhythmic.* New York: Knickerbocker Press.

Zachopoulou, E., Drri, V., Chatzopoulou, D., & Elinoudis, T. (2003). The application of Orff and Dalcroze activities in preschool children: Do they affect the level of rhythmic ability? *Physical Educator, 60*(2), 51–58.

Kodály

Choksy, L. (1981). *The Kodály context: Creating an environment for musical learning.* Englewood Cliffs, NJ: Prentice-Hall.

Choksy, L. (1999). *The Kodály method I: Comprehensive music education.* Upper Saddle River, NJ: Prentice-Hall.

Kodály, Z. (1965). *Let us sing correctly.* London: Boosey & Hawkes.

Kodály, Z. (1974). *The selected writings of Zoltán Kodály.* (Lily Halápy and Fred Macnicol, Trans.). London: Boosey & Hawkes.

Kodály, Z. (1965). *333 elementary exercises.* London: Boosey & Hawkes.

Kodály song web. (n.d.). Retrieved from http://www.kodalysongweb.net/songs

Shehan, P. K. (1986). Major approaches to music education: An account of method. *Music Educator's Journal*, February 72(6), 26–31.

Trinka, J. (n.d.). The Kodály approach. Retrieved from http://www.allianceamm.org/resources/dalcroze/

Gordon

Gordon, E. E. (2007). *Learning sequences in music: A contemporary music learning theory.* Chicago, IL: GIA.

Valerio, W. (n.d.). "The Gordon approach: Music learning theory." *The Alliance for Active Music Making.* Retrieved from http://www.allianceamm.org/resources/gordon/.

Suzuki

Scott, L. (1992). Attention and perseverance behaviors of preschool children enrolled in Suzuki violin lessons and other activities. *Journal of Research in Music Education, 40*, 225–235.

Suzuki, S. (1993). *Nurtured by love: The classic approach to talent education.* 2nd ed. New York: Alfred Music.

Suzuki, S., & Nagata, M. (1999). *Ability development from age zero.* NY: Alfred Music.

Reggio Emilia

Crisp, B. ,& Caldwell, L. (2007). Orff-Schulwerk and the Reggio approaches are interwoven successfully. *The Orff Echo, 39*(3), 26–30.

Edwards, C., Gandini, L., & Forman, G. (1998). Introduction: Background and starting points. In *The hundred languages of children: The Reggio Emilia approach—Advanced reflections* (5–26) (2nd ed.). Greenwich, CT: Ablex Publishing.

Smith, A. P. (2011). The incorporation of principles of the Reggio Emilia approach in a North American pre-school music curriculum: An action research. *Visions of Research in Music Education, 17* .

General Reference

Chosky, L., Abramson, R., Gillespie, A., Woods, D., & York, F. (2000). *Teaching music in the twenty-first century* (2nd ed.). Upper Saddle River, NJ: Pearson.

Alliance for Active Music Making. (n.d.). Retrieved from http://www.allianceamm.org/resources_elem_Orff.html

Moore, J. (n.d.). Philosophy of the Alliance for Active Music Making. Retrieved from http://www.allianceamm.org/philosophy/

Vocabulary

canon (Dalcroze): a eurhythmic exercise in which students echo back a pattern, but one measure later, and while they are performing their pattern, they are simultaneously listening and memorizing a new pattern

Curwen hand signs: hand symbols developed to represent the notes of the scale; i.e., do, re, mi, fa, sol, la, ti, do

drone: a continuous low tone produced by the bass pipes or bass strings of musical instruments

elemental music (Orff): is pattern-based music built on natural speech and body rhythms, familiar melodic patterns, and simple forms that can be readily understood and performed by children without extensive musical training

eurhythmics (Dalcroze): a method of instruction developed by Dalcroze to introduce rhythm, structure, and musical expression through movement; the ultimate goal of the method is to develop total cognitive and kinesthetic awareness through sound

follow (Dalcroze): a basic eurhythmics exercise in which the students physically respond to the sounds they hear

force: strength, energy, power, intensity

instrumentarium (Orff): instruments used to play Orff music

interrupted canon (Dalcroze): a eurhythmic exercise in which students imitate or echo a beat or pattern; a preparatory exercise for the canon

locomotor: movement through space

metallophone: any musical instrument consisting of a graduated series of metal parts that can be struck by hammers operated manually or played with a keyboard

mother-tongue approach (Suzuki): children are influenced by their surroundings with fine music

movement: moving the body to go with the rhythm or sound of the music

non-locomotor: movement in place

ostinato: a constantly recurring melodic fragment

quick reaction (Dalcroze): a eurhythmic exercise in which students react to verbal signs or cues

rhythm syllables: rhythm representations developed by Kodály

solfege: a syllable system used for sight singing; each note of the scale is represented by a syllable: do, re, mi, fa, sol, la, ti, do

space: the portion or extent of this in a given instance; the designed and structured surface of a picture

time: a limited period or interval, as between two successive events

xylophone: a musical instrument consisting of a graduated series of wooden bars usually sounded by striking with small wooden hammers

Chapter 5

Children Singing and Children's Songs

Chapter Objective: One of the most basic yet challenging activities to do with children is to teach them a song. This chapter focuses on the child's singing voice, including their vocal range, selection of appropriate musical material, and methods for teaching a song in a musically meaningful, cognitively stimulating way that lays the groundwork for future integration.

I. A Child's Voice

One common mistake that adults make when singing with children is that they tend to "pitch" the songs, (or sing them in a key), that is comfortable for themselves, but unfortunately, out of a comfortable singing range for the children. Adults sing in much lower range than children, therefore pitching a song too low causes children to be unsuccessful at reaching some of the lower notes.

Pitching a song in the wrong range can have significant negative consequences on a child's musical self-esteem. An incorrect key can take away the child's ability to sing the song well or sing the song at all. Singing in a key that is out of a child's range would be analogous to an art teacher giving a creative assignment to students and then placing all of the art materials up on a shelf out of reach for most of them. While a few might be tall enough, most won't be. After a while, they will give up trying to reach the material altogether. Similarly, these are the students who start to believe that they can't sing at all, and give up on music.

Good Singing

Although we are used to hearing and singing pop music, a child's voice is not yet ready to sing songs either with such a wide vocal range or with the sophisticated vocal stylings or timbre that he or she might try to imitate from pop singers. As children's voices are very light, they should not be pushed out of their vocal ranges too soon. Using a clear, clean, straight head voice rather than chest voice will help to avoid this, and will strengthen a child's vocal musculature for a lifetime of excellent singing.

One good habit to help children sing well is to ask them sing in their **head voice** rather than their **chest voice**. Although most songs children hear are pop songs that are placed in the chest, a child's voice is not yet developed, and should not be belting out or pushing from the lower range or chest voice. Head voice requires placing the sound higher up in the "vocal mask" or the face, as if singing from the eyes. Chest voice feels like the sound is emanating from the chest, which tends to create a lot of tension in the throat, particularly in younger singers. The head voice is lighter, more tension-free, and more natural and therefore more beautiful sounding.

Children's Vocal Ranges

Below are the general ranges of a child's voice.

Preschool–Kindergarten (3–5 years old), C to A

First–third grade (6–8 years old) C to C'

Fourth–sixth grade (9–11 years old) Bflat to E'

The strongest notes in a child's vocal range are right in the middle of their range, around pitches F and G. While they may be able to hit higher or lower notes, these few notes are where they can sing the loudest and most comfortably.

Vocal Warm-Ups for Children

Activities for helping children explore their voices and find their head voice:

Speech warm-ups

Activities for exploring the child's voice and finding the child's head voice:
   Helping children find their head voice
- Have children imitate the sound of a:
  - Wolf, coyote, ghost, owl, siren, train whistle, wind
- Have them "read" abstract notation (lines, dots, squiggles) experimenting with different vocal sounds and timbres in their head voice.

• What does a blue squiggly line sound like? Green bumps? Red jagged mountains?

Warm-up 1

Abstract notation: Example 1

Warm-up 2

Abstract notation: Example 2

Warm-up 3

Abstract notation: Example 3

Help children find their different types of voices
• Outside, inside/speaking, whispering, singing voice
  • This is my outside voice! (shouting)
  • This is my inside voice (speaking).
  • This is my *whispering voice* (whispering).
  • This is my singing voice (sung on Sol Sol Mi, Sol Sol Mi).

This   is   my   sing - ing   voice
S   S   M   S   S   M

- High, low, whisper, projecting
  - I take my voice up high (low to high),
  - I take my voice down low (high to low).
  - I send my voice out into space and (shouting/projecting)
  - I whisper all around, whisper all around (whisper).
- High, low, medium
  - Bow wow says the dog (medium voice),
  - Meow, meow says the cat (high voice),
  - Grunt, grunt says the hog (low voice),
  - Squeak, squeak says the rat (very high voice).
- High, low, medium
  - You must pay the rent (low, Landlord).
  - But I can't pay the rent (high, young girl Tenant) (Repeat these first two lines 3 times).
  - I'll pay the rent (medium, young male, Hero).
  - My hero! (high)
  - Curses, foiled again (low).

Singing warm-ups

Doing warm-ups not only helps children explore their vocal range but expand it as well. As with all pitched warm-ups, start at the bottom of the range and move up in half-step increments and then back down. Some of the warm-ups are quite cognitively challenging.

Number the scale

This is a cognitively challenging exercise. The easiest way to sing it is to write the pattern for the exercise on the board, telling students that each number corresponds to a note on the major scale (1 = middle C, 2 = D, etc.). After singing from a low C to a high C, reverse the pyramid, and begin and high C and descend downward (i.e. 8, 878, 87678).

1 1
1 2 1
1 2 3 2 1
1 2 3 4 3 2 1
1 2 3 4 5 4 3 2 1
1 2 3 4 5 6 5 4 3 2 1
1 2 3 4 5 6 7 6 5 4 3 2 1
1 2 3 4 5 6 7 8 7 6 5 4 3 2 1

One, One, One, Two, One Vocal Warm-up

Bubble Gum Vocal Warm-up

Double bubble gum, double bubble gum, double bubble

gum, double bubble gum, double bubble gum, double

bubble gum, double bubble gum gum.

triple double bubble gum, triple double bubble gum,

triple double bubble gum, triple double bubble gum,

triple double bubble gum, triple double bubble gum,

triple double bubble gum gum.

Selecting and Performing Songs

Children are certainly capable of singing very complicated rhythms and melodies just by listening and aural imitation, but when selecting a song to sing, it is important to find a song that matches the **vocal range** and the **tessitura** of the children. A song's *range* concerns all of the notes in a song from lowest to highest, while the *tessitura* concerns the part of the register that contains the *most* tones of that melody. For example, you might have a song with a few pitches that are too high or too low for the child's voice, but the majority of the song lies within a proper singing range for the child. Consider the 1857 song "Here We Go Round the Mulberry Bush." The song contains a few notes on middle C, which is a bit low for young children, but the tessitura of the entire song contains notes from F to a C', all of which are easily accessible. The traditional Scottish folk song "My Bonnie Lies Over the Ocean" has a range of an entire octave from C to C', but most of the song lies within a Major 6th from E to C'.

My Bonnie Lies Over the Ocean

Scottish folk song

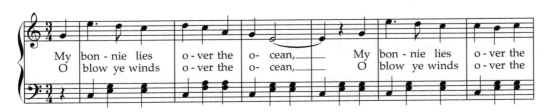

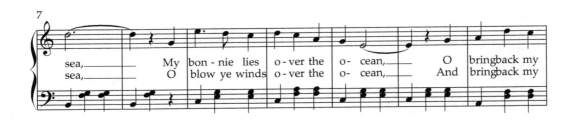

II. Teaching a Song at the Elementary Level

The Fundamentals of a Song

After finding songs with the appropriate range and tessitura, it is critical to analyze a few additional musical components before you teach it. The important things to assess are: the song's meter and then the phrases and sections of the song. The final step is to have the song down cold before attempting to teach it. The same goes for any material you want to teach children. If you yourself don't really know it, you will not be able to teach it successfully.

Finding a Song's Meter

If the song is notated, you can just look on the music to find the meter (e.g. 2/4, 3/4, 4/4, 6/8, etc.). However, if you don't have the song written in notation, you will need to determine the song's meter by ear. To find a song's meter, first find the downbeat (the strongest beat) and the weaker beats of each measure. Begin tapping on a desk while singing the song. If you tap slightly harder on the downbeat (the first beat of the group of two or three or six in each measure of the song) and begin singing, it will help you to find the meter. Groups of beats in Western music are mostly either in duple (two or four beats for a measure) or triple (three or six beats in a measure), so try tapping in groups of two first to see if that fits, and then try three.

For example, consider the song "Take Me Out to the Ballgame." Is it in duple or triple meter?

Sing and tap:		1	2	1	2	1	2	1	2
		>		>		>		>	
Then try:	1	2	3	1	2	3	1	2	3
		>			>			>	

Which meter fits the song better? The first is in duple, the second is in triple feel. The triple feel probably feels better—as it should because the song is in a 3/4 meter. In addition to the downbeat and meter, you will also need to determine whether the first note of the song begins directly on the downbeat or on a pickup. Songs that begin on a pickup (i.e., a note that is not on the first beat of the measure) are more difficult and require a stronger preparation from the teacher (for examples of this, see the section "Prepare" on page 104.)

Identifying the Sections of a Song

Children's songs are usually simple in form, often containing only one or two sections or parts; A one-part song (unitary) is designated with the letter A for purposes of analysis, while two-part songs (AB) are referred to as binary, verse-refrain, or verse-chorus. Songs in which the first section returns again at the end are known as ternary, three-part or ABA.

Examples of song forms:

1-part songs (A):
  a. "A Tisket, A Tasket"
  b. "Mary Had a Little Lamb"
  c. "The People on the Bus"
  d. "If You're Happy and you Know It"

2-part songs (AB)
  e. "Yankee Doodle"
  f. "Oh Susanna"
  g. "Home on the Range"
  h. "Oats, Peas, Beans and Barley Grow"
  i. "Erie Canal"

3-part songs (ABA)
  j. "Shoo-fly don't bother me"
  k. "Twinkle, Twinkle Little Star"
  l. "We Wish you a Merry Christmas"

Activity 5A

TRY THIS

Now try singing and tapping each line above while singing "Old MacDonald Had a Farm." Which meter best fits the song? Think of some other children's songs you know and sing them to find which meter is most appropriate.

Techniques for teaching a song

While it may seem quite intuitive to teach a song to children, there's actually a great deal to consider. The different ways to teach a song are related to children's different learning styles, such as *aural* and *visual* learning, and the child's appropriate cognitive development; e.g., age and grade development. The first method is to teach a song by rote, a technique also known as aural learning, or "by ear." Rote usually requires a great deal of repetition. The second method is a hybrid known as rote-note, where the song is taught mostly by ear, but also involves the addition of some type of visual element, such as showing some notation. The third method is known as note, which is teaching the song using written in notation (e.g. sheet music). These three styles of teaching not only relate to aural and visual learners, but also correlate to the basic cognitive development theories of Jerome Bruner's *modes of representation* and Jean Piaget's *four stages of cognitive development*.

Song teaching styles

Song Teaching Style	Primary Learning Style	Developmental Level	Bruner	Piaget
Rote/Aural Teaching (Sing by ear, no notation)	Aural	Any age, but appropriate for early childhood	Enactive (action-based)	Sensorimotor (learning through senses)
Rote-Note Teaching (Mostly aural, partial notation)	Aural-Visual	Appropriate for lower elementary students (K–2)	Iconic (image-based)	Pre-Operational
Note Teaching (Teaching a song through written notation)	Visual	Appropriate for upper elementary (3–6)	Symbolic (language-based)	Concrete Operational

Rote/aural teaching is **enactive** (action-based) and can be used at any age through adulthood, but is particularly appropriate for preschool through early childhood (into the lower elementary grades). Motor skills can be added to a song to increase the learning dimensions.

Rote-note teaching is partially **iconic** (image-based) and appropriate for lower elementary students (K–2) just learning to read as it involves some type of iconic or image-based representation of music, such as using abstract notation or modified rhythmic or pitch notation.

Note teaching is **symbolic** (language-based) and more appropriate for upper elementary grades.

Teaching the whole song vs. phrase-by-phrase

The next decision is whether to teach the song as a whole or by one phrase or line at a time. This consideration will happen regardless of which teaching style—rote, rote-note, or note—is used. Note that the term **phrase** refers to the music, while **line** refers to the lyrics or poem.

Whole song: Teaching a whole song is exactly what it sounds like…singing the whole song at once and having the students echo the whole song right back. This is good for very short, simple songs; songs that have a lot of repetition either in the words or music; or call and response songs with few variables. The benefit of this is, according to Edwin Gordon's approach, to have the child experience the whole piece first, and then learn what the song comprises in detail.

Phrase-by-phrase teaching is best when the song is longer or has a lot of lyrics or complex melodies. This is the most common method for teaching more complicated or lengthy songs. In this technique, each phrase is sung by the teacher and then immediately echoed back by the students.

For example, consider the song "A Tisket, a Tasket":

A Tisket, A Tasket

American children's game song, late 19th century

A tis - ket, a tas - ket, A green and yel - low bas - ket, I

wrote a let - ter to my love, and on the way I dropped it, I

dropped it, I dropped it, and on the way I dropped it.

Phrase by phrase or line by line:
Teacher: A tisket, a tasket
Students: A tisket, a tasket
Teacher: A green and yellow basket
Students: A green and yellow basket
Teacher: I wrote a letter to my love
Students: I wrote a letter to my love
Teacher: And on the way I dropped it
Students: And on the way I dropped it

If there is more than one **verse** to a song, after teaching one verse, make sure to repeat the first verse several times with the students before moving on to the next verse.

Activity 5B

TRY THIS

You are teaching a group of kindergarteners. Which songs would you be more likely to teach 1) as a whole song; 2) phrase by phrase?
- "Rain, Rain, Go Away"
- "Oh, Susanna"
- "A Tisket, a Tasket"
- "Michael Row the Boat Ashore"

Rain, Rain Go Away

Traditional children's song, 17th century

Rain, Rain, go a - way, come a - gain some oth - er day

Oh! Susanna

American minstrel song, Stephen Foster, 1848

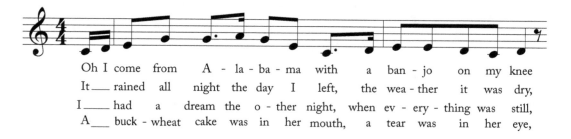

Oh I come from A - la - ba - ma with a ban - jo on my knee
It __ rained all night the day I left, the wea - ther it was dry,
I __ had a dream the o - ther night, when ev - ery - thing was still,
A __ buck - wheat cake was in her mouth, a tear was in her eye,

I'm goin' to Loui - si - a - na my ____ true love for to see.
The sun so hot I froze to death, Su - san - na don't you cry.
I __ dreamed I saw Su - san __ na, a co - min' down the hill.
Says I, "I'm co - min' from the south, Su - san - na don't you cry.

Oh Su - san - na, oh don't you cry for me, I've

come from A - la - ba - ma with a ban - jo on my knee.

Michael Row the Boat Ashore

African American spiritual, South Carolina Sea Islands, 1860s

Song Analysis

Of course singing a song is fun, but it can also be highly educational. In preparation for integration, and for using music with other art and subject areas, train yourself to explore the full potential of each song.

Having students identify or "analyze" what is going on in the song is educationally sound and cognitively effective. They are listening, analyzing, visualizing, sequencing, and applying concentrated brainwork to understand what they are singing.

Music vs. lyrics

When most people think about "song" they tend to think of the lyrics *plus* the music together, and often don't realize that the music is a separate entity with its own cohesiveness and structure. Getting students to understand the musical differences between phrases is actually less challenging than you might imagine. For example, if I asked you which lines of "A Tisket, A Tasket" are the same, you would say none if you thought of only the lyrics. But what if I asked you which musical phrases are the same? If you have trouble, remove the lyrics and hum the melody. Now how many are the same? Three of them—the first, second, and fourth. For example, the melody for "A Tisket, A Tasket" looks like this, with lines 1, 2, and 4 being basically the same. Line 3 is different.

1. A tisket, a tasket

2. A green and yellow basket

I   wrote   a   let - ter   to   my   love,

3.   I wrote a letter to my love

and   on   the   way   I   dropped   it,

4.   And on the way I dropped it

Having students hum the melody rather than singing words helps them hear the melody separately from the lyrics. Holding up fingers as they sing each phrase marks where they are in the song. Better still, have them sing the solfege for the different lines instead of the words or humming. In terms of analysis, solfege instantly informs the listener or singer which lines of music are the same and helps them compare and contrast each line rather quickly!

Steps for Introducing a New Song

While many children's songs are relatively easy to sing, most will need to be broken down into smaller parts (phrases) to learn easily. Breaking a song into "chunks" helps exercise children's cognitive and analytical abilities to understand, compare, and contrast the different parts or phrases of a song. Below are some important strategies for teaching a song either for the first time, or even to review a song or help children analyze an old and familiar song.

1.   Provide an opportunity for students to hear the song first, preferably by you singing it.
2.   Always ask students to listen FOR something. Before teaching it, ask students to listen carefully to something in the song's phrasing, repetition, rhythm, melody, timbre, lyrics, dynamics, rests, mood or affect, etc.
3.   Using a piano/keyboard, pitch pipe, or some other melodic instrument, find the correct starting pitch for the range of students in your class.
4.   Teach the song by rote using **song phrase, whole song, note-rote,** or **note** technique (use note technique in fourth or fifth grades).
5.   Develop a style for indicating that it is your turn to sing or their turn to sing.
6.   In phrase-by-phrase technique, teach each phrase (or line) of the song separately. Usually phrases vary from four to eight beats in length. For example, see "Rain, Rain Go Away," "A Tisket, a Tasket," and "Oh, Susanna" above.
7.   Try not to sing too loudly while the class is repeating each phrase; strive for singing independence among students.
8.   Ask the class to repeat the song while you mouth the words (do not sing).
9.   Finally, let the class sing with no support from you.
10. Variation: Sing each phrase one at a time. Rather than having student echo you, have them sing the phrase silently, and point to them when it is their turn to sing aloud.

Teaching a Song: The 4 Ps

Imagine that you are at the beginning of a track race. You are at the starting gate, and are anxiously waiting for the signal to begin running. You hear a count, then a starting shot, and you're off. Now imagine you are at a race in which no count or starting signal is given, but a chosen leader just decides to start running and you are expected to jump in and catch up. In some ways, beginning a song is similar. Many adults begin a song with no preparation and expect children to just jump in, requiring children to figure out the tempo, the starting pitch, and the lyrics all at the same time, and on their own.

It takes just a few seconds to prepare students before they begin a song. Counting them in gives them the tempo, and singing the counts on the opening pitch gives them the starting note. Below are a few hints for starting a song that will help students be successful right from the first note!

- Pulse
- Pitch
- Prepare
- Point

Pulse

The pulse indicates the tempo at which you would like to sing the song, as well as the song's meter.

- First, check the song's meter to see whether it is in 2/4, 4/4, 3/4, or 6/8 (see above for how to find which meter you are in).
- Then internally feel the pulse or **beat** of the song. Maybe tap your toe or hit your thigh as you sing the song in your head to find the appropriate tempo.

Pitch

Find the starting **pitch** for the song on any pitched instrument (i.e., piano, xylophone, recorder, or pitch pipe). Keep in mind the child's vocal range and the range/tessitura of the song.

Prepare

When bringing in the children to sing, you need to be aware of whether or not the song begins on a **downbeat** or **upbeat** (aka **pickup**). Many songs begin directly on the downbeat such as "Jingle Bells" or "Here We Go Round the Mulberry Bush," while others such as "Oh, Susanna!" or "The People on the Bus Go Up and Down" begin with an upbeat or pickup (see below).

- How do you find out if your song begins on an upbeat or downbeat? Clap or tap to the beat of a song for a few measures, tapping louder on the downbeat and lighter on the other beats in the measure, then begin singing. If you start singing while your hand is hitting the downbeat (first and strongest beat of the measure), the song starts on a downbeat. If your hand is in the air when you start singing, or the song's entrance falls on the weaker beats, that's an upbeat.

- Many pickups begin on a lower note than the rest of the song. For example, "The People on the Bus" starts on a pickup or upbeat note that is a 4th lower from the key of the song.

The Wheels on the Bus

upbeat and
starting note of "C" - a 4th below "F" which is the key of the song

The peo-ple on the bus go up and down, Up and down, Up and down, The

peo - ple on the bus go up and down, All through the town.

Now you have to take all of the above information and somehow transmit it to the children before you sing. Develop a preparatory phrase that you feel comfortable with which gives children the pulse and pitch of a song. The following preparations work very well for songs in duple meter if you sing them on the starting pitch that you want the children to come in on.

For duple meter (2/4 or 4/4) songs:

| | | |
1-2-3 sing

| | || |
1-2 here we go

|| | | |
Ready and sing now

For triple meter (3/4 or 6/8) songs:

| | | || |
1-2-3 | 1-2-sing

| | | | | |
Here we go | read-y now

Point

Add a pointing motion to start them off, such as an arm or hand gesture that lets them know it is their turn to sing. Use this same gesture when echoing during the phrase-by-phrase method to help students enter at the right time.

Below are some examples of preparations to sing a few well-known songs.

Mary Had a Little Lamb

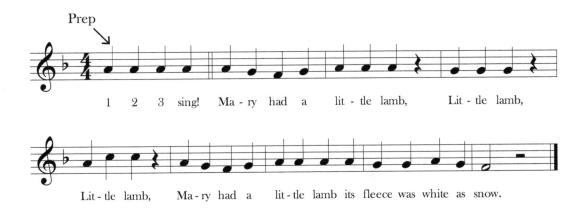

Home on the Range

Daniel E. Kelley

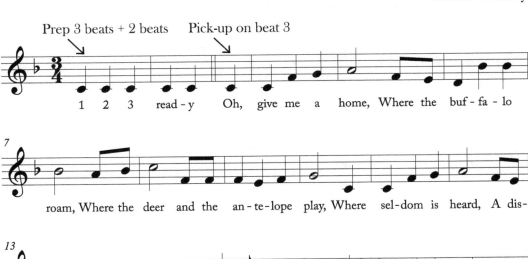

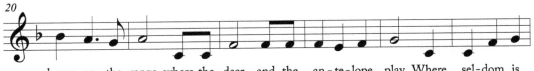

If You're Happy and You Know It

Activity 5C

TRY THIS

How would you prepare students to begin singing the following songs? What is your starting pitch? Meter? Tempo? Is there a pick-up/upbeat?
- "Frère Jacques"
- "A Tisket, A Tasket" (see above)
- "Hush Little Baby Don't Say a Word"
- "Three Blind Mice"

Frère Jacques

French folk round, 18th century

Frè - re   Jac - ques,   Frè - re   Jac - ques,   Dor - mez   vous?
Are   you   sleep - ing?   Are   you   sleep - ing?   Bro - ther   John?

Dor - mez vous?   Son - nez les ma - ti - nes,   Son - nez les ma - ti - nes,
Bro - ther John?   Morn - ing bells are ring - ing,   Morn - ing bells are ring - ing,

Ding Daing Dong,   Ding Daing, Dong.

Hush Little Baby, Don't Say a Word

American lullaby song

Hush lit - tle   ba - by don't say a word   pa-pa's gon-na buy you a Mock - ing - bird.
If   that   Mock-ing - bird won't sing,   pa-pa's gon-na buy you a   dia - mond ring.

Three Blind Mice

English children's song attributed to Thomas Ravenscroft, 1609

Three blind   mice,   Three blind   mice,   See how they run,

See how they run, They all ran aft-er the farm-er's wive who

cut off their tails with a car-ving knife, Did you e-ver see such a

sigh in your life, As three blind mice.

Resources

Folk songs for children
  • http://musiced.about.com/od/lessonsandtips/tp/folksongs.htm
Proper Vocal Ranges for Children (Kathie Hill Music)
  • http://www.youtube.com/watch?v=pyXaQURviAs

Vocabulary

aural learning: learning music "by ear"—learning by hearing only (no use of written notation)

beat: a pulse in a piece of music; the basic unit of time in music

binary form: a song in with two discernible sections; also referred to as verse-refrain or verse-chorus and designated as AB.

chest voice: singing when the sound feels like it is emanating from the chest or throat

downbeat: the first beat in the measure; beat in a measure that is most accented

duple: two or four beats per measure

head voice: placing the sound higher up in the "vocal mask" or the face, as if singing through the eyes

line: reference to a line of the lyrics or poem when learning music; usually corresponds to a musical phrase

note: learning music by reading the notes; reading the music or score in order to play or learn

note-rote: song is taught mostly by ear or repetition, but also shows some iconic notation (written notation)

phrase-by-phrase: teaching a song one line at a time; breaking down the song into individual phrases

pickup: a note or series of notes that preceded the first downbeat of the first measure; also called *anacrusis*

pitch: the frequency of the sound based upon its wavelength; the higher the pitch, the higher the frequency

pulse: in learning music, the pulse indicates to the children the tempo at which you would like to sing the song as well as the song's meter; "feel the beat"

range: all of the notes in the song from lowest to highest

rote: learning through repetition; learning without use of written music or a score

song phrase: reference to a group of notes in learning music, usually equivalent to a sentence or the length of one line of poetry

tempo: pace in which the notes of a song are sung or played

ternary form: as song with 3-sections, where the first section returns at the end in exact form and the middle section is different or contrasting; designated as ABA.

tessitura: the part of the register in which most of the tones of the melody or voice part lies

triple: three or six beats per measure

unitary: a song with only one section, and no refrain; can be labeled as A.

upbeat: pickup beat (see above)

verse-refrain: a verse corresponds to a poetic stanza of a song; usually distinguished from the chorus or refrain of a song, which has repeated lyrics (e.g., in "Oh, Susanna" the verse begins with "oh I came from Alabama" and the chorus or refrain begins with "Oh, Susanna, oh don't you cry for me...")

whole song: teach the whole song at once without breaking it into individual phrases; useful technique for very short songs

Chapter 6

Creative Activity and Lesson Planning

Chapter Summary: This chapter looks at creative ideas for approaching and planning a successful music lesson, including a guided outline, models of full lessons, and classroom management tips.

I. Lesson Plans as a Creative Activity

At some point or other, students in education programs are required to write lesson plans.Often, however, the meaning of writing a lesson plan becomes lost in the academic process, and the lesson's grade becomes the goal rather than the meaningful construction of the lesson and learning the technique of organizing your thoughts. Often students believe that writing a lesson plan is only used in a classroom setting. The reality is, however, that *all* professions require the organization of a plan of action to be carried out, including an articulation of goals and objectives to reach them, followed by a reflection or assessment of the effectiveness. In other professions, you might be asked for a plan of action composed of three inherent questions: 1) What are you going to do? 2) How are you going to do it? and 3) How will you assess what you've done? In education, a lesson plan is nothing more than a plan of action with the same three questions: 1) What are you going to teach? 2) How are you going to teach it? and 3) How will you assess what you have taught?

Lesson Plan Preparation: Start With (Musical) Inspiration!

Much of the time as a teacher, you will be required to teach a certain set curriculum in the classroom that conforms to the Common Core State Standards (see Chapter 3). However, this doesn't mean that the lesson has to be devoid of inspiration. Whatever your content area, there is probably an arts-related activity that can be applied or integrated (see Chapter 12 for Arts Integration information). It is much easier to create a good lesson plan if you are inspired. Your inspiration for a music or integrated lesson plan can be a song, an instrument, timbre, vocal sound, poem, story, rhythm, speech pattern, etc.

Creative problem solving requires that you be able to see and manipulate your lesson material in unique ways to reach all types of student learners. The music education methods of Orff, Dalcroze, Kodály, etc., offer easily implemented solutions to add layers of cognitively challenging musical activities to something as simple as a song. When developing your lesson, start by thinking outside of the box.

Activity 6A

TRY THIS

How can I make the lesson interesting? Challenging? What might I be able to add to a lesson to increase its effectiveness for the learner—e.g., movement? rhythm? instruments?

Below are a few ways to challenge students physically, cognitively, and multi-modally just with a simple song. The first rule is not to be afraid of experimenting with sound, using either your own voice, various instruments, or maybe even the walls, doors, floors, chairs, and surroundings, all of which have their own unique timbres to explore!

Musically creative lesson planning

Musically Creative Lesson Planning
Begin with the list of music elements and vocabulary from Chapter 2. Select a song, then brainstorm different ways of performing the song using what you've learned. For example:
Vocal
• Sing the song *a capella* (without instrumental accompaniment)
• Add a speech rhythm ostinato
• Add a melodic ostinato using voices
• Add a drone using voices
Dynamics, Tempo, Form
• Sing the song changing tempos on different sections, phrases, or measures
• Sing the song changing dynamics on different sections, phrases, or measures
• Sing the song alternating phrases or sections between two groups of singers
Body Percussion
• Add a beat or ostinato by clapping
• Add a beat or ostinato by patching
• Add a beat or ostinato by tapping
Instruments
• Add a beat or ostinato on an unpitched percussion instrument
• Add a bordun ostinato or drone on a pitched percussion instrument
• Add more than one bordun on multiple instruments

• Play only metal instruments, or wood instruments, etc.	
Conclusion	
• Do endless combinations of all of the above	

Creative Exploration of Classroom Instruments

Inspiration can come from anywhere, including the arsenal of classroom and children's instruments available. Classroom instruments are much more than noisemakers to accompany songs. There are many creative ways to use these inexpensive instruments to help and inspire you, and which will fire up a child's imagination. Here are a few instruments typically found in classrooms, or that can be purchased inexpensively at a music store or online. This list is by no means exhaustive, but it does provide a wide range of commonly used instruments from Western and world cultures.

Typical classroom instruments

Xylophones	Metallophones
Glockenspiels	Boomwhackers
Recorders	Slide whistles
Jingle bells	Kokoriko
Castanets	Bells
Agogo bells (African double bell)	Shekere (African gourd shaker)
Maracas	Triangle
Cymbals (finger, crash, suspended)	Tambourines
Timpani	Gongs
Bongos	Temple blocks
Steel drum	Hand drum
Conga drums	Claves
Cowbell	Djembe
Rainmaker	Rhythm blocks
Sand blocks	Panpipes
Ocarina	Piano
Mbira (thumb piano)	Guiro
Tick tock	Tone block
Vibra slap	Wood block
Guitar	Violin
Chimes	

Thinking about the source of sound production and materials will lead you to the field of **organology,** or the classification of musical instruments. Instruments all over the world can be grouped into five categories based on the Sachs-Hornbostel instrument classification system. This system groups the instruments by the way in which sound is produced. They are:

Aerophones: Instruments that produce sound by using air as the primary vibrating means. (e.g., flutes, horns, whistles).

Membranophones: Instruments that produce sound by means of vibrating a stretched membrane (e.g., drums)

Chordophones: A term used for stringed instruments. Refers to an instrument sounded by bowing, plucking, or striking a string that is stretched between two fixed points. (e.g., violins)

Idiophones: Instruments that produce sound from the material of the instrument itself. Idiophones produce sounds from the following methods and represent the largest category of classroom instruments.

- **Percussion**: instrument caused to vibrate by striking it with a non-vibrating object such as a mallet or stick
- **Shaken**: sound produced by small particles contained within the instrument
- **Scraped**: sound produced by scraping the instrument with a stick
- **Plucked**: instruments with a flexible tongue that is plucked to vibrate
- **Concussion**: two similar objects struck together to create sound
- **Stamping**: striking the object on a hard surface to vibrate the object

Electrophones: Refers to electronic instruments that either have their sound generated electronically or acoustic instruments that have their sounds amplified

The Sachs-Hornbostel list, however, is only one way to think about instruments. Children often come up with very imaginative ways to group instruments based on characteristics other than sound production. Children can explore the timbre, production, and material of the instruments to come up with their own ways of categorizing them. After students explore and group instruments, they can develop their own instrumentation for a piece, then vary it. Below is a list of other ways to think about instruments besides the way the sound is produced, such as its timbre or similar sound; physical attributes, etc.

Examples of different ways children can categorize instruments.

	Terminology	Explanation
By Physical Attributes: e.g. Color, size, shape	round, tube, big, medium, small, rectangular, long, short, hollow, solid, jingles, ridges, skin/membrane, brown, silver, red, low pitch, high pitch	For younger children, one of the most obvious types of recognition belongs to color, shape, and size—attributes they are identifying in other subjects. They may want to group instruments by their color, how big or small, and their shape. Musically, the shape of the instrument is important since the shape is directly related to sound and sound production. The smaller the instrument, the higher the pitch, for example.
By Material	Metal, wood, metal and wood, plastic, wire, string, skin	This type of grouping brings students to another level of understanding in terms of discussing the sound of the instruments. What an instrument is made of has a direct effect on its timbre. The challenge here is that some instruments, such as the tambourine, contain more than one type of material. Ask students how they might label such instruments.
By Timbre	Rattly-sounding, woody, metallic, jingly, high, thin, low, loud, soft, hollow, smooth, rough	An instrument's timbre is directly related to its size, material, and even shape. All of the above properties affect the sound production of an instrument
Melody-Making Ability	plays a song, doesn't play a song; pitched, unpitched	Children may find other unique ways of classifying instruments such as whether the instrument can play a melody. This classification concerns Pitched instruments or Unpitched instruments.
Culture of Origin	Sub-Saharan Africa, North America, South America	Another way of classifying is to know the country or culture of origin for the instruments. This related to musical instruments and their community
Multi-Purpose Use	Used for activities other than music making	While most classroom instruments only have one use, there are many instruments that serve other purposes such as for cooking. The cowbell, for example, is an instrument that has another purpose besides its musical one.

Activity 6B

TRY THIS

The instruments on the Typical Classroom Instrument list above are random, and not categorized purposefully in any way. See if you can develop other ways of classifying these instruments in addition to the ways listed. How could you use this classification to create a lesson on science? Physics? Math? History? Social science? World history?

Start thinking scientifically and creatively about this list. How might you *approach* or *use* these instruments when creating a lesson plan? Here are a few questions that might help in thinking about the instruments.

Suggested Questions
- What do the instruments have in common?
- Where do the instruments come from (culture of origin)?
- What materials are they made of? *(wood, metal, plastic)*
- How are they played? *(shaken, hit, struck with mallet, scraped, blown, pulled, etc.)*
- What special sounds can they make? *(jingles, shakes, thumps, scrapes)*
- Where is the sound coming from (how is the sound produced)? *(a hollow tube, the instrument itself vibrates, a vibrating string)*
- What do the instruments sound like? *(harsh, metallic, hollow, soft, smooth, mellow, high, low, etc.)*

II. Lesson Planning

Below are some guidelines for creating a lesson plan. Regardless of subject, method, and additional requirements, all lesson plans contain the same basic structure and four core components:

1. Goals and objectives: What will students be able to do when I've finished teaching my lesson?
2. Standards: Common Core or National Standards: Which state content and developmental standards are addressed in my lesson?
3. Procedure: A step-by-step listing of your actions—core lesson in which you creatively assemble and format the material to present to your students in order to achieve your goals and objectives.
   a. What types of instructional input will I use (e.g., lecture, demonstration, modeling, guided practice, independent practice)?
   b. Which educational theories will I include (e.g., Bloom, Gardner, different types of learners)?
   c. How will I capture learners' attention and engage them?
   d. What critical thinking will I implement?

e. Close the procedure section with a wrap-up and find ways to extend the lesson concepts in future activities

4. Assessment: How will I know my students learned the material? How might I modify the material if I did not reach my goals or if students need accommodation?

Preparing for the Lesson

Gather your thoughts and materials on the following before beginning your lesson:

- Prerequisites: What do the students already know?
- Concept(s), vocabulary, experiences: What new concepts am I going to teach? Where do I want to take them?
- Materials: What materials will I need?

Parts of a Lesson

General Information

- Lesson plan title
- Grade level
- Length of class (time)
- Type of class: Regular, inclusive

Materials and Resources

- List the materials you will need to teach the lesson or cite the location of any resources.

Goals and Objectives

- What will the students be able to do as a result of this lesson that they couldn't do before?
- What concepts and vocabulary will be taught?
- What processes will you use to teach those concepts and vocabulary?

Common Core Standards

- Which Common Core standards are addressed in the lesson?

Core Lesson Procedures

- *Opening activity/Energizer/Warm-up*
  - Sometimes called an "energizer," the opening statement provides an attention-grabbing focus and an *invitation* to the lesson.
- *Main lesson*
  - Includes instructional input such as a lecture, demo, modeling, guided practice, etc.
  - Outline all of the steps that the teacher will do to get the students to achieve the goals (use action words).
- *Closure and extension*
  - Wrap up the lesson with a summary or question.

- Think of ways to extend your lesson.

Assessment

- How will you know if the lesson was effective?
  - Observe students as they work or perform. Ask questions, get feedback, check for facial expressions and body language, etc.
- Did your lesson meet your goals and objectives above?
- *Modifications/accommodations*
  - Adjust for any special needs students in the class.

Lesson Plan Example #1: Teaching a Song

General Information

Title: Teaching "Oats, Peas, Beans, and Barley Grow" Using Rote

Grade level: Kindergarten–first grade

Length of class: 40 minutes

Type of class: Regular

Materials
- Game song: "Oats, Peas, Beans, and Barley Grow"

Learning/Behavioral Objectives

Students will be able to:
- Sing the folk song "Oats, Peas, Beans, and Barley Grow"
- Recognize the long-short, long-short ♩♪♩♪ "horse trot" rhythmic patterns in the song
- Patsch the rhythm ♩♪♩♪ on their legs while saying long-short long short
- Gallop/move to the long-short rhythm ♩♪♩♪

National Common Core Arts Standards in Music
- With (limited) guidance, perform music with expression. MU: Pr6.1.Ka/1a
- With guidance, explore and demonstrate awareness of musical contrasts (such as high/low, loud/soft, same/different) in a variety of music selected for performance. MU:Pr4.2.Ka/1a

Oats, Peas, Beans and Barley Grow

Oats, peas, beans and bar-ley grow, oats, peas, beans and bar-ley grow, can
Here's the farm-er sow-ing seed, then he stands and takes his ease, ___

you____ or I or an - y - one know how oats, peas, beans and bar - ley grow?
stamp-ing his foot and clap-ping his hands, he turns a - round and views his lands.

Refrain

Wait - ing for a part - ner, wait - ing for a part - ner,

o - pen the ring and bring one in while we all gai - ly dance and sing.

Warm-up Rhythms

Procedures: Opening Activity (Note: T = Teacher; S = Student)

- T claps various measures of warm-up rhythms to establish 6/8 meter. Students echo.
- T claps the long-short, long-short pattern ♩♪♩♪ and chants "long-short-long-short-long" etc. Students echo.
- T: "What type of animal does this remind you of when it's moving? What animal move like this?" Students reply with horse or pony.
- T plays this rhythm on an instrument, piano, drum, or recording, or claps it while students gallop around the room.
- T asks students to sit down, and claps the rhythm ♩♪♩♪ again, adding the words "oats, peas, beans, and barley grow." Students echo.
- T goes back to warm-up rhythms, playing them on a drum or other instrument, and asks students to identify the long-short-long-short rhythm by raising their hands when they hear it.

Oats, Peas, Beans and Barley Grow (with additional verses)

1. Oats, peas, beans and bar - ley grow, oats, peas, beans and bar - ley grow, can
2. Here's the farm - er sow - ing seed, then he stands and takes his ease, ___
3. Next the farm - er waters the seed, then he stands and takes his ease, ___
4. Next the farm - er hoes the weeds, then he stands and takes his ease, ___
5. Last the farm - er harvests his seed, then he stands and takes his ease, ___

you ___ or I or an - y - one know how oats, peas, beans and bar - ley grow?
stamp-ing his foot and clap-ping his hands, he turns a - round and views his lands.
stamp-ing his foot and clap-ping his hands, he turns a - round and views his lands.
stamp-ing his foot and clap-ping his hands, he turns a - round and views his lands.
stamp-ing his foot and clap-ping his hands, he turns a - round and views his lands.

Wait - ing for a part - ner, wait - ing for a part - ner,

o - pen the ring and bring one in while we all gai - ly dance and sing.

Procedures: Teaching the Song

Song: "Oats, Peas, Beans, and Barley Grow"

- T: "Okay, now we're going to learn a song to go with this rhythm. This song is about oats, peas, and beans. Does anyone know what those are? Has anyone ever eaten them?" (T may want to bring in different kinds of oats, peas, beans, and barley to show the class or bring in pictures if foods are not available. If foods are available, have students touch them and answer questions about them (e.g., do they eat any of these for breakfast? dinner?).
- T: "This song goes along with the rhythm we were just moving and clapping to. Echo after me."
- T claps, sings lyrics, or uses solfege and hand signs to teach the song in a phrase-by-phrase approach as follows: A single phrase equals six beats. T may repeat each line a few times until students get the rhythm.

Phrase 1

Oats,   peas,   beans   and   bar - ley grow,

Phrase 2

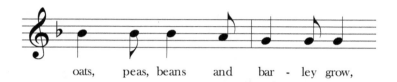

oats,   peas,   beans   and   bar - ley grow,

Phrase 3

can   you___   or   I   or   an - y - one know

Phrase 4

how   oats,   peas,   beans   and   bar - ley grow?

- T: "Now I'm going to put two lines together." T then doubles the phrases (12 beats for each phrase).

Phrases 1 and 2

Oats, peas, beans and bar - ley grow,   oats, peas, beans and bar - ley grow,

Phrases 3 and 4

can   you   or   I   or   an-y-one   know   how   oats,   peas,   beans   and   bar-ley   grow?

- T: "Now can we put this much of the song together?" T and students sing Verse 1. Repeat until students are singing confidently.
- T then selects one child to be the farmer, and has children hold hands and walk in a circle around the farmer while singing Verse 1.
- T: "Now let's learn how to change farmers." T then teaches the refrain "Waiting for a partner," line by line. After students have learned this, the old farmer selects a new farmer to be in the middle.
- T: "There are a few more words to the song, and they show the kinds of activities a farmer does to grow food." T then teaches Verse 2, "Here's the farmer…," line by line. T then adds the motions to go along with the lyrics (e.g., stamping, turning, viewing). T explains what a "hoe" is and the motions to pull up weeds, etc.
- T: "Now let's sing the whole song and do the movements that we're singing about."
- Students play game until everyone has had a chance to be the farmer.

Closure and Extension

- Review what it was that the farmer was doing. Ask students to think about what other kinds of foods come from seeds that we eat.
- Ask students to think about what other songs they know that have the long-short-long-short rhythm.

Assessing Your Lesson Plan

Assessing the execution of the lesson:

Observe students as they are performing by themselves and their ability to move to the rhythms successfully and sing the song successfully.

- Are only a few students able to perform? Are most students able to? Do students look puzzled or confused?

Assessing the content of the lesson:

Did the lesson address different types of learning? Multiple intelligences? Common Core Standards? Learning objectives? Did it contain various modes of instructional input and modalities (e.g., lecture, demonstration, etc.)?

"Oats, Peas, Beans" Lesson

1. Addresses different types of learning—Visual, aural, tactile/kinesthetic
2. Addresses multiple intelligences—Bodily/kinesthetic, musical/rhythmic, etc.
3. Contains appropriate Common Core or National Standards—Musical analysis
4. Contains clear and age-appropriate learning objectives—Circle game with rhythm
5. Uses a variety of music methods/techniques—Singing, rhythm, movement
6. Incorporates a variety of instructional modalities—Question/answer, kinetic, and linguistic activities

Lesson Plan Example #2: Teaching a Song and Musical Concept(s)

General Information

Title: Teaching the Song "Li'l Liza Jane" using Rote-Note Methods

Grade level: Second grade

Length of class: 40 minutes

Musical Concept(s)
- Synco-pa (syncopation) ♪♩♪
- One octave

Materials
- Song: "Li'l Liza Jane"
- Chart of scale (solfege)
- Rhythm cards of rhythms using only quarter and eighth notes
- Rhythm cards with various rhythmic patterns from the song

Learning/Behavioral Objectives

Students will be able to:
- Sing the American folk song "Little Liza Jane"
- Recognize the synco-pa rhythmic patterns in the song
- Clap the synco-pa pattern when it occurs
- Sing the synco-pa pattern on solfege pitches
- Recognize an octave jump in a folk song from Do to Do'
- Sing an octave jump on solfege

National Standards
- Sing independently or in a group, singing correctly (1)
- Identify simple music forms when presented aurally (6)
- Use appropriate terminology in explaining music (6)
- Use a system (syllables) to read simple rhythmic notations (5)

Li'l Liza Jane

American folk song, late 19th century

M		M	R	D	M	S	S		L	S	M		S		M		M	R	D	M	S	S		M	M	R	D

1.Come my love and go with me Li'l Li-za Jane, Come my love and go with me Li'l Li-za Jane

ti   ti ti   ti ti ti ta syn-co-pa ta   ti   ti   ti ti ti ti ta syn-co-pa ta

Refrain

D' S L S   L S M S   D' S L S   M M R D
O, E - li - za, Li'l Li - za Jane,   O, E - li - za, Li'l Li - za Jane.
tai - i ta ta   syn - co - pa ta,   tai - ti ta ta   syn - co - pa ta

Warm-up Rhythms

Song Rhythm Practice

syn - co - pa ta   syn - co - pa taa,   syn - co - pa ta ta   syn - co - pa taa,

tai - ti ta ta   tai - ti taa   tai - ti ta ta   syn - co - pa ta

Procedures: Opening Activity

- T claps four beats of warm-up rhythms using only quarter and eighth notes. Students echo.
- T claps a syncopated pattern.
- T asks, "How is this rhythm different from the first rhythm?" (short long short instead of a steady beat).
- T then clap rhythms containing synco-pa.
- T asks students to alternate a syncopated rhythm, with the straight quarter/eighth note rhythms.
- Students put the syncopated rhythms into body percussion (e.g., patsch on lap).
- T then asks students to march to a steady beat played on a drum. When students hear the syncopated rhythm, they should walk to the rhythm short-long-short-long, freeze in place, or clap.

Procedures: Teaching the Song "Li'l Liza Jane"

- T: "Okay, now we're going to learn a song. Echo after me."

- T uses solfege and hand signs to teach the song in a phrase-by-phrase approach as follows: Single-phrase (four beats for each phrase).

♪ ♪ ♪ ♪ ♪ ♪ ♩

M M R D M S S

Come my love and go with me

♪ ♩ ♪ ♩

L S M S

Li'l Liza Jane

♪ ♪ ♪ ♪ ♪ ♪ ♩

M M R D M S S

Come my love and go with me

♪ ♩ ♪ ♩

M M R D

Li'l Liza Jane

♩ ♪ ♩ ♩

D' S L S

O Eliza

♪ ♩ ♪ ♩

L S M S

Li'l Liza Jane

♩ ♪ ♩ ♩

D' S L S

O Eliza

♪ ♩ ♪ ♩

M M R D

Li'l Liza Jane

- Double phrases (eight beats for each phrase)
- T sings the song and asks how many phrases there are (eight).
- T: "Did you notice which notes we have that were missing from our song? Which solfege notes didn't we sing?" (F and T)
- T: "What is the highest note in our song?" (High Do')
- T: "What is the lowest?" (Do)
- T: "There is a name for the distance between a note and that same note higher up. It is an interval of an octave. Octave means eight notes. There are eight notes

between low Do and high Do. Do you know of any other words meaning eight with *oct* in it?" (octagon, octopus). "*Oct* is the Latin root for eight. So the space between low D and high D is one octave. Can you all show me and sing low D to high D?" (Sing and show hand signs a few times.)

- T: "Now, at the beginning of class, we learned a rhythm. Can you remember that rhythm?" (♪♩♪ synco-pa)
- T: "Let's sing the song again, and this time, listen for that rhythm in this song."
- T: "How many times did you hear the rhythm in the song?" (Four)
- T: "On which word did this rhythm occur in the song? Was it on the same or on different words?"
- T: "This rhythm looks like this (show card ♪♩♪), but instead of saying ti ta ti, it has its own word, 'synco-pa.' Repeat that please, and then let's clap ♪♩♪ synco-pa and say it. The reason it's called synco-pa is that it is short for the word syncopation, which means to have a rhythm that is 'off-beat' or doesn't fall right on the beats of a song."
- Sing the song again, this time holding up the card each time the ♪♩♪ synco-pa rhythm occurs.
- T: "Now let's sing some of the verses of the song."
- T: "What can you tell me about Liza Jane? Who is singing the song? What does this person want?"

Closure and Extension

- Ask students to sing the song without teacher help while clapping the synco-pas.
- As students to find syncopated rhythm in other songs.
- Use the syncopation as an ostinato pattern throughout the song.

Assessing Your Lesson Plan

Assessing the execution of the lesson:

Observe students as they are performing by themselves and their ability to clap the rhythm successfully or identify the rhythm and octave successfully.

- Are only a few students able to perform and identify? Are most students able to? Do students look puzzled or confused?

Assessing the content of the lesson:

Did the lesson address different types of learning? Multiple intelligences? National Standards? Learning objectives? Did it contain various modes of instructional input and modalities (e.g., lecture, demonstration, etc.)?

Li'l Liza Jane Lesson

1. Adresses different types of learning—Visual, aural, and kinesthetic
2. Addresses multiple intelligences—Musical, logical/mathematical, linguistic, etc.
3. Contains appropriate Common Core or National Standards—1, 5, and 6
4. Contains clear and age-appropriate learning objectives—Synco-pa, octave
5. Uses a variety of music methods/techniques—Singing, rhythm, instruments, some written notation

6. Incorporates a variety of instructional modalities—Lecture, demonstration, question/answer, call and response, and kinetic and linguistic activities

Lesson Plan Example #3: Teaching a Song and Musical Concept(s) Plus English Language Arts Standards (Integrated)

General Information

Title: Teaching the Song "Erie Canal" Using Note Method

Grade level: Fourth or fifth grade

Type of class: Regular

Materials
- Sheet music of "Erie Canal"
- Visual notation of major and minor scales; various other familiar songs in major and minor ("Hey Ho Nobody Home," "Johnny Has Gone for a Soldier," etc.
- Map of Great Lakes/New York

Learning/Behavioral Objectives (Music and Language Arts/History)

Students will be able to:
- Sing the American folk song "Erie Canal"
- Differentiate between major and minor mode/scales used in the song and recognize a *fermata*
- Understand the song as a binary form (AB form)
- Deduce information about life in early 20th-century America (New York) from the song lyrics
- Use geography to understand the canal as an important mode of 19th- and early 20th-century transportation
- Distinguish the difference between the use of the two modes in the song and the lyrical/emotional meaning

Common Core Music Standards (Fourth/Fifth)
- Demonstrate and explain how intent is conveyed through interpretive decisions and expressive qualities (such as dynamics, tempo, and timbre). MU: Pr4.3.4a/5a
- Perform music, alone or with others, with expression and technical accuracy, and appropriate interpretation. MU: Pr6.1.4a/5a
- Demonstrate and explain how responses to music are informed by the structure, the use of the elements of music, and context (social and cultural). MU: Re7.2.4a/5a

Common English Language Arts Standards (Fourth/Fifth)

- Determine one or more main ideas of a text and explain how they are supported by key details; summarize the text. CCSS.ELA-Literacy.RI.4.2/ CCSS.ELA-Literacy.RI.5.2
- Explain the relationships or interactions between two or more individuals, events, ideas, or concepts in a historical, scientific, or technical text based on specific information in the text. CCSS.ELA-Literacy.RI.4.3/CCSS.ELA-Literacy.RI.5.3

Procedures: Opening Activity

- T: "Today we're going to learn about the Erie Canal. Does anyone know what the Erie Canal is, where it is, or what it was used for?"
- T: "Let's learn the song and see what we can find out. I'd like you to pay attention to both the lyrics of the song and the melody, because the music is also giving you a lot of information about what's going on in the song."
- T plays a recording, passes out sheet music, or sings song in its entirety. Students sing song by looking at the sheet music (by note).

Erie Canal

Thomas S. Allen, 1905

Low bridge 'cuz we're co-min' to a town. And you al-ways know you're neigh-bor, you

al-ways know your pal if you're e-ver na-vi-ga-tin' on the E-rie Can-al.

Procedures: Music Analysis

- T: "First, let's think about the music. Can anyone tell me how many sections there are to the song? Where does the second section begin?" *T plays or sings again if necessary, and students also sing.* (Second section begins at "Low bridge.")
- T: "This is known as AB form, which means that the music contains two distinct sections. How can you tell that the sections are musically different?" (There is a slowing down at the end of the first section. It sounds different than the first. The pitches and scale sound different.)
- T: "The 'slowing down' is caused by two *fermatas*, which means 'hold' in Italian. The symbol looks like an eye. When a note has a *fermata* on it, you hold it for about twice the length of time."
- T: "Let's sing 'Buffalo' again to practice the *fermatas*."

to___ Bu-fa-lo.___

- T: "The other musical clue that you're hearing is that the song is actually in two different modes or scales. The first part is minor, usually associated with sadness or melancholy, and the second part is major, which is usually associated with happiness or joy."
- T: "Can you think of another song that's in minor that is an unhappy one?" ("Hey Ho Nobody Home," "Johnny Has Gone for a Soldier," etc.)
- T: "What do all of these songs have in common emotionally?" (Sadness, loneliness, melancholy)
- T plays and shows the pitches of the major and minor scales. Students sing D R M F S L T D' for major and L, T, D R M F S L for minor. If T has an instrument, have students guess which scale is being played. If not, T can play clips from other songs or have them sing other short songs to reinforce the concepts of major and minor.

F Major   *D Minor*

D R M F S L T D'   L, T, D R M F S L

- T: "Why do you think the composer chose to end the first section with two *fermatas*?" (To help the singer recognize the two sections, and to distinguish between the minor and major parts of the song)

Procedure: Literary Analysis

- T: "What's happening in the song?" (Various answers summarizing the text)
- T: "What was the Erie Canal used for? Why do you think the Erie Canal was built?" (To transport things easily on water as there were no trains, or trucks at the time)
- T: "What types of things?" (Lumber, coal, and hay)
- T: "Which towns does the canal connect in New York?" (Albany and Buffalo)
- T: "Why does the composer write about a mule? What was the mule used for?" (Hauling barges)
- T: "Good! Does anyone know what a barge is?" (A flat-bottomed boat for carrying freight)
- T: "How do the barge and mule drivers know they are coming to a town?" (Because they cross under a low bridge)
- T: "How does the singer feel when they are coming to a town?" (Happy)
- T: "How do you know this?" (Because they talk about meeting neighbors and pals)
- T: "Is there something in the music that also tells you that the singer feels happy when coming to a town?" (Yes, the major scale is used in the second part of the song)
- T: "Good, what in the music tells you that the singer is not happy about losing their work hauling the barges?" (The minor mode)

Procedure: Integrated Context

- T: "When thinking of the lyrics and the music, why might the composer have set the first part of the song to sad or minor music, and the second part to happier or major music?" (The first part is talking about work and hauling barges, and the second is talking about coming to a town and meeting your neighbors.)
- T: "There's also another part to the history of this song. It was written just as the last mules were being used to haul or pull the barges and were being converted to steam power. If this is the case, why does the singer talk about the mule as a 'friend' or 'pal'?" (Because they've been working together for years, and now they aren't going to be working any more pulling the barges.)
- T: "Now I'd like you to deduce something first by *not* looking at the map. We know that the canal goes from Buffalo to Albany, but can you tell me which great lake the canal connects to? Think! The song tells you." (Lake Erie)
- T: "Now, let's look at the map. Can anyone see which waterway the canal connects to in Albany?" (The Hudson River, leading to the Atlantic Ocean through New York City)
- T: "Albany is not on the Atlantic Ocean, so the Hudson River was used to connect the two waterways."

Closure and Extension

- T: "So, to summarize, what impact might this have had on the city of New York in the 19th century to have it be one of the largest seaports in the U.S.?" [This made New York City one of the most important ports and cities in the country, and helped the city grow and become home to many immigrants, workers, etc.]
- T: "What do you think happened to all of the mules and mule drivers after they were replaced? Is there a musical indication that things turned out all right?" [The switch to major mode and the sense of community and belonging at the end]

Assessing Your Lesson Plan

Assessing the execution of the lesson:

Observe students as they are performing by themselves and their ability to sing the song and identify the modes and binary form successfully.

- Are only a few students able to perform and identify? Are most students able to? Do students look puzzled or confused? Are they not engaging with the music or the questions?

Assessing the content of the lesson:

Did the lesson address different types of learning? Multiple intelligences? National Standards? Learning objectives? Did it contain various modes of instructional input and modalities (e.g., lecture, demonstration, etc.)?

"Erie Canal" Lesson

1. Addresses different types of learning—e.g. Visual, aural
2. Addresses multiple intelligences—e.g. Musical, logical/mathematical, linguistic, etc.
3. Contains appropriate Common Core or National Standards
4. Contains clear and age-appropriate learning objectives—Analysis of musical and literary ideas
5. Uses a variety of music methods/techniques—Singing, rhythm, notation analysis
6. Incorporates a variety of instructional modalities—Lecture, demonstration, question/answer, written word

III. Classroom Management

While lessons on paper are an integral and necessary step, the actual implementation of the lesson in front of a live class is quite another matter. Teachers all over the world have their own tips and hints as to what makes a good teacher and what makes a lesson successful, and reviewing a few ideas on classroom management is an extremely helpful first step. If the students aren't focused on the lesson, all of your preparatory work is for naught. Below are a few basic classroom management ideas to use when teaching music.

Classroom Behavior Management Techniques

- Don't be afraid to be the teacher!

- Tell students what you expect them to do. Don't ask them what they want to do. You are the teacher, and you set the agenda.
- Use positive reinforcement whenever possible.
  - Don't be afraid to point out places where students can improve. Show them the next level and let them strive to get there.
- When disciplining, select one person to stand out as a role model
  - "Look how well Suzie, Frank, and Leticia are doing at…let's see if we all can do that!"
- Pay attention to the *singing voice*! Check whether you yourself are singing correctly and check that the students are singing correctly as well.
- Use *magic*, *wonder*, and *surprise* whenever possible!
  - "Guess what will happen next?"
  - "What does this sound remind you of?"
- Add movement whenever possible
  - Hand gestures, small body movements, large body movements
- Keep sweeping the room, checking to see that they are all "getting it."
- Do not talk or give directions over the music; they won't hear you or the music.
- When handing out instruments, develop an orderly system for distribution and have a system in place to keep instruments quiet while you're talking.
- Talk less and do more.
  - Sing, play, and instrument or mime as meaningful substitutions for words and directions.
- Most importantly, have fun! If the material excites you, your students will be engaged as well.

Resources

- Instruments Website: Sachs-Hornbostel Instrument Classification List
- National Standards in Music: http://www.educationworld.com/standards/national/arts/music/k_4.shtml
- Writing Lesson Plans: http://www.huntington.edu/dept_interior.aspx?id=2217

Vocabulary

aerophones: instruments that produce sound by using air as the primary vibrating means (flutes, horns, whistle)

chordophones: a term used for stringed instruments referring to instruments sounded by bowing, plucking, or striking a string that is stretched between two fixed points (violins)

concussion: two similar objects struck together to create sound

electrophones: electronic instruments that either have their sound generated electronically or acoustic instruments that have their sounds amplified

idiophones: instruments that produce sound from the material of the instrument itself; probably the largest category of classroom instruments; sounds produced through shaking, scraping, plucking, etc.

instrumentation: source of sound and music that a child develops from hearing rhythm and a melody

membranophones: instruments that produce sound by means of vibrating a stretched membrane (drums)

organology: the classification of musical instruments around the world

percussion: instrument caused to vibrate by striking it with a non-vibrating object such as a mallet or stick

pitched instruments: instruments capable of making distinct notes and pitch changes while simultaneously following a rhythm (e.g., a piano, clarinet)

plucked: instruments with a flexible tongue that is plucked to vibrate

scraped: sound produced by scraping the instrument with a stick across grooves

shakers: sound produced by small particles contained within the instrument

stamping: striking the object on a hard surface to vibrate the object

syncopation: to have rhythm that is "off-beat" or doesn't fall right on the beats of a song

unpitched instruments: instruments incapable of making distinct notes and pitch changes, but have one pitch only; usually used to keep the rhythm and tempo steady (e.g., wood-block, claves)

Chapter 7

Music and the Brain

Chapter Summary: Scientists are only recently beginning to investigate the relationship between music and the brain as the field of neuroscience develops. This chapter covers some of this research in terms of music processing, active listening, and benefits of the music-brain connection.

The brain is malleable from childhood to adulthood. If musical training is found to have a beneficial effect on brain function beyond that involved in musical performance, this may have implications for the education of children, for life-long strategies to preserve the fitness of the aging brain…

—C. Pantev (Baycrest, 2002)

Dr. Christo Pantev made the above statement over 10 years ago, when embarking on a groundbreaking study to show that musicians' brains hear music differently from those of non-musicians. This began a wave of neurological studies on music and the brain, all of which point to the same conclusion: that musical study and training are indeed beneficial to the human brain.

Brain research is proceeding at an amazing pace, with countless new studies and discoveries appearing every year. With that said, let's take a look at what we currently know about the impact of music on the brain and beyond, keeping in mind that this information will become more and more detailed and specific in the coming years. In this chapter, we will examine the following questions: Is music innate to humans? How does the brain process music? How does the brain respond to music making? Music listening? What are some of the overall benefits of music?

I. Are We Hardwired for Music?

Music is a human universal. In order to determine if a certain human trait is part of the brain's hardwiring, scientists submit it to a set of criteria. Some of the questions concerning the biological evidence of music's hardwiring include 1) whether or not it is present in all cultures; 2) if the ability to process music appears early in life, i.e., it is found in infants; 3) if examples of music are found in the animal world; and 4) if there are specialized areas of the brain dedicated to it. Music fulfills all of these criteria, and is definitely hard-wired in the human brain.

All Cultures Have Music

For thousands of years people have sung, performed, and enjoyed music. World travelers and social scientists have consistently observed that all of the people in the world have some type of music, and all people recognize music when they hear it, even if they have different names and categories for what they hear. While the music of other cultures will sound different and have different meanings and emotions associated with it, every culture makes it.

Researchers in different fields have summarized conclusions about the nature of music and culture after many years of observing human behavior and music. Alan Merriam, an anthropologist and one of the founders of ethnomusicology, created a list of ten commonalities of musical behavior after travelling extensively among many different people. His list, known as the "Ten Functions of Music," is included in his landmark study *The Anthropology of Music* (1964).

1. Emotional expression
2. Aesthetic enjoyment
3. Entertainment
4. Communication
5. Symbolic representation
6. Physical response
7. Enforcing conformity to social norms
8. Validating social institutions and religious rituals
9. Providing continuity and stability of culture
10. Facilitating social integration

Everett Gaston, a psychologist, music educator, and founding father of music therapy, developed a similar list containing eight fundamental considerations of the impact of music on humans concerning his work on music and therapy in *Music in Therapy* (1968).

1. All humans need aesthetic expression and experiences
2. Musical experiences are culturally determined
3. Music has spiritual significance
4. Music is communication
5. Music structures reality
6. Music is derived from the deepest and most tender human emotions
7. Music serves as a source of personal gratification
8. The potency of musical effects are greatest in social interactions

Physiological and Cultural Functions of Music

It is impossible to separate what we now know about the role of the body in the creation of music from cultural musical behaviors. Just how much of a role the neurological plays in music making and perception and how much is governed by music as a cultural institution remains to be seen. However, it is valuable to consider the implications of both when discussing music's impact on humans. After several decades of research, I have developed a set of functions for music that takes into account the role of neurology and physiology as well as culture in its relationship to music.

Socially connects
- Integrates, mobilizes, controls, expresses, unites, and normalizes.

Communicates
- History, memory, emotions, cultural beliefs, and social mores. It educates, creates the status quo, and also protests against it.

Coordinates and instigates neurological and physical movement
- Work/labor, military drills, dance, ritual, and trance.
- Songs and chants use the beat to maintain a group's tempo and coordinate movements, or it stimulates entrainment found in trance by lining up the brain's frequencies with that of sound.

Stimulates pleasure senses
- Excites, emotes, entertains, and elicits neurochemical responses, such as sweaty hands and a rapid heartbeat.
- It's addictive, creating cycles of expectation and satisfying that anticipation. It stimulates the pleasure center in the ancient part of the brain responsible for re-warding stimuli such as food or sex.
- We get a "chill" when listening to music from a dopamine release anticipating a peak emotional response.

Alters perception
- Regulates and changes mood/emotion. It's therapeutic, cathartic, and allows transcendence.
- Fosters flexible experiencing of time.
- Increases focus and attention and stimulates large areas of the brain.

Constructs identity (cultural and personal)
- Defines, represents, symbolizes, expresses, and transforms (Sarrazin, 2014).

Activity 7A

TRY THIS

In our culture, we tend to think of music primarily as entertainment. After studying the lists of music's functions on the previous page, think of some of your own uses and examples of music. What do you use music for? When do you use it? How? Have you used music to create, foster, and support relationships with others? To communicate? To restructure reality? For your health, well-being, and emotional support?

Musical Ability in Infants

According to recent neurological research, "the ability to perceive and enjoy music is an inborn human trait" (Sousa, 2011, p. 221). If music is an inborn and biological component, it should be found in infants, as well as in other animal species. Musical ability is indeed found in infants, who at only a few months old can manipulate an object in response to hearing certain songs. Infants can also differentiate between sounds as well as recognize different melodies. They are well aware of their mother's voice and will turn their heads towards it when she speaks.

Musical Use in Animal Culture

Another approach scientists take to determine if we are hardwired for music is looking for examples in the animal world. We are all aware of the presence of birdsong and the musical patterns emitted by dolphins and whales to communicate, but so far, it has been difficult to determine if animals have the ability for abstraction required to understand music and art. However, there are growing examples in animal research demonstrating that animals do indeed use music, and that monkeys and other animals use musical patterns and can hear abstractions in music as well. A study by Kaplan (2009) indicates that animals are responsive to music and may even engage in music activity.

Specialized Areas of the Brain

The final clue as to music's innateness is that there are many areas of the brain that process music. The auditory cortex has areas that process pitch, while other areas of the brain combine biology and culture to stimulate the limbic system to respond emotionally to music.

II. How the Brain Processes Music

Neurologists have long known that there were areas of the brain specifically dedicated to music, but through fMRIs and Pet scans conducted in live time, they've discovered that music's reach is far more extensive. When listening to music, sound vibrations enter the auditory cortex and are instantaneously broken down into elements of pitch, timbre, spatial relations, and tone duration. The data is then sent to other parts of the brain and compared against stored sound associations (do I run or stay) and emotional responses (do I like it or not), stimulating many parts of the brain in both hemispheres.

The auditory cortex is the brain's primary region for hearing and processing sound, and is part of the brain's cerebral cortex. As we might expect, the auditory cortex helps us discern different sounds processed by the cochlea. It processes frequencies (pitch), and contains numerous neurons organized from low to high (known as a frequency map), which are dedicated to specific pitches. The auditory cortex also recognizes the location of different sound sources in space, and can identify and segregate different auditory objects.

Another aspect of the auditory cortex's function is how it groups or perceives musical information. Diana Deutsch (2010) writes that the auditory cortex performs fusions and separations of sound components according to the music fundamentals of pitch (frequency) and timing. Pitch information is one of the most significant and most well-understood aspects of the musical brain. Pitch information includes the related concepts of intervals, melody, and harmony. The brain processes pitch information both locally and globally, where local music refers to the intervals between pitches, while global processing refers to the entire contour of the melody. This type of processing may have implications for teaching, and awareness of the brain's reaction to music can help inform teaching strategies and techniques.

Time information, which includes rhythm, tempo and meter, timbre, meaning, and emotion is less understood. Musical timbre is one of the most critical of all components of music, yet remains one of the most mysterious of all human perceptual attributes. In a 2012 study, Patil et al. examined the neural underpinnings of musical timbre in order to understand the underlying processes of timbre recognition. They observed how timbre is recognized at the mammalian primary auditory cortex to predict human sound source recognition. The primary auditory cortex is one of the oldest and first developed areas of the human brain, suggesting that recognizing timbre is an extremely important function in human evolution. Although neurologists are still exploring how the auditory cortex functions, they now believe that music processing is actually much more complex then initially imagined, and involves many more parts of the brain than previously thought.

Activity 7B

WATCH THIS

In 2009, the World Science Festival "Notes and Neurons: In search of the common chorus" features Bobby McFerrin and an array of scientists discussing music's impact on the human brain.

III. Benefits of Learning Music

Music's influence on the brain is significant, and includes therapeutic improvements, healing, educational, and cognitive benefits. According to Campbell (2011b), author of the book Healing at the Speed of Sound: How What We Hear Transforms Our Brains and Our Lives, "A child who is moving, dancing and singing learns coordination between their eye, ear and sound early on. And [the experience of participating in music education] helps integrate the social, the emotional and the real context of what we're learning. There are studies that show children who play music have higher SAT scores, that learning to control rhythm and tempo not only help them get along with others but plants seeds for similar advantages when we get much older."

Music not only helps increase children's verbal memory and reduces memory loss during aging, but aids people in healing faster after a stroke, reduces stress and anxiety, increases memory retention, helps transplant recipients, and soothes pain.

Music shows a positive impact on a person's
- vision, body awareness, and gross and fine motor skills;
- directionality—moving expressively in response to directions and use of musical instruments;
- acquisition of receptive and expressive language, voice in singing;
- cognitive abilities of memorization, sequencing, imitation, and classification; making relationships and choices affects each child's ability to create new lyrics, melodies, harmonies, and rhythms and express perceptions of dynamics, mood, form, and timbre;
- and ability to pay attention.

In a 2006 study, Tallal et al. suggest relationships between musical training, auditory processing, language, and literary skills. The study shows that music training and musical aptitude improves or correlates positively with:

- **Music Processing** (melody, rhythm, meter, timbre, harmony, etc.)
- **General Auditory Processing** (pitch discrimination, pitch memory, auditory rapid spectrotemporal processing)
- **Language and Literary Skills** (reading, phonological awareness, pitch processing in speech, prosody perception, verbal memory, verbal fluency)

The study also indicates that after musical training, there was an improvement in attention, sequencing skills, and processing literary components such as syllables, language skills, and literacy skills.

A two–three-year-long study concluded that children attending a musical play school exhibited significant differences in auditory discrimination and attention compared to children not involved in music. Children with exposure to more musical activities showed more mature processing of auditory features and heightened sensitivity in temporal aspects of sounds, while surprising sounds were less likely to distract the children's attention (Putkenin et al., 2013).

Study after study records significant findings regarding brain changes in musicians, particularly instrumental musicians' motor, auditory, and visual-spatial regions (Gaser, 2003). These same brain changes occur at very early ages for young children who play music. Children with only 15 months of musical training demonstrated structural brain changes in early childhood, which correlated with improvements in relevant motor and auditory skills (Hyde et al., 2009).

Activity 7C

LEARN MORE

7. What does music have to do with creativity? This TED talk by Charles Limb discusses just that and more.
8. "How music changes our brains": An article on how music affects the brain.
9. An incredible video showing a three-year-old child conducting Beethoven.
10. An article and video on the psychological effects of music on health and to help the body sleep.

The "Mozart Effect"

In the past decade, scientists have become very interested in studying the effects of sound on the human brain, and parents have rushed to embrace and apply any possible benefit to the development of their children. One of the early studies that spurred a rather heightened curiosity of the benefits of music was dubbed the "Mozart Effect." In 1993, a study by Rauscher et al. was published, which looked at the possible correlations between listening to different types of music and intelligence. Soon after, the study erroneously credited with the notion that listening to classical music, particularly the music of Mozart, made you more intelligent. As a result, people started buying and playing Mozart to their children thinking that this would increase their intelligence. Georgia Governor Zell Miller, in 1998, proposed sending every newborn in the state a copy of a classical CD based on this supposed "effect." The Baby Einstein toy company was also launched in reaction to this study. However, the study only demonstrated a small benefit in the area of spatial reasoning as a result of listening to Mozart, and the limited results showed that a person's IQ increased for only a brief period of time—no longer than 15 minutes, after which it returned to normal. Other studies have not been able to replicate even the 15-minute bump in IQ.

READ THIS <u>GOVERNOR MILLER'S REACTION TO THE "MOZART EFFECT"</u>

IV. Listening to Music vs. Creating Music

Both listening to and creating music are crucial factors in engaging a child's brain with music. There is, however, a clear difference in what happens in our brains when we listen to music and when we make music.

In terms of listening to music, there is a difference between the intensity and focus required to simply hear music (or hearing anything for that matter) and *listening* to music. Hearing is the act of perceiving sounds by the ear. In other words, if you are not hearing impaired, your ear will pick up and receive sounds. Good and active *listening*, on the other hand, is something that is done consciously, and requires some type of focus or engagement on behalf of the individual. Most of us are well aware of the fact that we can hear something without really listening to it or understanding it.

It is also true that all listening is not the same. In terms of our daily interactions with sound, we are constantly bombarded with all types of sounds, both chosen and unchosen. Kassabian (2013) calls the constant presence of music in modern life "ubiquitous listening." Children are also inundated with sounds that enhance life or distract from it, dividing children's already fragile attention and making it difficult for them to filter out unwanted noises and focus.

Understanding the full range of listening possibilities begins with what Peterson (2006) identifies as three types of listening: passive listening, responsive listening, and active listening.

- **Passive listening** means that music is in the background, and usually the person is doing something else while the music is playing. There is very little in the way of interaction or engagement with the music.
  - Classroom examples: Playing music while children are doing homework.
- **Responsive listening** means that music creates an atmosphere. The listener responds with heightened emotion.
  - Classroom examples: Playing calming music after an active event; playing music before the school day starts.
- **Active listening** means that music is the main focus. The listener interacts with the music in a cognitive, emotional, and meaningful way.
  - Classroom examples: Finding the meaning of the piece through the lyrics, recognizing musical patterns, and finding elements such as phrases, direction of the melody, and rhythm.

These three types of listening are not ranked in any way, nor are these categories concrete. There are specific times when one type will fulfill the goal of an activity more effectively than another, and, as Peterson points out (2006), sometimes you find yourself actively listening to a piece of background music or even a ring tone, or you might just as easily disengage from a live concert recital as an audience member. All music listening can't be active listening. It is important to keep in mind that simply exposing children to music in and of itself is already extremely beneficial and highly influential in terms of developing extended musical tastes, and connects music to the well being of the child on an emotional and cognitive level. Creating active listeners who can focus, concentrate, and direct their attention should be one of the main goals of teaching, and one in which music can play a vital role.

While music listening is wonderful for our brains, it turns out that music performance is really where the fireworks happen.

- **Performing music involves all regions of the brain** such as the visual, auditory, motor, sensory, and prefrontal cortices; corpus callosum; hippocampus; and cerebellum. It speeds up communication between the hemispheres and affects language and higher-order brain functioning.
- **Music increases brain plasticity**, changing neural pathways. Musicians tend to have greater word memory and more complex neural brain patterning, as well as greater organizational and higher-order executive functioning.
- **Playing an instrument influences generalized parts of the brain used for other functions.** People who receive music training demonstrated increased efficiency in many other skills, including linguistic processing ability, and increased motor, auditory, and visual-spatial brain regions (Gaser and Schlaug, 2003).

In short, scientists say that nothing we do as humans uses more parts of our brain and is more complex than playing an instrument.

But until very recently, we didn't have proof of music's extensive cognitive benefits. Yet some innate imperative to make music has guaranteed its existence—a remarkable feat considering that music requires such intense cultural investment. But of all of music's contributions to the human condition, its ability to create social cohesion and communicate emotion has ensured its longevity. Evolutionary psychologists Kirschner and Tomasello strongly suggest that music fosters social bonding and empathy (2010). Children who had previously made music together were significantly more likely to spontaneously help each other than those who had not.

Activity 7D

TRY THIS

Create lesson ideas that involve *passive, responsive,* and *active* listening with children.

Active Listening to Music

Guiding children towards more deliberate and *active* listening that engages the brain and all of its neural connections is highly beneficial. Children should hopefully be able to not only comprehend the musical elements, but also uncover cognitive meaning and the memory aspects of the song in order to stimulate all of the parts of the brain mentioned in the previous section.

Music listening is, of course, closely related to brain function. **Auditory stimulation** through simple activities can enhance attention in children, exercise the brain, and create a flexible and responsive brain. **Auditory discrimination** exercises work the child's ability to hear differences in sound in order to organize and make sense of sound. These exercises provide focal points for children's active listening and response, working *local* listening.

Although these exercises were developed for children with special needs, they are highly applicable in developing crucial musical listening skills and for helping children recognize categories of music, instruments, and timbre of sounds.

Exercises for engaging in auditory discrimination.

Adapted from Callandar and Buttriss (2007)

Exercises for engaging in Auditory Discrimination
Aural-visual identification • Children listen to sounds on a CD and point to a picture of the object making the sound and name it. • Point to a real object that makes the sound and then try it out. • Sound walk: pupils draw pictures or write down the names of the sounds they hear on the walk. • Show children picture-noun cards and have them clap the syllable beats. • Aural identification: Listen to the sound of real objects with eyes closed. Children guess and name. • Sound bingo: Listen to sounds and cover the correct picture. • Clap or tap rhythms of children's names and have them identify them.
Grouping sounds • Ask children to group similar sounds by source (animals, musical instruments, vehicles); by timbre (rough, airy, scratchy); or by material (wooden, metallic, electronic). • Odd one out: ask the pupils to identify the sound that is not part of a group of sounds (e.g. dogs barking, pig grunting, cow mooing, musical instrument playing).
Musical discrimination • Discriminate between loud/quiet, high/low, fast/slow, rough/smooth, contrasting phrases or sections.

Activity 7E

TRY THIS

Think of some activities that incorporate the above exercises. How might you adapt some of these to a language arts lesson? A social studies lesson? An art lesson?

References

Baycrest Center For Geriatric Care. (2002). Study to look at possible benefits of musical training on brain function in young and old. *Science Daily.* Retrieved April 19, 2013, from http://www.sciencedaily.com/releases/2002/01/020110074219.htm

Callandar, A., and Buttriss, J. (2008). *A-Z of special needs for every teacher* (2nd ed.). London: Optimus Education.

Campbell, D., and Doman, A. (2011a). *Healing at the speed of sound: How what we hear transforms our brains and our lives.* New York : Hudson Street Press.

Campbell, D. (2011b, October 23). How music changes our brains / Interviewer: Thomas Rogers. *Salon.* Retrieved from http://www.salon.com/2011/10/23/how_music_warps_our_minds/

Deutsch, D. (2010). Hearing music in ensembles. *Physics Today*, 63(2), 40–45.

Edwards, R. (2008). *The neurosciences and music education: An online database of brain imaging neuromusical research* (Doctoral dissertation). Retrieved from ProQuest UMI (NEED ACCESSION or ORDER NO.).

Gaser, C., & Schlaug, G. (2003). Brain structures differ between musicians and non-musicians. *The Journal of Neuroscience,* 8 October 23 (27): 9240–9245.

Gaston, E. T. (1968). *Music in therapy.* New York: Macmillan.

Hyde, K., Lerch, J., Norton, A., Forgeard, M., Winner, E., Eans, A., & Schlaug, G. (2009). The effects of musical training on structural brain development: A longitudinal study. In S. Dalla Bella et al. (Eds.), *The neurosciences and music iii: Disorders and plasticity* (182–186). New York: Annuals of the New York Academy of Science, 1169.

Jensen, E. (2002). *Arts with the brain in mind.* Alexandria, VA: Association for Supervision and Curriculum Development.

Kaplan, G. (2009). Animals and music: Between cultural definitions and sensory evidence. *Sign Systems Studies*, 37, 3(4), 423–451.

Kassabian, A. (2013). *Ubiquitous listening: Affect, attention, and distributed subjectivity.* Berkeley, CA: University of California Press.

Kirschner, S., & Tomasello, M. (2010). Joint music making promotes prosocial behavior in 4-year-old children. *Evolution and Human Behavior* 31, 354–364.

Merriam, A. (1964). *The anthropology of music.* Chicago, IL: Northwestern University Press.

Overy, K., Norton, A., Cronin, K., Winner, E., & Schlaug, G. (2005). Examining rhythm and melody processing in young children using fMRI. In G. Avanzini et al. (Eds.), *Neurosciences and music ii: From perception to performance* (210–218). New York: Annals of the New York Academy of Sciences, 1060.

Pantev, C., Oostenveld, R., Engelien, A., Ross, B., Roberts, L. E., & Hoke, M. (1998). Increased auditory cortical representation in musicians. *Nature 392*, 811–814.

Patil, K., Pressnitzer, D., Shamma, S., & Elhilali, M. (2012). Music in our ears: The biological bases of musical timbre perception. *PLoS Comput Biol 8*(11), e1002759. doi:10.1371/journal.pcbi.1002759

Peterson, E. (2006). *Inspired by listening: Teaching your curriculum while actively listening to music: Strategies for all teachers.* Hampton Falls, NH: Yeogirl Press.

Putkinen, V., Teraviemi, M., & Huotilainen, M. (2013). Effects of informal music activities on auditory discrimination and attention in 2–3-year-old children. *European Journal of Neuroscience 37*(4), 654–61. Video presentation on the research.

Schellenberg, E., & Hallam, S. (2005). Listening and cognitive abilities in 10- and 11-year-olds: The blur effect. In G. Avanzini et al. (Eds.), *Neurosciences and music ii: From perception to performance* (202–209). New York: Annals of the New York Academy of Sciences, 1060.

Schlaug, G., Norton, A., Overy, K.; & Winner, E. (2005). Effects of music training on the child's brain and cognitive development. In G. Avanzini et al. (Eds.), *Neurosciences and music ii: From perception to performance* (219–230). New York: Annals of the New York Academy of Sciences, 1050.

Sousa, D. (2011). *How the brain learns.* Thousand Oaks, CA: Corwin Press.

Tallal, P., & Gaab, N. (2006). Dynamic auditory processing, musical experience and language development. *TRENDS in Neuroscience, 29*(7), 382–390.

Vaughn, K. (2000). Music and mathematics: Modest support for the oft-claimed relationship. *Journal of Aesthetic Education 34*, 149–166.

Warren, J. (2008). How does the brain process music? *Clinical Medicine: Royal College of Physicians 8*(1), 32–36.

Vocabulary

active listening: music is the main focus; the listener interacts with the music in a cognitive, emotional, and meaningful way

auditory discrimination: the ability to hear differences in sound in order to organize and make sense of sound

auditory stimulation: stimulating the brain through sound such as music

hearing: the act of perceiving sounds through the ear

passive listening: music is in the background, and usually the person is doing something else while the music is playing; there is very little in the way of interaction or engagement with the music

responsive listening: means that music creates an atmosphere; the listener responds with heightened emotion

Chapter 8

Music in Early Childhood Development

Chapter Summary: This chapter focuses on the role of music in early childhood, including the importance of musical experience in early childhood, the musical abilities and enjoyment of infants and children, and the vocal ranges of the young child. It also explores musical activities and repertoires appropriate for young children.

What a child has heard in his first six years of life cannot be eradicated later. Thus it is too late to begin teaching at school, because a child stores a mass of musical impressions before school age, and if what is bad predominates, then his fate, as far as music is concerned, has been sealed for a lifetime.

—Zoltán Kodály, Children's Day Speech, 1951

Arts as a Means of Expression for Young Children

How important are the arts as a mode of expression for children? Children, especially very young children, cannot express themselves fluently either through speech or writing—two modes of communication that adults use almost exclusively. Instead, children express themselves through movement, sound, and art. If they can express themselves through these modes, it is logical that they can learn through them as well.

Many times, however, adults are at a loss to understand or interpret what it is children are saying to us, or to appreciate how profound it might be. Mark E. Turner (2008), building upon the work of Edwin Gordon and Reggio Emilia, thought considerably about children's representation through the arts. He sought to provide authentic ways for children to express themselves and developed scaffolding to better harness and understand children's musical development. As Turner states, the idea that the "performing arts" must always be performed onstage to be valid detracts from their use to develop and explore the emotional, cognitive, social development and human potential.

Activity 8A

READ MORE

Children, Meaning-Making, and the Arts, Susan Wright ed. 2nd ed., Pearson, 2012.

Music for Young Children

Any of the music methods (e.g., Kodály, Orff) mentioned in Chapter 4 offer sequential learning for children. Kodály in particular spent a great deal of effort on developing beautiful singing voices for young children. Children's voices, after all, are their first instrument—a child's first exceptionally pleasant musical experience is likely to be hearing lullabies from a parent or guardian, and then vocally experimenting with his or her own voice. Kodály graded learning in small steps for the very beginner learners, starting with three-note songs (sol, mi, la) and expanding gradually to four, five, and six notes and beyond. For the youngest, songs with three notes are an excellent place to start, because these children will not have much difficulty imitating or matching these pitches and can be successful from the outset.

I. Music for Children Birth to Three Years Old

Music activity for infants and toddlers engages the child's aural and physical being. Such age-old activities include tickling, wiggling, bouncing, and finger playing.

At this level, musical play creates and reinforces the special personal bond between an adult (or older child) and infant, while also introducing music to the child. For newborns and very young children, speaking a rhyme and wiggling toes connects sound to a pleasurable and intimate act, as well as introducing the idea of rhythm and phrasing to newborns and young children.

Below are a few of the rhymes and songs particularly good for newborns and toddlers. They include some very familiar nursery rhymes and action games appropriate for this age group. Keep in mind that almost any nursery rhyme can be used for these activities, as long as they have a steady beat, which luckily most of them do.

Bounces

For newborns to three-year-olds, having them feel the beat in their bodies, aided by adults, are called "bounces," based on the experience of bouncing a child up and down on a knee or lap.

Bumpity Bump

O - ver the road we bump - i - ty bump,   O - ver the road we bump - i - ty bump,

O - ver the road we bump - i - ty bump,   How we love to bump - i - ty bump!

Tommy O'Flynn

Tom - my O' - Flynn and the   old grey mare, Went to see the coun - try fair. The

bridge fell down and the bridge fell in, and   that was the end of Tom - my O' - Flynn.

Tommy O'Flynn and the old grey mare (bounce child on knees)
Went to see the country fair
The bridge fell down and the bridge fell in (open knees and let child drop a bit)
And that was the end of Tommy O'Flynn

Wiggles

Wiggles are those activities involving the wiggling of fingers or toes. "This Little Piggy Went to Market" is another wiggle with which you may be familiar.

The first little pig danced a merry, merry jig
The second little pig ate candy
The third little pig wore a blue and yellow wig
The fourth little pig was a dandy
The fifth little pig never grew to be big
So they called him Tiny Little Andy

Tickles

Tickles involve exactly that—tickling the child either all over or just in the stomach, usually ending in lots of giggles!

Slowly, slowly, very slowly up the garden trail (*crawl hands up baby starting from feet*)
Slowly, slowly, very slowly creeps the garden snail (*continue crawling*)

Quickly, quickly, very quickly all around the house (*tickle all over*)
Quickly, quickly, very quickly runs the little mouse (*continue tickling*)
My father was a butcher (*make chopping motions on child's body*)
My mother cuts the meat (*make cutting motions on child's body*)
And I'm a little hot dog
That runs around the street (*tickle all over*)

Pizza pickle pumpernickel

Pizza, pickle, pumpernickel (*flash one hand wide, then the other, then roll arms*)
My little one shall have a tickle! (*tickle child*)
One for your nose (*tickle child's nose*)
And one for your toes (*tickle child's toes*)
And one for your tummy, where the hot dog goes! (*tickle child's tummy*)

Finger Play

Finger play songs can also be types of *tickles*. The most common finger play song is the "Eensy, Weensy Spider."

Eensy Weensy Spider

Tapping

For an infant, the parent would take the child's foot or hand and tap it to the beat of the music. If the child can tap by him- or herself, that will work also.

Cock a Doodle Do

English nursery rhyme, 1765

Cock-a-doo-dle-do, My dame has lost her shoe, My mas-ter's lost his fid-dling stick and

does-n't know what to do. And does-n't know what to do, And does-n't know what to do,

My mas-ter's lost his fid-dling stick and does-n't know what to do.

> Cock-a-doodle doo (tap one foot)
> My dame has lost her shoe
> My master's lost his fiddling stick
> And doesn't know what to do.
> Cock-a-doodle doo (tap other foot)
> What is my dame to do?
> Til master finds his fiddling stick
> She'll dance without a shoe.
> Cock-a-doodle doo (tap both feet)
> My dame has found her shoe
> And master's found his fiddling stick
> Sing doodle, doodle, doo.

Clapping (Nine+ Months)

As children develop physically, they can clap their hands either together or against those of another. The well-known "Patty Cake" is a good example.

Patty Cake

> Patty cake, patty cake, baker's man
> Bake me a cake as fast as you can
> Roll it and pat it and mark it with a "B"
> And put it in the oven for baby and me!

Hot Cross Buns

> Hot cross buns
> Hot cross buns
> One a penny, two a penny
> Hot cross buns.

Pease Porridge Hot
   Pease porridge hot
   Pease porridge cold
   Pease porridge in the pot
   Nine days old.

Responding to the Beat: Moving to Music

Responding to a musical beat is an innate part of what it means to be human, and even the youngest children can begin to feel music, either by moving to the beat or having an adult help a child move to the beat (Feierabend, 2001).

The simplest thing to do is to find recordings of quality music and play songs with an even, steady beat and have children move, clap, tap, patsch, hit an instrument, or walk to that beat.

An extended possibility is to create a story, miming movements that reflect a steady beat while telling a simple narrative. For example, a leader begins by miming actions such as teeth brushing, bouncing a ball, or eating food from a bowl, and the group imitates them. All movements are done to the beat (e.g., teeth brushing, up down up down). At the end of the leader's turn, the children have to remember the "storyline."

Lullabies

Bye Baby Bunting

English lullaby, 1784

All the Pretty Little Horses

African American lullaby

When you wake,   you shall have,   All   the pret - ty   lit - tle   hors - es

Blacks and   bays,   Dap - ples and   grays,   All   the Pret - ty   lit - tle   hors - es.

Hush - a - bye,   don't you   cry,   Go   to sle - ep   lit - tle   ba - by.

Hush Little Baby, Don't Say a Word

American lullaby song

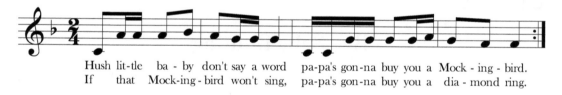

Hush lit-tle   ba - by don't say a word   pa-pa's gon-na buy you a Mock - ing - bird.
If   that   Mock-ing - bird won't sing,   pa-pa's gon-na buy you a   dia - mond ring.

II. Music for Children Three to Five Years Old

Three- to five-year-olds are capable of singing more complicated songs, doing more complicated games and rhymes, and, of course, capable of more sophisticated listening. They can also understand some of the basic vocabulary and building blocks of music. It is appropriate to introduce a few concepts when performing songs and games with children, and also to experiment with these concepts, such as changing tempos and dynamics. Some vocabulary to use when pointing out these concept to younger children include:
- High—Low (pitch)
- Loud—Soft (dynamics)
- Fast—Slow (tempo)
- Smooth—Detached (articulation)
- Duple—Triple (meter)
- Steady Beat (tempo)
- Timbre (the quality of sound)

For slightly older children, Feierabend (2001) identifies activities that help children develop spontaneous music ability and original music thinking under his "Arioso" category, as well as a detailed array of vocal- and motor-based experiences with music.

Feierabend's music readiness approach in his series *First Steps in Music*

An 8-part music readiness curriculum for 3–8 year old children (Feierabend, 2006)

Singing/Tonal Activity Categories	
1. Pitch Exploration/Vocal Warm-up	Discovering the sensation of the singing voice • Vocal glissandos
2. Fragment Singing	Developing independent singing • Echo songs • Call-and-response songs
3. Simple Songs	Developing independent singing and musical syntax • Three–five-note songs • Expanded range
4. Arioso	Developing original musical thinking • Spontaneous created songs by the child
5. Song Tales	Developing expressive sensitivity through listening • Ballads for children
Movement Activities Categories	
6. Movement Exploration/Warm-up	Developing expressive sensitivity through movement • Movement with and without classical music accompaniment
7. Movement for Form and Expression	Singing/speaking and moving with formal structure and expression • Non-locomotor (finger plays, action songs, circle games, with recorded music) • Locomotor (circle games, with recorded music)

8. Beat Motion Activities	Developing competencies in maintaining the beat in groups of two and three
	• Child-initiated beat motions
	   • Non-locomotor or locomotor
	• Teacher-initiated beat motions
	   • Non-locomotor or locomotor

Vocal Activities for Three to Five Years Old

Preschoolers (three-, four-, and five-year-olds) have a range of six notes between a middle C and the A above it. Their most comfortable notes are in the middle between E and F.

Most comfortable notes

The goal is to have them not sing too far below the staff or too low in their voices, and to not push or strain their voices too far above this range either. Singing should be light, in the child's head voice, never forced or pushed, and beautiful music-making should be stressed.

Initially, children need to explore their voices to find out what they are capable of, and to start hearing that their voices do indeed have a range to them. It is very good for children to make light, airy, and smooth sounds in their head voice as they find their individual sound.

Begin with some vocal exploration with speech, just getting them to loosen up and find their high, light head voice.

Voice exploration speech exercises

1. I take my voice up high
I take my voice up high (start low, and slide voice up)
I bring my voice down low (Start high, and slide voice down)
I send my voice out into space (Cup hands around mouth and project)
I whisper all around, whisper, whisper (Whisper line and whisper to neighbors)

2. Bow wow
Bow wow, says the dog (medium voice)
Meow, meow says the cat (high voice)
Grunt, grunt says the hog (low voice)
Squeak, squeak says the rat (very high)

3. Elevator
Have the children pretend their voice is an elevator sliding up and down between floors. They can accompany their vocal exploration with physical moving up and down as well, or the teacher may want to have a focal object like a puppet moving up and down that they can follow with their voice.

Pitch matching songs and games

Begin with simple but interesting songs with small ranges. These songs can be varied and repeated, and help children sing accurately. "Who's Wearing Blue" is an excellent warm-up or opening activity in a music class. What did the children wear? do? see? There are endless, creative opportunities to ask them about their lives in a few notes.

Sol, mi, la songs

Who's Wearing Blue?

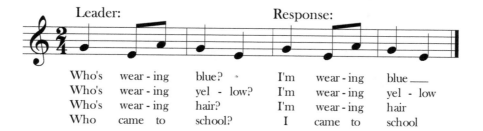

We are Dancing in the Forest

SCALE: S, M, L

One child is the wolf, who hides. All other children hold hands in circle, and move in circle while singing.

We are dan-cing in the for-est, Who knows what will hap-pen to us,

While the wolf is far a-way, If he finds us at our play.

Mi, re, do songs

Hot Cross Buns

English traditional street cry, 1733

Hot cross buns! Hot cross buns! One ha' pen-ny, Two ha' pen-ny,

Hot cross buns! Hot cross buns! Hot cross buns! One ha' pen-ny, Two ha' pen-ny,

Hot cross buns!

Simple songs in a limited range

Rain, Rain Go Away

Traditional children's song, 17th century

Rain, Rain, go a-way, come a-gain some oth-er day

Snail, Snail

Children form a single line, holding on the waist of the child in front of them. The child at the front of the line is the snail's head, who holds up and wiggles both index fingers on the forehead representing the snail's eyestalks. The line shuffles around the room imitating the slow, fluid motions of a snail.

Scale: S, M, L

Snail, snail, snail, snail, round and round, and round and round.

Little Sally Water

Scale S, M, L   Traditional American circle game song

Lit-tle Sal-ly Wa-ter, Sit-ting in a sau-cer, Rise, Sal-ly rise, Wipe out your eyes,

Turn to the east, Sal-ly, Turn to the west, Sal-ly, turn to the one that you like the best, Sal-ly.

See Saw, Margery Daw

English nursery rhyme, 1765

See - saw Mar-ger-y Daw, Jack shall have a new mas-ter.

He shall get a pen-ny a day Be-cause he can't work an-y fast-er.

I Have Lost my Closet Key

American folk song

I have lost my clos-et key In my la-dy's gar-den.
found

I have lost my clos-et key In my la-dy's gar-den.
found

Accompanying game for "I Have Lost my Closet Key": Children sit in a circle. One child hides a key in their hand while another child walks around the circle trying to guess who has the key while all sing Verse 1. After finding the key, all sing Verse 2. That person then becomes "it" and another is chosen to hide the key.

Au Clair de la Lune

French folk song

Au Clair de la Lu - ne, Mon a - mi Pier - rot.
In the eve - ning moon - light, My dear friend Pier - rot.

Pre - tes - moi ta plu - me, Pour e - crire un mot.
Lend to me a pen - cil, so that I may write.

Ring Around the Rosy

English song attributed to 1665 Black Plague, but sources only go back to 19th century

Ring - a - round - the ros - ie a po - cket full of po - sie,

ash - es　ash - es　we　all　fall　down.

Sally Go Round the Sun

Scale: D, R, M, S, L

Sal - ly　go　round　the　sun,　Sal - ly　go　round　the　moon,

Sal - ly　go　round　the　sun - shine,　Ev - ery aft - er - noon,　Boom!

Rocky Mountain

Appalachian folk song

Scale: D, M, S, L

Rock - y　moun - tain,　rock - y　moun - tain,　rock - y　moun - tain　high.

When　you're　on　that　rock - y　moun - tain,　Hang　your　head　and　cry.

Do,　do,　do,　do,　do　re - mem - ber　me.

Do,　do　do　do,　do　re - mem - ber　me.

No Bears Out Tonight

One child is the "bear" who hides while others count one o' clock to midnight.
Children search for the bear, then run back to "home" when the bear is found.

No   bears   out   to-night,   No   bears   out   to-night,

No   bears   out   to-night,   They've   all   gone   a - way

The Mulberry Bush

English nursery rhyme, 1840s

Scale: D, R, M, S, L, T

Here   we   go 'round   the   Mul-ber-ry   bush,   the   Mul-ber-ry   bush,   the   Mul-ber-ry   bush.

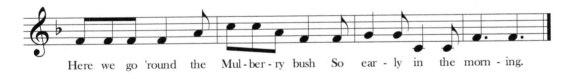

Here   we   go 'round   the   Mul-ber-ry   bush   So   ear-ly   in   the   morn-ing.

Instrumental Music Activities for Three to Five Years Old

High/Low Pitches: You or a child plays a low instrument (drum, bass xylophone, etc.) and children respond by moving in low space. Then try the same for high-pitched instruments (triangle, tambourine, etc.), having them move through high space.

Fast/Slow Tempo and Loud/Soft Dynamics Game: Similar to above, play instruments in different tempos and dynamics. Switch and mix them up (fast and loud, soft and slow, fast and soft, slow and loud), and if the child doesn't switch, he or she is out.

Contrasting Timbres: Assign a different movement to different timbres. For example, a wood block corresponds to a hop, a xylophone glissando is a leap, a shaker means to shake. Create an orchestra with half of the class playing and the other half responding. For more advanced children, create a choreographed and composed piece from the game.

Musical Simon Says: Review concepts learned such as loud/soft, high/low, or fast/slow. Simon says yell loud, Simon says whisper, Simon says sing high, Simon says groan low, etc.

Rhymes and Games

Poetry and rhymes are among the most basic forms of human expression, and both children and adults use poetry, rhymes, and games to tell stories, remember history, fantasize, dream, and play. For young children, the rhyme is magical as they first encounter the powerful sound of rhyming words. Words create rhythmic patterns that captivate a child's attention. The natural rhythms inherent in rhyming can become the basis for exploration, improvisation, vocalizations, and instrumental creativity.

Rhymes with actions, in particular, are enjoyable to children because children live through all of their senses and their whole body. Adding movement helps reinforce the linguistic content of the rhyme or song. Movement and rhymes build cognitive abilities in terms of sequencing physical and linguistic activity, imitation, and internalization.

Adding Movement to Rhymes

There are many types of movement to add to rhymes and games. There are **narrative** movements, which are mimetic actions that help to illustrate certain words and tell the story (e.g., "I'm a Little Teapot"); **abstract** movements, which do not carry any specific linguistic meaning, such as waving arms or jumping; and **rhythmic** movements, which can either emphasize the beat of the rhyme or the rhythm of the text, such as clapping or body percussion.

Narrative Movements: It is easy to add narrative movements to most children's rhymes as these poems often tell some type of story. Consider the rhyme "I'm a Little Ducky." Adding swimming and flapping motions would be an obvious activity to add. Narrative motions not only bring the story to life, but also significantly help children to remember the words to a rhyme or song.

> I'm a little ducky swimming in the water
> I'm a little ducky doing what I oughter
> Took a bite of a lily pad
> Flapped my wings and said, "I'm glad"
> I'm a little ducky swimming in the water
> Flap, flap, flap

Abstract Motions and Rhythmic Motions: Almost any non-locomotive or even some locomotive motions would work here. Abstract motions can easily be rhythmic as well (e.g., swaying to the beat, nodding the head to the beat, tapping the rhythm of the words or beat, etc.).

Walking to the Beat: While a seemingly simple-sounding exercise, walking to the beat requires a physical awareness and near-constant mental and physical adjustment to the walking stride in order to fit the beat and tempo of the rhyme.

> **Example:** Take any standard, well-known nursery rhyme. Walk to the beat while saying the rhyme. End precisely on the last beat of the rhyme and freeze!

Advanced: This game can be further developed for older or more advanced children. Once they are walking to a steady beat and stopping precisely on the last beat, have children drop the recitation of the rhyme, and just walk the beat. See if they can all still stop on the last beat! This helps students internalize the beat and phrases of the song.

Steady Beat Games

Pass the Beat: Begin with a simple rhyme or song. While sitting in a circle, have students pass a beanbag around the circle *on the beat.* If the child misses, they are "out" or "in the soup" in the middle of the circle.

Bouncing Beat: Another game is to bounce a ball to the beat of a simple song such as "Bounce High." This is a little more challenging because they have to keep control of their bodies, voices, and a ball.

S, M, L song

Bounce High

Action Songs

Head and Shoulders (Key of F)

Shoo Fly

American folk song, 1863

Shoo fly, don't bo - ther me, Shoo fly, don't bo - ther me.

Shoo fly don't bo - ther me, for I be - long to some - bo - dy.

I feel, I feel, I feel like a morn - ing star,

I feel, I feel, I feel like a morn - ing star.

Do You Know the Muffin Man?

English folk song, 1820

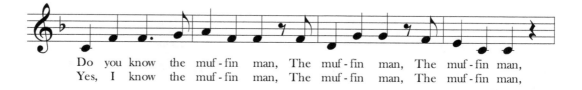

Do you know the muf - fin man, The muf - fin man, The muf - fin man,
Yes, I know the muf - fin man, The muf - fin man, The muf - fin man,

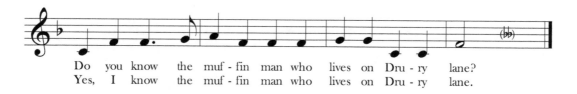

Do you know the muf - fin man who lives on Dru - ry lane?
Yes, I know the muf - fin man who lives on Dru - ry lane.

Did You Ever See a Lassie?

American folk song, late 19th century

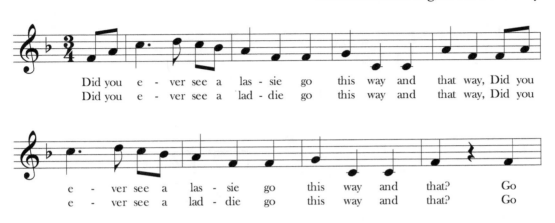

Did you e - ver see a las - sie go this way and that way, Did you
Did you e - ver see a lad - die go this way and that way, Did you

e - ver see a las - sie go this way and that? Go
e - ver see a lad - die go this way and that? Go

this way and that way, go this way and that way, Did you
this way and that way, go this way and that way, Did you

e - ver see a las - sie go this way and that?
e - ver see a lad - dit go this way and that?

Go to Sleep

Go to sleep my lit - tle ba - by, Go to sleep and do not cry.

Mo - ther's arms will gent - ly rock you, As she sings this lul - la - by.

If You're Ready for Music

If you're read - y for mu - sic stand on up,
If you're read - y for mu - sic clap your hands,
If you're read - y for * * * * *

stand on up, stand on up, If you're read - y for mu - sic
clap your hands, clap your hands, If you're read - y for mu - sic
* * * * * * If you're read - y for * *

stand on up, stand on ____ up!
clap your hands, clap your ____ hands!
* * * * * * *

Rhymes

Deedle, Deedle Dumpling
Deedle, deedle dumpling, my son John
Went to bed with his stockings on
One shoe off and one shoe on
Deedle, deedle dumpling, my son John

Oliver Twist
Oliver Twist, Twist, Twist
Can't do this, this, this
Touch his nose, nose, nose
Touch his toes, toes, toes
And around he goes, goes, goes

Rub, Rub
Rub, rub, rub
_____'s in the tub
Rub her/him dry
Hang her high
Rub, rub, rub

Jingle Jive
Jingle, jingle, jingle jive

Move until you count to five
1, 2, 3, 4, 5

Open Shut Them

This is an action game song where the lyrics are imitated through movement using simple actions in both hands.

Open Shut Them

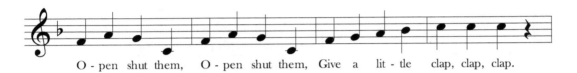

Open, shut them, Open, shut them, (*open and shut both hands*)
Give a little clap, clap, clap (*clap on each "clap"*)
Open, shut them, Open, shut them, (*open and shut both hands*)
Put them in you lap, lap, lap (*tap open hands on thighs*)
Creep them, creep them, creep them, creep them, (*crawl hands up to chin*)
Right up to your chin, chin, chin (*tap on each "chin"*)
Open wide your little mouth (*open mouth*)
But do not put them in, in, in (*tap on each "chin" again*)

III. Musical Developmental Milestones in Young Children

Although we might not have thought of it, children's linguistic development is related to their musical development. Research shows a direct correlation between the development of children's speech and their musical/singing ability, with music skills correlating significantly with both phonological awareness and reading development (Anvari et al., 2002).

While teachers of preschool children may have a sense of the linguistic milestones for children, they are less aware of the musical milestones. Since music and language development have a high correlation in terms of development, it is helpful to know what activities children are developmentally ready for musically, and when are they ready for them. For example, most four- and even five-year-olds are not yet able to play a steady beat on an instrument. Expecting them to will only frustrate both the children and yourself. The following chart indicates musical developmental ability by age, and will guide you in introducing musical skills and material that children are developmentally ready for.

Musical Abilities by Age.

Age	Musical Behaviors	Appropriate Activities	Limitations
0–1 year old (Infants)	Enjoy hearing: • Melodic contour in voice • Being sung to • Hearing a variety of styles of music	Enjoy: • Being rocked, patted, and stroked to music • Responding to rhythmic play and body touch songs • Bouncing or jumping to music • Experimenting with gestures, clapping, and pointing • Playing with rattles and bells	Cannot use language or sing
1–2 years old (Toddlers)	• Are aware of musical sounds • Demand repetition • Delayed response during music time	• Create their own made-up songs • Sing simple 1–2 word songs • Enjoy voice inflection games • Enjoy making random sounds on instruments • Improvise their own lyrics to traditional songs • Respond to musical stimuli • Perform rhythmic movement and movement patterns • Clap to music, steady beat • Move and respond to signals and sound and silence games	Cannot sing "in tune" but can maintain melodic contour Developmental Issues: "Centering" (pre-operational stage) can fix a child's attention on one perceptual feature. Difficulty seeing the larger transformational picture of some activities as attention is diverted by one feature.
3-year-olds	• Prefer to sing beginning on their own pitch • Increasing ability to match pitches • Sense of musical phrasing • Increasing expressiveness in voice • Find it easier to pat thighs rather than clap Enjoy: • Manipulating objects while creating songs • Repeated songs • Having their own movements/ideas copied by others	• Reproduce recognizable songs • Explore musical sounds with their voices and instruments • Random exploration of xylophones, percussion instruments, and voices • Maintain steady beat • Handle mallets and drum beaters • Move spontaneously to music • Respond to sound and silence games	• Cannot reverse thought (i.e., can't reason back to the beginning) • Cannot play a repeated xylophone pattern Developmental Issues: • Responds to abstract or iconic musical notation: • Pictures • Hand signs • Movement/motions • Cannot respond to formal music notation (i.e., notes on a staff)

4-year-olds	• Awareness of beat, tempo, volume, pitch, and form • Sings a wide variety of songs • Sings in D–A range • Critique their own song-making efforts • Aware of tonal center	• Perform individualized musical exploration and play; large motor movement is best. • Have the ability to step to beat • Repeat short movement sequences, simple rhythms, echo, pitch contour, melodic fragments, formality within phrases, key stability, and categorization of instruments • Symbolic "pretend" play, songs with stories, acting/pretending • Can perform some musical analysis such as hearing form (AB, ABA) or distinguishing song phrases	• Group musical activities or coordinated instrumental play is difficult • Cannot perform a steady beat on xylophones • Have trouble discriminating between musical genres
4–5-year-olds	Able to classify sounds as: • High-low • Loud-soft • Fast-slow • Smooth-disconnected (legato-staccato)	• Can reproduce sounds and patterns vocally and with instruments • Able to play simple, repeated instrumental accompaniments to songs and improvise on simple classroom instruments • Improvement in stepping to the beat • 5-year-olds can learn simple dance steps • Organize sounds that express a story or accompany a song Prefer: • Action songs and finger plays (imagination) • Silly word and rhyming songs	Require many opportunities to match pitches and order direction of musical sounds in terms of going up, going down, and staying the same

---

Activity 8B

TRY THIS

Based on the chart above, answer the following in terms of what age is appropriate for each activity.
1. Analyzing/hearing the different sections of a song.
2. Responding vocally using different tones and inflections.
3. Singing the song "I'm a Nut."
4. Echoing/responding to short, clapped rhythms.
5. Playing a steady beat on the xylophone or other percussion instrument.
6. Seeing abstract images and performing them either on voice or instruments.

Resources

Feierabend, J. (2011). *Music and early childhood.* Chicago: GIA Publications.

Songs for Teaching: Using Music to Promote Learning, Gari Stein http://www.songs-forteaching.com/teachingtips/benefitsofmusicwithyoungchildren.htm

Early Childhood Music and Movement Association (ECMMA) https://ecmma.org/

Children's Camp Songs https://www.care.com/c/stories/3343/50-great-camp-songs-for-kids/

Music Notes: Music You Can Read http://musicnotes.net/SONGS/02-SARAS.html

Preschool Rhymes for Self and Family Themes (finger plays, action poems, songs and nursery rhymes) http://www.preschoolrainbow.org/family-rhymes.htm

References

Anvari, S., Trainor, L., Woodside, J., & Levy, A. (2002). Relations among musical skills, phonological processing, and early reading ability in preschool children. *Journal of Experimental Child Psychology*, 83(2), 111–130.

Chen-Hafteck, L. (1997). Music and language development in early childhood: Integrating past research in the two domains In *Early Child Development and Care* 130 (1): 85-97.

Deliège, I. and Sloboda, J. (Eds.). (1996). *Musical beginnings: Origins and development of musical competence.* Oxford: Oxford University Press.

Feierabend, J. (2001). *First steps in classical music: Keeping the beat.* Chicago, IL: GIA Publications.

Feierabend, J. (2006). *First steps in music for preschool and beyond : The curriculum.* Chicago, IL: GIA Publications.

Gordon, E. E. (2007). *Learning sequences in music: A contemporary music learning theory.* Chicago, IL: GIA Publications.

Gordon, E. E. (2007). *Learning sequences in music: A contemporary music learning theory: Study guide.* Chicago, IL: GIA Publications.

Gordon, E. E. (2007). *Lecture cds for learning sequences in music: A contemporary music learning theory.* Chicago, IL: GIA Publications.

Gordon, E. (2000). *Jump right in: Grade 1 teacher's guide—The general music series* (2nd ed.). Chicago, IL: GIA Publications.

Haroutounian, J. (2002). *Kindling the spark: Recognizing and developing musical talent.* Oxford: Oxford University Press.

Jensen, E. (1998). *Teaching with the brain in mind.* Alexandria, VA: ASCD Publisher.

Jordan-DeCarbo, J., and Galliford, J. (2011). The effect of an age-appropriate music curriculum on motor and linguistic and nonlinguistic skills of children three to five years of age. In S. Burton & C. Taggart (Eds.), *Learning from young children: Research in early childhood music* (pp. 211–230). Lanham, MD: MENC and Rowman Littlefield.

Moore, R. S. (1991). Comparison of children's and adults' vocal ranges and preferred tessituras in singing familiar songs. *Bulletin of the Council for Research in Music Education*, Winter, 13–22.

Reynolds, A., Bolton, B., Taggert, C., Valerio, W., & Gordon, E. (1998). *Music play: The early childhood music curriculum guide.* Chicago, IL: GIA Publications.

Suzuki, S., and Nagata, M. L. (1981). *Ability development from age zero.* Athens, OH: Suzuki Method International.

Turner, M. E. (2008). *Listen, move, think: Communicating through the languages of music and creative movement.* Retrieved from http://www.listenmovethink.com/#intro

Vocabulary

abstract movements: movements do not carry any specific linguistic meaning, such as waving arms or jumping

articulation: the approach to playing a note and style of playing in terms of its smoothness, detachment, accents, etc.

dynamics: how loud or soft the music is

meter: meter determines where the stresses in music are, or how music stresses are grouped. A triple meter, for example, will have groups of 3 with a stress on the first beat of the group. A duple meter will have groups of 2 with a stress on the first beat of the group.

narrative movements: mimetic actions that help to illustrate certain words and tell the story (e.g., "I'm a Little Teapot")

pitch: how high or low a note is

rhythmic movements: movements that can either emphasize the beat of the rhyme or the rhythm of the text, such as clapping or body percussion

tempo: how fast or slow the music is played

timbre: the quality of sound

Chapter 9

Music and the Older Child

Chapter Summary: This chapter explores the uses of music with older elementary-aged children. It covers their vocal ranges, preparation for multi-part singing including echo songs, ostinato patterns, drone and multi-part performing including polyphony (multiple melodies) such as rounds, partner songs, harmony and descants, as well as other age-appropriate repertoire such as cumulative songs, play-party songs, and African-American songs.

Older children, ages 6 and up, have listened to a great deal of musical material in their short lives. The songs and sounds they've absorbed are part of western musical style, and are now part of the musical *lingua franca* or the music that is "normal" for them. They're familiar with the musical genres, timbres, modes, and instruments, rhythmic and melodic patterns, and have learned the culturally acceptable cadences, harmonies, texture, and so forth. The lower to middle elementary-aged child is ready for more complex listening, singing, and music making. This chapter will offer music suggestions to inspire older children, including cultural games, songs, and dances.

I. Singing Voices of Older Children

Developmental Abilities

Just as children's aptitude to learn a foreign language stabilizes after the age of 9, Music researcher Edwin Gordon (2007) found that children's musical aptitude is also developmental, fluctuating until age 9, and stabilizing afterwards. This doesn't mean that children can't learn music after the age of 9, of course, but that the language of musical enculturation is well under way by that age. It is important to keep in mind that a rich musical environment at home and at school will greatly benefit a child's musical and cognitive abilities at any age.

In terms of the voice, both boys and girls should remain singing in their head voice or **falsetto**. Falsetto is a light, high, head voice that is not pushed, yelled, or forced in any way. Younger boys can switch easily into falsetto or head voice, as their voices have not yet begun to change. A good falsetto produces a clear, clean "boy's choir" type of sound, and is where children should try to sing in order to maintain a healthy voice.

Singing Ranges for Older Children

As we recall from the previous chapter, children's singing ranges expand year by year. Older children may have an expanded vocal range, but it is important to remember that the pitches that are most comfortable to sing are in the middle of their range.

Six to Eight Years Old

Grades first through third, or six to eight-year-olds, can sing about an octave from C to C', with their most comfortable notes from E to G.

Eight to Eleven Years Old

Children aged eight to eleven can sing from the B flat below middle C to about an E flat or E, 3 notes above high C'. Their most comfortable notes are between D and G.

Selecting a Song in the Proper Singing Range

When selecting a song for older children, first check the pitch range appropriate for the child given the guidelines above. Most of the notes of the song should match the child's most comfortable pitches right in the middle of their range. Children start to become weaker when singing around middle C. Try to avoid songs that sit in a lower range such as middle C or D, and instead pitch or place the song slightly higher up around E, F and G. Most of the songs in this book are transposed to the key of F so that most of the pitches of the song are around the tonic, or F.

Another important thing to keep in mind is that where an adult feels most comfortable singing, is probably not where the child feels most comfortable. Remember that many times, classroom teachers pitch the song in their own range, not thinking about where the song would work best for the children, and children struggle to sing well.

Activity 9A

TRY THIS

Select the notation below that best fits the vocal ranges for children ages 3, 4 and 5.
How about 6-8? 8-11?

If You're Happy and You Know It (Keys of E flat Major, C Major, F Major)

E♭ Major

C Major

II. Advanced Musical Experiences

Beginning at around eight years of age, children are ready for more advanced musical experiences vocally, instrumentally, and theoretically, and more complex musical subject matter. This section will explore different types of songs appropriate for older children, and the process for introducing more complex musical experiences.

Repertoire

Most of us are surrounded by pop music culture, and children at this age are particularly aware of and influenced by the pop scene. They hear pop music, watch singing competition shows on television, have pop idols, and want to sing pop music. The challenge with older children is their desire to vocally imitate the pop singing style. This music, of course, is very familiar and accessible to them, and it is only normal that they are inspired by and want to mimic their favorite pop star. However, keep in mind that a child's vocal apparatus is still developing, and imitating adult singing with scoops, chest voice, or belting is *affected* singing and not natural. Not only does it inhibit the child's sense of ownership of their own vocal instrument and musicality, it also inhibits their ability to explore the natural timbre of their own voices, and find their own unique musical style. These songs are intended for adult voices, and are often out of the comfortable singing range of children. Belting or pushing a developing voice too far can be detrimental to the child's voice, and can result in permanent damage.

Subject Matter

Luckily, there is an enormous children's repertoire of songs, including folk songs, historical songs, play party songs, story and game songs, classical pieces, and popular songs written for children's voices with subject matters that appeal to their developing sense of morality and worldview, and are steeped with sociohistorical meaning.

Many songs for older elementary children are highly appropriate for use in the classroom curriculum, including core subject songs (math, social studies, science), national songs, cultural and historical songs, language arts songs, holiday songs, etc. The songs presented in this book are folk and popular songs, some of which are not only historically important, but culturally significant as well. These songs are part of a potentially rich musical experience for the child—exposing them to material with inherent sociocultural meaning that can contribute to excellent lessons and, most importantly, enhance integration activities.

Multiple Part Performance: Introducing Texture and Layers

By the age of seven or eight, children are ready for some type of vocal multiple part performing. Multi-part performing includes both instrumental and vocal music making, and can refer to the performance of more than one melody at the same time (i.e. a round), vocal harmony, or any type of accompaniment. Playing two or more parts on instruments is far easier and children can begin this type of multi-part performance much earlier. Vocally, however, children find it quite difficult to sustain their own vocal part against that of another singer or singers before the age of 8.

Multi-part performance in either the vocal or instrumental milieu is cognitively beneficial, and will increase a child's musical competence. Older children appreciate and are capable of singing complex songs, particularly those that include multiple parts and simple harmony. Musical texture (performing multiple lines of music simultaneously) not only creates more intricate and interesting music, but it provides significant cognitive benefits. Multi-part performance of any kind requires the child to focus intensely on their part, training the brain to produce one part while acknowledging additional auditory stimuli coming from the other parts. The brain then must process the whole piece at once while still remaining focused on the one performing part.

Children, who may not yet ready for harmony, can be prepped for harmony at much earlier ages through the use of layered speech pieces, rhythmic instrumental or vocal patterns (see *ostinato* below). Keep in mind that children are performing in multiple parts even when they are singing a song and doing any other simultaneous activity such as tapping the beat, playing a pattern on an instrument or performing body percussion (snapping, stomping). Any rhyme can be made more complex by adding a body percussion pattern or simple instrument pattern.

Deedle Deedle Dumpling

English nursery rhyme

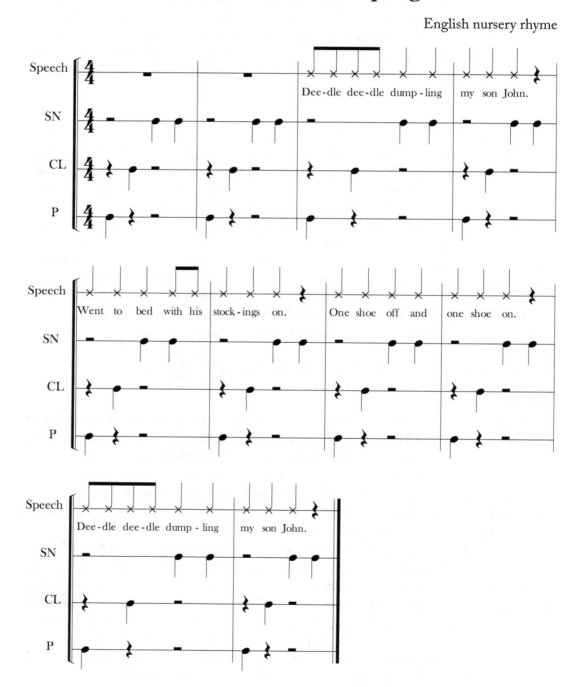

Any familiar song can be used to teach two parts, such as taking a simple melody and adding a vocal ostinato. The song "A Ram Sam Sam," for example, is a traditional Moroccan folk song that contains many simple repeating patterns. Begin by learning the song and performing it in unison. Then sing several times as a two part round.

A Ram Sam Sam

Traditional Morrocan folk round

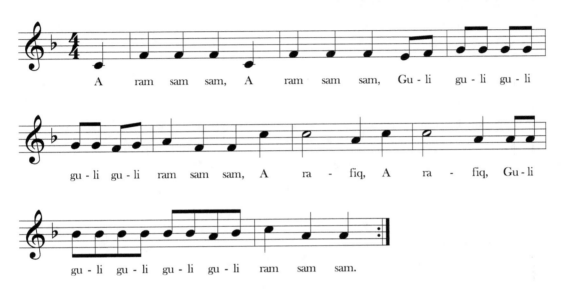

Creating ostinati patterns

Ostinati are short patterns, repeated persistently throughout a piece often at the same pitch. Ostinati (pl. of **ostinato**) can be either vocal or rhythmic. The easiest way to find an ostinato is to take a short pattern right from the song itself. Ostinati can also be composed. Using short patterns from the song is a simple way to create vocal or rhythmic ostinati. Start by finding a short, simple, fun or interesting pattern in the song. An ostinato can be performed using body percussion, instruments or with the voice.

If the children are not ready to sing the song with a sung vocal ostinato, begin by chanting the song as a speech piece and adding one or more speech ostinato patterns.

A Ram Sam Sam (Speech with one ostinato)

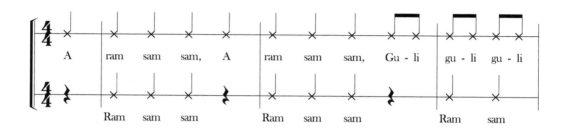

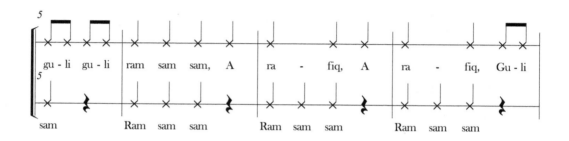

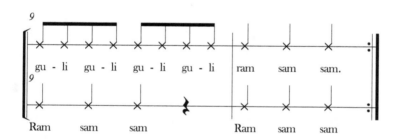

Begin with a simple ostinato. In this case, the rhythm of the very last phrase "Ram Sam Sam" (ta ta ta rest), works very well. Have children clap and say the words simultaneously.

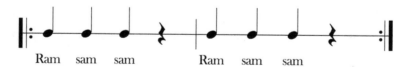

Two additional ostinati for this song with more complex rhythms include "ra-fiq a ra-fiq" ("ta-a ta, ta ta-a ta") or "gu-li gu-li gu-li gu-li" (ti ti ti ti ti ti ti ti). Have children clap and say their ostinati. Notice, however, that "a ra-fiq" begins on a pickup beat, which can be tricky for entrances. To avoid that, begin with "ra" on the downbeat so that both ostinati (ra-fiq and gu-li gu-li) begin in simultaneously.

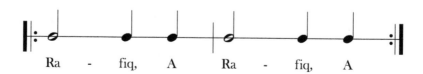

Divide the class into four equal parts, one group chanting and clapping the "melody" rhythm and the other three chanting and clapping the ostinati. After a few times through, have the students drop the chanting and perform the piece using clapping only.

A Ram Sam Sam (Speech with vocal ostinato)

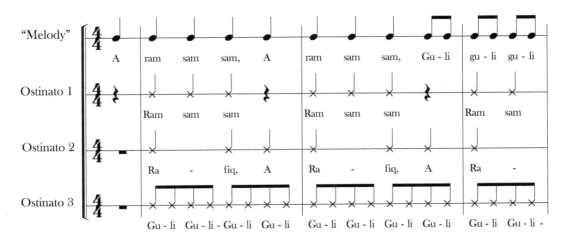

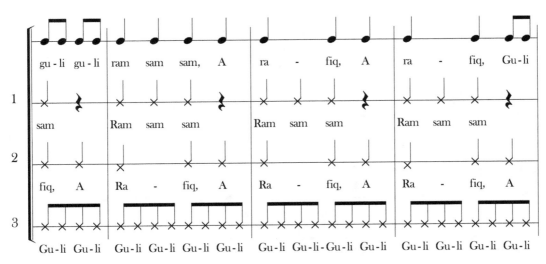

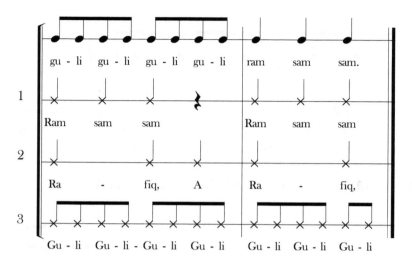

Depending on the level of the class, the switch to singing the song with all of its ostinati can be done all at once or by using a combination of spoken and sung. Using a combined approach, begin by having the melody group sing the melody, while the ostinati groups come in one at a time using speech only.

A Ram Sam Sam (With one ostinato)

Gradually add the other two ostinati patterns, one at a time.

A Ram Sam Sam (With two ostinati)

A Ram Sam Sam (With three ostinati)

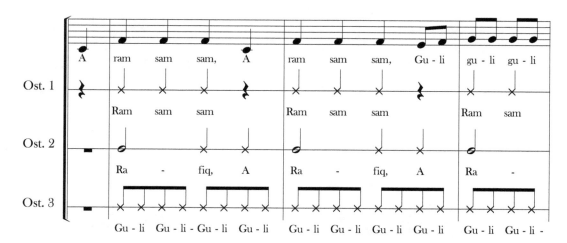

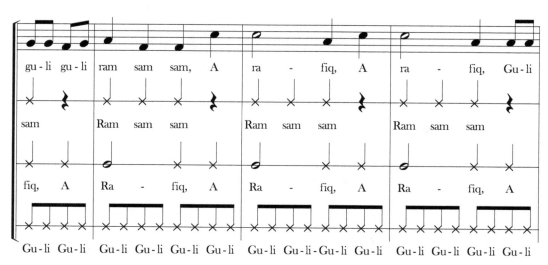

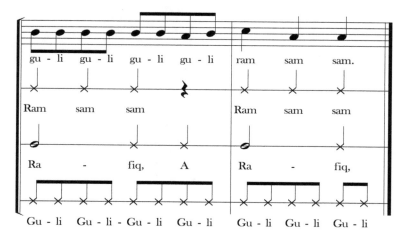

Move from using rhythmic ostinati to melodic ones. Be sure to have them learn the song very well before adding a sung ostinato. Divide the group in half and have half sing "Ram Sam Sam" while the other half sings the melody. These are examples of pitched ostinati that are taken directly from the melody of song (measures 2 and 9). The easier of the two is 1a, but if the class is advanced, use 1b.

Vocal Ostinato ex. 1a

Vocal Ostinato ex. 1b

The other two ostinati can also be sung. For more advanced groups, try dividing into three parts, with the melody in one part and sung ostinati in the other groups.

Vocal Ostinato #2

Vocal Ostinato #3

A Ram Sam Sam (With three sung ostinati)

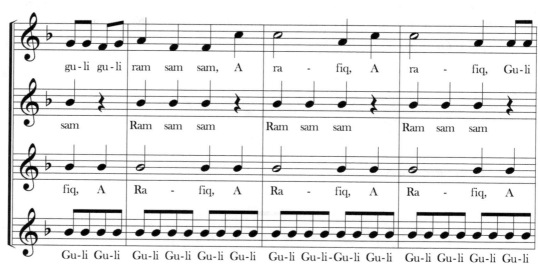

Note: In order for the harmony to work with the song, the pitches for "gu-li gu-li" need to be changed in measures 3 and 7 to a "B♭" rather than "A." If this is too difficult, remain on the "A."

Drone

A drone is usually a single pitch, usually held or repeated underneath a melody. The simplest type of accompaniment is to add a single note drone to a melody. Songs such as "Amazing Grace," "Bow, Wow, Wow," "Tideo," are all pentatonic songs that work well with a drone accompaniment. Drones can also be several pitches, but they repeat throughout all or most of a song. Children may be tempted to speak or chant the drone part, but it is important that they sing it, maintaining a constant pitch and good tone.

Tideo

Traditional American play party song

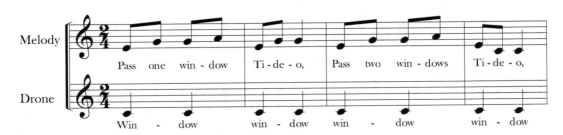

More complex part singing

Older children are ready for singing in two, three and four parts, and also performing on instruments layering many different patterns together. In singing, there are two types of basic part-singing appropriate for children: **polyphony** and **harmony**.

Polyphony is a word that refers to multiple independent lines of music sung at the same time. Polyphony can happen in many different ways. **Rounds** and **partner songs** are two good examples of polyphony.

In a round, all of the voices are singing the same melody but at slightly different times, and in a partner song each part is singing a different melody. The important element is that all of the parts or "voices" are equal, and there isn't a single dominant melodic line. Although we associate rounds with children, there are many complex and lengthy rounds with more serious topics for adults.

Rounds

Rounds or canons have been around for hundreds of years, and play a significant role in European and American society. Group singing played a major role in society, for emotional expression, entertainment, social cohesion, and so forth. In a round, everyone contributes equally in terms of melody. The oldest polyphonic song known is the Medieval English song "Sumer Is Icumen In" dated from the mid-13th century. This round, which is about the arrival of summer, actually has two "melodic ostinati," which are known as "grounds," at the end, which can be sung along with the melody.

Sumer Is Icumin In

Medieval English song, 13th century

Su - mer is i - cu - men in___ Lhu - de sing cuc - cu.

Gro-weth sed and blo-weth med and springth the wu-de nu. Sing cuc - cu.

A - ve ble - theth af - ter lomb, louth af - ter cal - ve cu.

Bul - luc ster - teth, buc - ke ver - teth mur - ie sing cuc - cu.

Cuc - cu cuc - cu___ wel sing-es thu cuc - cu ne swik thu na - ver nu.

Ost. 1 "ground": Sing cuc - cu nu.__ Sing cuc - cu.

Ost. 2: Sing cuc - cu. Sing cuc - cu nu.__

More simple rounds that most people know include: "Row, Row, Row Your Boat," "Frère Jacques," and "Scotland's Burning."

Row, Row, Row Your Boat

American folk song and round, 1852

Row, row, row your boat, Gent - ly down the stream.

Mer - ri - ly, mer - ri - ly, mer - ri - ly, mer - ri - ly, Life is but a dream.

Frère Jacques

French folk round, 18th century

Frè - re Jac - ques, Frè - re Jac - ques, Dor - mez vous? Dor - mez vous?
Are you sleep - ing? Are you sleep - ing? Bro - ther John? Bro - ther John?

Son - nez les ma - ti - nes, Son - nez les ma - ti - nes, Ding Daing Dong, Ding Daing, Dong.
Morn - ing bells are ring - ing, Morn - ing bells are ring - ing,

Scotland's Burning

Traditional American round, 19th century

More complex rounds include: "Oh How Lovely Is the Evening," "Dona Nobis Pacem," "Hey, Ho, Nobody Home," which is in minor, and "Viva la Musica," a 16th century round written by the Renaissance composer Giovanni Palestrina.

Oh, How Lovely

German folk round

Dona Nobis Pacem

Text from "Lamb of God," Latin Mass

Hey Ho, Nobody Home

Chrismas round

Viva la Musica!

Michael Praetorius (1571-1621)

Partner songs

Partner songs are another way to experience multiple-part (polyphonic) singing. In a partner song, two or more songs, which are musically compatible, are sung together. Similar to a round, everyone contributes a melody. Partner songs are slightly more challenging to sing in that they use different melodies. A good example is the song "One Bottle of Pop" in which three separate melodies work well together.

One Bottle of Pop

Below are some additional examples of individual songs and their potential "partners" that blend well and go together. The songs "This Old Man," "Skip to My Lou," "Shoo Fly," "Bow Belinda," and "Sandy Land," for example, are all able to be sung simultaneously.

This Old Man

English game song, 19th century

This old man, he played one, He played knick - knack on my thumb,

Knick-knack, pad-dy whack,* give a dog a bone, This old man came roll-ing home.

Skip to My Lou

Traditional American play party song

Flies in the but - ter-milk, Shoo fly shoo, Flies in the but - ter-milk, Shoo fly shoo,
Lost my — part - ner, what'll I do? Lost my — part - ner, what'll I do?
I'll get a - noth-er one, better than you! I'll get a - noth-er one, better than you!

Flies in the but - ter milk, shoo fly shoo, Skip to my Lou my dar - ling.
Lost my — part - ner, what'll I do? Skip to my Lou, my dar - ling.
I'll get a - noth - er one, better than you! Skip to my Lou, my dar - ling.

Shoo Fly

American folk song, 1863

Shoo fly, don't bo - ther me, Shoo fly, don't bo - ther me.

Shoo fly don't bo - ther me, for I be-long to some-bo-dy. I

feel, I feel, I feel like a morn - ing star, I

feel, I feel, I feel like a morn - ing star.

Bow Belinda

Bow, bow, bow, Be - lin - da, Bow, bow, bow, Be - lin - da,

Bow, bow, bow, Be - lin - da, You're the one my dar - ling.

Sandy Land

Traditional folk song, Texas

Make my li - vin' in San - dy land, Make my li - vin' in San - dy land,

Make my li - vin' in San - dy land, La - dies fare you well

This Old Man and Sandy Land

Bow Belinda and This Old Man

All of the songs together:

Bow Belinda, This Old Man, Shoo Fly, Sandy Land

List of children's songs and partner songs

The list below consists of suggested songs that work well when sung together. Each box represents a group of songs that can be sung in pairs as partner songs, or even layered as three or more songs.

Partner songs: groups of commonly known songs that can be paired or layered.

Row, Row, Row, Your Boat Here Comes a Bluebird Frere Jacques/Are you Sleeping? Three Blind Mice London Bridge The Old Grey Mare Mary Had a Little Lamb Merrily We Roll Along Boola, Boola The Farmer in the Dell Here We Go Looby Loo Go Tell Aunt Rhody Hot Cross Buns Where is Thumbkin? He's Got the Whole World in His Hands Rock-a My Soul	Bow Belinda Sandy Land This Old Man 10 Little Indians Skip to My Lou Paw, Paw Patch Mulberry Bush Oh, Dear, What Can the Matter Be? Irish Washerwoman Liza Jane Old Brass Wagon Michael Finnegan	Good Night Ladies Pickalittle, Talkalittle (Music Man) When the Saints Go Marching In Swing Low Sweet Chariot This Train Nobody Knows the Trouble I've Seen Gospel Train She'll be Comin' Round the Mountain All Night, All Day Rock-a My Soul
Joshua Fought the Battle of Jericho Hey Ho, Nobody Home When Johnny Comes Marching Home Wondrous Love Kookaburra Wade in the Water	Juanita Santa Lucia Bicycle Built for Two Sidewalks of New York In the Good Old Summertime	Arkansas Traveler Oh, Susanna Turkey in the Straw Camptown Races (verse)
Humoresque Old Folks at Home Put on Your Old Gray Bonnet	Child of God Mary Had a Baby Sing Hallelu	One Bottle of Pop Don't put your Dust Fish and Chips and Vinegar
My Bonnie Lies Over the Ocean (refrain) Cielito Lindo (refrain) Man on the Flying Trapeze	Home on the Range My Home's in Montana	Old Texas Old Chisholm Trail
Ta-Ra-Ra-Boom-De-Ay Long, Long Ago	All Night, All Day Swing Low Sweet Chariot	I Love the Mountains Heart and Soul
Bluetail Fly (refrain) Shoo Fly (refrain)	Dixie Yankee Doodle	Zum Gali Gali Shalom Chavarim
I am a Poor Wayfaring Stranger Scarborough Fair	Land of the Silver Birch My Paddle	Be Bow Wow Wow Hot Cross Buns
Sally Go Round the Sun See Saw, Margery Daw	We Wish You a Merry Christmas O Christmas Tree	Mango Walk Sweet Potatoes
Lida Rose (Music Man) Will I Ever Tell You?	Go Tell It on the Mountain Some Folks Do	Mr. Frog Went A-Courtin' Goin' Down to Cairo
Jubilate (Hark! The Vesper Bells are Ringing) Chumbara	Haul Away Joe Early in the Morning	Hush-a-bye Lullaby
What Shall We Do with a Drunken Sailor Sinner Man	Sing a Song of Peace This is My Country	Little Red Caboose Sourwood Mountain

Harmony

After success singing rounds and partner songs, children may be ready to sing in harmony. **Harmony** is the sounding of two notes simultaneously. When singing harmony, one voice usually has the melody and is dominant, while the harmony parts take a "back seat" so to speak. The melody notes are usually the highest notes, with the harmony supporting underneath. Singing in harmony is quite a bit more challenging than partner songs or rounds.

Harmony lines are often the interval of a third (3rd) or a sixth (6th) below the melody line. Singing a 3rd or 6th away from the melody is very challenging, as the tendency is for singers to slip from their parts into unison with the melody.

Preparation for vocal harmony

Singing a drone is excellent preparation for harmony (see "Tideo" above). Here is a scale warm-up that also helps prepare students to hold onto their part against another moving part.

Warm-up for Harmony

N. Sarrazin

Sarasponda

Attributed as a Dutch spinning song

Sa - ra - spon - da, Sa - ra - spon - da, Sa - ra - spon - da ret set set, Sa - ra -

Oom-da oom-da oom-da oom-da oom-da oom-da oom-da oom-da oom-da

spon-da, Sa - ra-spon-da, Sa - ra-spon-da ret set set, Ah do - ray - o, Ah

oom-da oom-da oom-da oom-da oom-da oom-da oom-da oom-da oom-da oom-da oom-da oom-da

do - ray boom-day - o,   Ah do - ray boom-day ret set set,   Ah say - pa - say o.

oom-da oom - da oom-da oom-da oom - da oom - da oom-da oom-da oom-da oom-da oom-da

Ah, Poor Bird (with harmony)

Elizabethan English round

Harmony N. Sarrazin

Ah, poor bird,   take thy flight,   High a - bove the sor - rows of this fair night.
Ah, poor bird,   as you fly,   Can you see the dawn of to - mor-row's sky.

Descants are also a type of harmony, but are instead placed above the melody. Descants can have text, but are also sung on neutral syllables such as oh, or ah.

Ah, Poor Bird (with descant)

Elizabethan English round

Descant N. Sarrazin

ah, _____   ah, _____   ah, _____   ah _____

Ah, poor bird,   take thy flight,   High a - bove the sor - rows of this fair night.
Ah, poor bird,   as you fly,   Can you see the dawn of to - mor-row's sky.

III. American Children's Games and Game Songs

America's folk heritage is rich with songs from many cultures. Folk songs such as play party songs, African-American songs, story songs, and dance-songs are all a part of American music history and are excellent opportunities to discuss history and the role of music in our culture. The lyrics to these songs contain literary and social references, and are rife for inclusion in the interdisciplinary classroom. The songs can also fit into other aspects of children's lives and their school curriculum as well.

Many game songs originated in the Georgia Sea Islands, a series of over 100 islands off the coast of South Carolina, Georgia, and Florida. The Islands have a long and complex cultural history, but are most known for their rich African-American heritage as white plantation owners left the islands in the 19th century leaving their slaves behind. The result was the creation of a distinct Gullah/Creole language and culture, which can be found in many children's games.

Draw Me a Bucket of Water

Georgia Sea Islands singing game

Groups of four: Couples facing each other grab both hands and sway back and forth to the beat while singing. The inside of the circle represents the "bucket." As the numbers increase, a person is added to the bucket encircled by the clasped hands.

Draw me a buck-et of   wa - ter,   For my old-est   daugh - ter, There's

none in the buck-et, And	four out the buck-et,	Won't you come ov-er sis-ter	Sal	- ly.
one	three			
two	two			
three	one			
four	none			

Frog in the buck-et and you can't get him out,   Frog in the buck-et and you can't get him out,

Frog in the buck-et and you can't get him out,   Frog in the buck-et and you can't get him out.

Ridin' in a Buggy

Traditional American play party song, South Carolina

Ri-din' in a bug-gy Miss Ma-ry Jane, Miss Ma-ry Jane, Miss Ma-ry Jane,

Ri-din' in a bug-gy Miss Ma-ry Jane, You're a long way from home.

Who'll moan for me, Who'll moan for me, Who'll moan for me my dar-lin'

who'll moan for me.

Oh! Susanna

American minstrel song
Stephen Foster, 1848

Oh I come from A - la - ba - ma with a ban - jo on my knee
It __ rained all night the day I left, the wea - ther it was dry,
I __ had a dream the o - ther night, when ev - ery - thing was still,
A __ buck - wheat cake was in her mouth, a tear was in her eye,

I'm goin' to Loui - si - a - na my __ true love for to see.
The sun so hot I froze to death, Su - san - na don't you cry.
I __ dreamed I saw Su - san __ na, a co - min' down the hill.
Says I, "I'm co - min' from the south, Su - san - na don't you cry.

Oh Su - san - na, oh don't you cry for me, I've come from A - la - ba - ma with a ban - jo on my knee.

Doctor Knickerbocker

American game song

Doc - tor Knick - er - bock - er, Knick - er - bock - er num - ber nine

He got stuck on the rail - road line. Now let's get the rhy - thm of the

hands (clap, clap) Now you've got the rhy - thm of the hands. (clap, clap) (Now)
feet. (stamp, stamp)   feet. (stamp, stamp)
hips. (swing, swing)   hips. (swing, swing)

Here We Go Zudio

African American song

Here we go, Zu - di - o, Zu - di - o, Zu - di - o, Here we go, Zu - di - o,

all night long, Step back Sal - ly, Sal - ly, Sal - ly, Step back Sal - ly, all night long. I

looked o - ver yon - der and what did I see? A great big man from Ten - ne - see.

Bet - cha five dol - lars that you can't to this To the front, to the back, to the

side, side, side. To the front, to the back, to the side, side, side.

Play Party Games

Play parties are singing parties that evolved along with the rural frontier American experience. In the early 1800s in the southwestern and western states, there was a prohibition against playing musical instruments and dancing by certain religious organizations. Play parties were a way around this. They were a social activity in which young people sang songs while clapping, incorporating drama, and some swinging movements. Many songs we know such were play-party songs such as "Buffalo Gals," "Skip to my Lou," "Old Dan Tucker," "Old Brass Wagon," "Pop Goes the Weasel," "Weevily Wheat," and "B.I.N.G.O."

The movements to "Old Brass Wagon" have children in a circle, basically following the instructions in the song. Everyone holds hands and circles to the left on the first verse, right on the second, etc.

Old Brass Wagon

Traditional American play party song

Cir - cle to the left,   Old brass wa - gon,   Cir - cle to the left,
Cir - cle to the right,   Old brass wa - gon,   Cir - cle to the right,
Swing___ oh___ swing,   Old brass wa - gon,   Swing___ oh___ swing,
Skip - ping all a - round, Old brass wa - gon,   Skip - ping all a - round,

Old brass wa-gon,   Cir - cle to the left,   Old brass wa-gon, You're the one my   dar-ling.
Old brass wa-gon,   Cir - cle to the right,   Old brass wa-gon, You're the one my   dar-ling.
Old brass wa-gon,   Swing   oh___ swing,   Old brass wa-gon, You're the one my   dar-ling.
Old brass wa-gon,   Skip - ping all a - round, Old brass wa-gon, You're the one my   dar-ling.

The circle dance song "I've Been to Haarlem" requires a more sophisticated choreography. One child stands in the middle of a circle of partners who walk in a circle in promenade position. On the words "turn the glasses over," the partner on the outside of the circle turns under the inside partner's arms, thus changing direction. The partners let go, and circle in opposite directions until the words "lose your partner in the ocean." On this last word "ocean" the child in the middle quickly rushes around trying to find a partner and leaving one child "out" who is now the one in the middle.

I've Been to Haarlem

I've been to Haar-lem, I've been to Do-ver, I've tra-velled this wide world all   o - ver,

O - ver,   o - ver, three times   o - ver, Drink all the Bran-dy wine and   turn the glas-ses   o - ver,

Sail - ing   east,   Sail - ing   west,   Sail - ing   o'er the   o - cean,   You'd   bet - ter watch

out when the boat be-gins to rock or you'll lose your part - ner in the o - cean.

The song "Weevily Wheat" refers to wheat that is infested with beetles or weevils that destroy the plants. The game for "Weevily Wheat" requires children in small groups of four, with each child numbering off 1-2-3-4. The song begins with the children holding hands and moving clockwise. On "take some," everyone reverses direction. On the words "five times five" all stand in place and layer hands in the center of the circle to the beat of the song. Child 1 puts their left hand in, 2 put theirs on top, 3 and 4 continue the pattern. Then all layer their right hand in. When they run out of hands, the children pull their left hand out from the bottom of the pile in turn and place on top, continuing until the end of the verse. This song contains multiplication and can be used as an extension activity for math.

Weevily Wheat

Traditional American play party song

D'wan' none   your   wee-vi-ly   wheat,   d'wan' none   your   bar - ley,

Take   some   flour   and   half   an   hour   to   bake   a   cake   for   Char - lie.

Five   times   five   is   twen-ty   five,   Five   times   six   is   thir - ty,

Five   times   sev'n   is   thir-ty   five,   Five   times   eight   is   for - ty.

Cumulative Songs

Cumulative songs are those in which each verse adds on lyrics and music from the previous verse, and by the end of the song, the singer sings through all of the accumulated lyrics. The most well-known cumulative song is "The Twelve Days of Christmas," but there are many others. These songs provide an excellent cognitive workout, as the singer has to mentally catalog each verse, adding each verse as they progress through the song, but then singing all of the lyrics backward in a cumulative fashion.

Some examples of cumulative songs are "Hey Ho, the Rattlin' Bog," "There was an Old Lady who Swallowed a Fly," "The Green Grass Grew all Around," "Allouette," and "I Bought me a Cat."

The song "Rattlin' Bog" has a refrain with verses that accumulate. This Irish song is also meant to gradually speed up in tempo as you sing.

Activity 9B

LISTEN

Listen to the band <u>Irish Descendants</u> sing "Rattlin' Bog." What is your reaction to the tempo of the song? Are you able to sing along? How might you use this type of song in a lesson?

The Rattlin' Bog

Traditional Irish folk song

Hey, ho the rat - tlin' bog the bog down in the val - ley oh,

Rare bog the rat - tin' bog the bog down in the val - ley oh.

Now in the bog there was a hole A rare hole and a rat - tlin' hole, A

hole in the bog and the bog down in the val - ley oh.

And in that hole there was a tree, a rare tree and a rat - tlin' tree, a

tree in the hole, and a hole in the bog and the   bog down in the val - ley oh.

"I Bought Me a Cat" is a traditional American song arranged by the famous American composer Aaron Copland. This song does not have a refrain, but the verses themselves accumulate lyrics.

I Bought Me a Cat

Traditional American children's song

goose un - der yon - der tree, My goose says "quaw, quaw," My

duck says "quaa, quaa," My cat says "Fid - dle - i - fee."

I bought me a hen, My hen pleased me. I

fed my hen un - der yon - der tree, My hen says

"shim - my shack, shim - my shack," My goose says "quaw, quaw," My duck says

"quaa, quaa," My cat says "Fid - dle - i - fee."

I bought me a pig, my pig pleased me
I fed my pig under yonder tree,
My pig says "griffey, griffey"
My hen says "shimmey shack, shimmey shack"
My goose says "quaw, quaw"
My duck says, "quaa, quaa"
My cat says "fiddle-i-fee."
I bought me a cow, my cow pleased me
I fed my cow under yonder tree,
My cow says "baw, baw" (etc.)
I bought me a horse, my horse pleased me
I fed my horse under yonder tree,
My horse says "neigh, neigh" (etc.)
I got me a wife, my wife pleased me
I fed my wife under yonder tree,
My wife says "honey, honey" (etc.)

Songs Every Child Should Know

National Association for Music Educators (NAfME) (formerly known as Music Educators National Conference, MENC) developed a suggested list of 42 songs every child should know. The songs are culled from folk, stage musicals, patriotic songs, Tin Pan Alley songs, culturally diverse songs, film songs, and religious songs.

42 Songs Every Child Should Know
- Amazing Grace
- America
- America the Beautiful
- Battle Hymn of the Republic
- Blue Skies
- De Colores
- Danny Boy (Londonderry Air)
- Dona Nobis Pacem
- Do-Re-Mi
- Down by the Riverside
- Frere Jacques
- Give My Regards to Broadway
- God Bless America
- God Bless the U.S.A.
- Green, Green Grass of Home
- Havah Nagilah
- He's Got the Whole World In His Hands
- Home on the Range
- I've Been Working on the Railroad
- If I Had a Hammer (The Hammer Song)
- Let There Be Peace on Earth
- Lift Ev'ry Voice and Sing
- Michael Row the Boat Ashore
- Music Alone Shall Live
- My Bonnie Lies Over the Ocean
- Oh, What a Beautiful Mornin'
- Oh! Susanna
- Over My Head
- Puff the Magic Dragon
- Rock-A-My Soul
- Sakura
- Shalom Chaverim
- She'll Be Comin' Round the Mountain
- Shenandoah
- Simple Gifts
- Sometimes I Feel Like a Motherless Child
- Star Spangled Banner
- Swing Low, Sweet Chariot
- This Land Is Your Land
- This Little Light of Mine

- Yesterday
- Zip-A-Dee-Doo-Dah

Resources

Songs for Teaching http://www.songsforteaching.com/index.html
- An excellent resource that includes educational songs, mathematics, social studies, plus classroom transition songs, activity and game songs, and much more.

Music Educator http://digitalmusiceducator.wordpress.com/2010/02/08/15-resources-for-elementary-music-teachers/
- Contains 15 websites for music.

Kodály Song Web http://kodalysongweb.net/songs
- A database of hundreds of songs categorized to indicate appropriate age, meter, genre, origin, melodic and rhythmic elements.

Music Notes http://musicnotes.net/songs_ALPHA.html
- Alphabetical list of hundreds of songs classified by grade, keywords for connecting to other subject areas and musical elements (meter, form, pitches). Also contains pitch and rhythm warm-ups, recorder, and sheet music.

Mama Lisa's World, International Music and Culture http://www.mamalisa.com/?t=hes&p=1299
- Contains hundreds of songs and rhymes by country of origin, as well as English nursery rhymes, Mother Goose, children's poetry, a blog and book reviews.

National Institute of Environmental Health Science (NIEHS) Kid's Page http://kids.niehs.nih.gov/games/songs/index.htm
- Hundreds of children's song lyrics with audio files for listening. Includes educational children's songs, holiday songs, favorites, and songs for teaching English as a second language.

References

Gordon, E. E. (2007). *Learning sequences in music: A contemporary music learning theory.* Chicago, IL: GIA.

Vocabulary

cumulative songs: songs in which each verse adds on lyrics and music from the previous verse; by the end of the song the singer is singing through all of the accumulated lyrics

descants: a type of harmony that is placed above the melody; can have text, but can also be sung on neutral syllables such as "oh," or "ah"

falsetto: a light, high, head voice that is not pushed, yelled, or forced in any way; usually used by boys

harmony: sounding of two or more notes simultaneously

partner songs: two songs, which are musically compatible, are sung together, and everyone contributes to the melody; considered more challenging than rounds.

polyphony: refers to multiple independent lines of music sing at the same time

rounds: also known as canons; group singing in which everyone contributes equally in terms of their melody

ostinato (pl. ostinati): easily repeated short musical phrases, patterns, or fragments.

unison: all parts are the same and sung at the same time

Chapter 10

Children's Musical Play: Musicality and Creativity

Chapter Summary: Children's creativity is at the heart of this book, and is one of the most important factors to consider when creating pedagogical material. This chapter addresses children's creativity, and introduces different types of children's musical play and their associated repertoires as well as ideas for children's improvisation.

There is very little research on children's musical play or creativity, making it difficult to draw any large conclusions on the topic. What research exists on musical play is based on behaviors from two general categories of data: 1) observations of younger children's spontaneous musical behaviors in daycare or educational settings designed by adults, or 2) observations of older children in educational settings or outdoors (Marsh and Young, 2006). With a few exceptions, children were not taken seriously as the main subjects or creative agents in studies of musical cultures until Patricia Shehan Campbell's book *Songs in their Heads* (2005). Campbell, a noted music educator and ethnomusicologist, acknowledged, "Up until a decade ago, the music culture (or cultures) of children had been largely overlooked and under-researched by ethnomusicologists, and had rarely been studied ethnographically by educators" (2005, p. 17-18). As discussed in Chapter 7 on music and the brain, the capacity to make music is present in all humans, "and that musicality is as universal as linguistic ability" (Hallam, 2006, p. 104). Each child is born with different strengths and abilities, including different types of creative thinking.

This chapter will outline some of the characteristics and key elements of music and play, including a discussion of the innateness of musical creativity and suggestions for encouraging creativity.

I. Musical Intelligence and Creativity

What is creativity? Can musical creativity be taught? Are only brilliant people creative? One of the foundational questions regarding any talent or ability is whether it is innate or learned—in other words, are we born musical, or can musicality and creativity be taught? Recent research into creativity has begun to answer some of these questions.

As it turns out, creative thinkers do not need to have a high IQ. According to neuroscientists, what makes a creative thinker is the high activity in the association cortices sections of the brain—responsible for making new connections and for "eureka" moments. The more associations, connections, memories or meanings an individual is able to make, the more creative the individual (Andreasen, 2006).Measuring creativity often utilizes tasks that reveal **divergent** thinking versus **convergent** thinking. A divergent thinker can come up with many different answers to a question, while a convergent thinker will come up with the one correct answer to a problem. One example might be to think of as many ways as possible to play a musical instrument. There is, of course, one standardized way to play an instrument (convergent thinking), but any instrument can be struck, plucked, banged, or shaken to produce many, many different types of sounds.

Gardner's Multiple Intelligences

Another take on creativity and intelligence involves Howard Gardner's *Multiple Theories of Intelligence*, which posits that intelligences are complex in that they are influenced by a combination of factors such as environment and biology, and that they are **educable**, capable of being educated or taught (Gardner, 1999). In other words, variations in opportunities and experiences can affect a child's skill building and therefore impact their intelligences.

Learning styles and approaches.

Types of Learners:	How they learn
Visual/Spatial	learn by seeing (graphs, maps, pictures)
Aural	learn by hearing (oral instructions, music)
Tactile/kinesthetic	learn by touching (hands on activities)

Gardner's Theory of Multiple Intelligences (1999) is one of the most significant educational influences of the 20th century and even today. He developed the theory in order to distinguish between different "modes" of intelligences rather than thinking of intelligence as one unified ability. Understanding these distinctions can help to guide educators in addressing different learning needs of children.

Multiple Intelligences (Bogod, 1998).

Logical-Mathematical	Ability to use reason, logic and numbers. These learners think conceptually in logical and numerical patterns making connections between pieces of information. Always curious about the world around them, these learners ask lots of questions and like to do experiments. Skills: problem solving, classifying and categorizing information, working with abstract concepts to figure out the relationship of each to the other, handling long chains of reason to make local progressions, doing controlled experiments, questioning and wondering about natural events, performing complex mathematical calculations, working with geometric shapes.

Musical-Rhythmic	Ability to produce and appreciate music. These musically inclined learners think in sounds, rhythms and patterns. They immediately respond to music either appreciating or criticizing what they hear. Many of these learners are extremely sensitive to environmental sounds (e.g., crickets, bells, dripping taps). Skills: singing, whistling, playing musical instruments, recognizing tonal patterns, composing music, remembering melodies, understanding the structure and rhythm of music
Visual-Spatial	Ability to perceive the visual. These learners tend to think in pictures and need to create vivid mental images to retain information. They enjoy looking at maps, charts, pictures, videos, and movies. Skills: puzzle building, reading, writing, understanding charts and graphs, a good sense of direction, sketching, painting, creating visual metaphors and analogies (perhaps through the visual arts), manipulating images, constructing, fixing, designing practical objects, interpreting visual images.
Bodily-Kinesthetic	Ability to control body movements and handle objects skillfully. These learners express themselves through movement. They have a good sense of balance and eye-hand co-ordination. (e.g., ball play, balancing beams). Through interacting with the space around them, they are able to remember and process information. Skills: dancing, physical co-ordination, sports, hands on experimentation, using body language, crafts, acting, miming, using their hands to create or build, expressing emotions through the body.
Intrapersonal	Ability to self-reflect and be aware of one's inner state of being. These learners try to understand their inner feelings, dreams, relationships with others, and strengths and weaknesses. Skills: Recognizing their own strengths and weaknesses, reflecting and analyzing themselves, awareness of their inner feelings, desires and dreams, evaluating their thinking patterns, reasoning with themselves, understanding their role in relationship to others.
Interpersonal	Ability to relate and understand others. These learners try to see things from other people's point of view in order to understand how they think and feel. They often have an uncanny ability to sense feelings, intentions and motivations. They are great organizers, although they sometimes resort to manipulation. Generally they try to maintain peace in group settings and encourage co-operation. They use both verbal (e.g. speaking) and non-verbal language (e.g. eye contact, body language) to open communication channels with others.

Interpersonal (cont'd)	Skills: seeing things from other perspectives (dual-perspective), listening, using empathy, understanding other people's moods and feelings, counseling, co-operating with groups, noticing people's moods, motivations and intentions, communicating both verbally and non-verbally, building trust, peaceful conflict resolution, establishing positive relations with other people.
Verbal/Linguistic	Ability to use words and language. These learners have highly developed auditory skills and are generally elegant speakers. They think in words rather than pictures. Skills: listening, speaking, writing, story telling, explaining, teaching, using humor, understanding the syntax and meaning of words, remembering information, convincing someone of their point of view, analyzing language usage.
Naturalist	Ability to nurture and relate information to one's natural surroundings. Classifying natural forms such as plants, rocks, and animals.
Spiritualist/Existential	Ability and proclivity to pose (and ponder) questions about life, death, and ultimate realities.

Gardner's Musical Intelligence

Gardner understood that children are innately musical, and also that creativity can be nurtured and taught. To a larger extent, using music as a means of expression not only helps develop the child psychologically and internally as a whole human being, but any musical expression also develops a sense of community and group cohesion.

Musical intelligence is the capacity to discern pitch, rhythm, timbre, and tone. This intelligence enables us to recognize, create, reproduce, and reflect on music, as demonstrated by composers, conductors, musicians, vocalists, and sensitive listeners. Interestingly, there is often an affective connection between music and the emotions, and musical intelligence may share common thinking processes with mathematical intelligence. Young adults with this kind of intelligence are usually singing or drumming to themselves. They are usually quite aware of sounds others may miss. (Campbell, 2008, p. 3)

Utilizing All of the Intelligences Through Music

When developing a lesson or working with children in any capacity, the more dimensions of learning you address, the richer the lesson will be. Using all of Gardner's Multiple Intelligences, or as many as possible, allows educators to construct their lesson plans as a way to engage students with strengths in other intelligences and to expose students with musical intelligence to apply those abilities to other areas. The most obvious connections might be between music and logical-mathematical or spatial intelligences since music involves rhythm, counting, and working with time-space relationships.

Activity 10A

TRY THIS

- Are you a divergent thinker or a convergent thinker? If you are one type of thinker, can you practice being the other type at least once each day?
- Deconstruct Gardner's Musical Intelligence by listing any of the processes he mentions that include music—skills, abilities, and behaviors.
- Are you or is someone you know highly engaged with music? How do you know?

II. Children's Musical Cultures and Play

The general perception is that children are surrounded by a variety of musical experiences. There are often fewer and fewer opportunities for children to actively engage in music making themselves. They are inundated with music emitting from a wide array of electronic devices, toys, and computers offering a limitless number of musical selections. However, much of the music in children's lives is "unchosen," in other words they are passive recipients in much of the music in their lives, and not actively engaged in its selection. They experience background music in computer games, cartoons, TV shows, films, on iPads, radios, and ringtones. They listen to music choices of their parents or siblings, and even the schools they attend often play music before the school day begins or in classrooms while students are working. Studies are being conducted on the effects of the ubiquitous pre-recorded music they encounter and whether or not it is intruding on their desire to make their own music or interact with each other on the playground.

Traditionally, children have participated in music making in activities such as singing songs learned via media or in-person interactions (school, camps, peers, playground). Children's repertoires include countless game-songs and rhymes for play, jump rope, etc., that have been passed down and modified for generations. In addition to pre-composed children's songs or folk songs, children create their own make-believe dialog and songs while playing with each other, or their toys and dolls, or just while daydreaming.

In a study of pre-school children and their musical play, Berger and Cooper (2003) discovered that children needed extended, uninterrupted time for play episodes. They identified interruptions that resulted in unfinished play and extinguished children's musical play, as well as environments that enhanced play such as the presence of an adult valuing all of the children's musical utterances and flexibility within structured lessons. One area of concern is the shrinking playground time during the school day due to an emphasis on more test-driven curricula. This deprives children of much of the freedom and interaction and development that can occur during free time with each other and with their own selves.

Activity 10B

TRY THIS

Think of the music that you encounter in just one day, including all of the chosen vs. unchosen music listening or making that occurs. How much of your day included unchosen music? Chosen music?

What is considered children's musical play? Children's musical play differs from teacher-structured play in an educational setting. Children's play is child-centered, child-structured, child-motivated, and child-run. It is:

- Initiated by children of their own volition
- Participated in voluntarily
- Intrinsically motivated
- Controlled by the child or children
- Free from external rules or run from internally developed rules
- Involved in everyday forms of musical activity (Marsh and Young, 2006)

Recent studies have not only looked at the processes of musical play, but studied them in the child's own environment rather than in an isolated and adult-controlled setting. Studies from Marsh (1995) and Hargreaves (1998) look at children's ability to compose and create songs on the playground among their peers and in a child-controlled environment.

The more intriguing aspect of children's play is that it naturally incorporates the integration and multimodality that we attempt to instill during education such as dance, drama, and music. Adult-led learning situations may be able to tap into or approximate the multi-modality that may increase arts and learning connections for children.

Marsh and Young's musical play within four age groups (2006)

Birth–Age 3
• Interactions between adults and babies • Bounces, repetitious songs
Preschool (3–6)

• Two types of singing:
  • "Communicative chant-like, repetitive singing of short verbal and musical ideas" sung in groups (p. 294-5)
  • "Introverted, solitary, free-flowing" singing generally alone (p. 295)
• Instruments: Explore "sound makers," instruments, or really any object
• Movement: Respond to any music played

Mid-Childhood (6+)
• Display more complex rhythms and melodies than originally assumed by ethnomusicologists • Tessitura much lower, closer to natural speaking voice • Reaction to cultural environment (pop music, traditional music)

Early Adolescence
• Downloading music files and singing with them
• Change to more dance-oriented play from singing and clapping games

Characteristics of Musical Play

According to Marsh (2006), play is:
- Multimodal
  - Blends movement with singing, making sounds with objects and instruments
  - Visually, kinesthetically, and aurally active
- Unpremeditated and improvisational
  - Younger children are more spontaneous
  - Older children are more stylized, and base their play on other genres
- A form of social interaction
  - Highly collaborative

Gender and cultural differences in all play also relates to musical play. **Collaborative musical play** continues among both boys and girls in international locations, whereas collaborative musical play in the U.S. among boys tends to wane. Boys' handclapping games are also more private, whereas girls will openly play jump rope games. (Marsh, 2006)

The Singing-Game: Children's Musical Creativity in Play

Children's singing game songs are one of the most profound examples of their creativity. Found the world over, children's song repertoires are some of the most imaginative and interesting cultural examples of any genre and are important expressions of children's lives in different cultures and eras. These games are creative and meaningful social artifacts embedded with children's culture, history, social mores, attitudes, and relationships.

Many folklorists speculate that children's songs actually began as adult games and songs, and then were adapted by children, since many cultures have shifted away from adults using music and dance as acceptable or valued social events and instead have turned toward other forms of entertainment. Nonetheless, games and songs were developed in their entirety or at least greatly enhanced by the creativity of children. Hand-clapping songs, circle games and dances in which narrative movements are used were performed and elaborated on generation after generation by children and youngsters. Below are a few examples.

A **singing game** is an activity based on a song verse, which has actions or movements associated with it. Some children's singing games have their roots in circle dances, while others reflect social traditions of courtship and marriage, friendship, overcoming childhood fears, or just expressing the fun and merriment of childhood.

Chapter 9 introduced the **play party game** and **cumulative songs**, appropriate for older children, but there are many other types of older children's game songs such as the Circle Game Songs, Handclapping songs, Jump rope songs, Counting out rhymes, Nursery rhymes, Chants, and Sea Chanteys.

Many of the children's games in the U.S. originated from Europe, and immigrants carried their ancestral heritage through songs and games, which in turn influenced childhood in the U.S.

The song "Farmer in the Dell" for example, reenacts the importance of agricultural life, animal and family relationships in early 19th century Germany by having participants imitate the types of animals and family existence common in rural areas.

The Farmer in the Dell

Traditional German singing game song

Circle songs from England that we are familiar with include "Here we go Round the Mulberry Bush" or "Ring Around the Rosie," as well as what is known as a "catching" game like "London Bridge" in which two children facing each other, join hands high above as a stream of children pass underneath. Suddenly, the two children drop arms and catch one child. Many folklorists trace these songs back for centuries. "London Bridge" might go as far back as the Middle Ages in London, as it describes the disrepair of the famous bridge.

London Bridge is Falling Down

English children's game song, 17th century

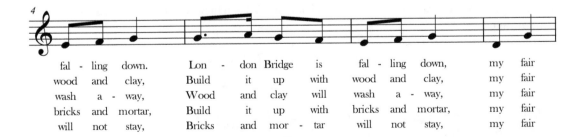

la   -   dy.
la   -   dy.
la   -   dy.
la   -   dy.
la   -   dy.

Many simple children's games actually carry complex musical attributes. For example, the camp song B-I-N-G-O appears to be a relatively straightforward spelling song. However, musically, it is quite advanced in that as you gradually silence the letter of the word B-I-N-G-O, the brain compensates for the missing pitch and rhythm using the inner ear.

B-I-N-G-O

American play party song

There   was   a   far - mer   had   a   dog   and   Bin - go   was   his

name - o,   B - I - N - G - O,   B - I - N - G - O,

B - I - N - G - O,   And   Bin - go   was   his   name - o.

Clapping and jump rope games are also widespread in the U.S. and around the world, and range from simple clapping patterns found in "Pat-a-cake, pat-a-cake baker's man," on to the complex and multi-versed rhymes such as "Miss Mary Mack" or "Miss Mary Had a Steamboat."

Miss Mary Mack

Miss Ma - ry Mack, Mack, Mack, All dressed in black, black, black, With sil - ver

buttons,   buttons,   buttons,   All   down   her   back,   back,   back.

Miss Mary Mack, Mack, Mack
All dressed in black, black, black
With silver buttons, buttons, buttons [butt'ns]
All down her back, back, back.
She asked her mother, mother, mother
for fifty cents, cents, cents
To see the elephants, elephants, elephants
Jump the fence, fence, fence.
They jumped so high, high, high
they reached the sky, sky, sky
And didn't come back, back, back
Till the fourth of July, ly, ly!

Counting Songs

Counting Songs are another important type of children's songs, particularly counting elimination games like "Eeny Meeny Miny Moe," or just counting rhymes such as "One-Two Buckle My Shoe."

"Eeny Meeny Miny Moe" in its modern version (oldest version found in 1815 or 20).

Eeny, meeny, miny, moe,
Catch a tiger by the toe.
If he hollers, let him go,
Eeny, meeny, miny, moe.

Counting songs are also found around the world as well. Here is one from India.

Ginti Geet (literally "Counting Song")

Ek do, kabhi na ro
teen chaar, rakhna pyar
paanch che, mil kar rakh
saath aat, pad le paat
nau das, zor se hans.
One Two, do not cry
Three Four, have love
Five Six, join and live
Seven Eight, read your lessons
Nine ten, laugh out loud.

In certain cultures, both adults and children play games. Two games from India are *kabbadi* and *antarkashi*. *Kabbadi,* a game similar to tag, involves the pursuer repeatedly chanting the word *kabbadi* in an uninterrupted stream without a breath while trying to tag someone. If the stream of breath is broken before they tag someone, they're out. (There are also World Cup Championship matches of *Kabbadi* in Asia.) *Antarkashi* is a challenging game involving song lyrics, where one team sings lines from a song and the other team must begin their song with the first letter of the last word from the previous team's selection. The first team to miss coming up with a response loses.

Activity 10C

THINK ABOUT IT

How is creativity perceived and valued in the U.S.? Among adults? Among children? How is children's play perceived? Is children's creativity given adequate importance in the curriculum?

TRY THIS

Try to play *Kabbadi* (*kuh-bah-dee*) using either the word *Kabbadi* or substituting an English word. *Kabbadi* means "holding hands" in Tamil.

In preparation for longer, narrative stories in which sound effects and music are incorporated, there are many children's rhymes that tell stories and incorporate fun sounds. One of them is "Bear Hunt" in which children make the sounds of footsteps, swishing through tall grass, splashing through a river, etc.

Start by patsching on your lap, L R L R L R while speaking the rhyme.

Bear Hunt
We're goin' on a bear hunt,
We're going to catch a big one,
I'm not scared
What a beautiful day!
Oh look! It's some long, wavy grass!
Can't go over it,
Can't go under it,
Can't go around it,
Got to go through it!
(Make arm motions like you're going through long grass and make swishing sounds.)
We're goin' on a bear hunt,
We're going to catch a big one,
I'm not scared
What a beautiful day!
Oh look! It's a mushroom patch.
Can't go over it,
Can't go under it,
Can't go around it,
Got to go through it!
(Pretend to go through the patch making popping sounds by clasping fingers together and clapping hands.)
We're goin' on a bear hunt,
We're going to catch a big one,
I'm not scared
What a beautiful day!

Oh look! It's a wide river.
Can't go over it,
Can't go under it,
Can't go through it,
Got to swim across it.
(Pretend to swim and make splashing sounds.)
We're goin' on a bear hunt,
We're going to catch a big one,
I'm not scared
What a beautiful day!
Oh look! A deep, dark cave.
Can't go over it,
Can't go under it,
Can't go through it,
Got to go in it.
(Pretend you're in a cave, and cup your hands around your mouth to make an echo-ey sound.)
Uh, oh! It's dark in here.
I feel something,
It has lots of hair!
It has sharp teeth!
It's a bear!
Hurry back through the river,
(Pretend to swim and make splashing sounds)
Back through the mushroom patch,
(Make popping sounds)
Back through the long grass
(Make motions like you're going through grass and make swishing sounds)
Run in the house and lock the door.
(Make a loud clap sound.)
Phew! That was close!
I'm not afraid!

Encouraging Musical Creativity through Improvisation

As educators, we are in a position to facilitate music making with children and encourage them to explore their musical selves, including their originality, intelligence, and musical capacity. A study by Koutsoupidou and Hargreaves (2009), found that improvisation had significant effects on the development of children's creative musical thinking, and that musical originality—the way the child manipulates musical sounds in a unique fashion—increased along with the child's musical flexibility. One of their significant findings reiterates the common sense idea that, "encouraging children to be creative in the classroom can promote creativity, while preventing them from engaging in creative activities might inhibit their creative potential" (p. 265-266).

One of the ways of fostering creativity is to encourage students' improvisation. . The term **improvisation** is often misunderstood to mean, "making something up on the spot." Even the Merriam-Webster definition, which states "to speak or perform without preparation," is highly misleading. In fact, improvisation is an advanced and highly sophisticated skill in which the musician must draw upon all of their previously practiced knowledge and techniques in order to compose "in the moment." Musicians must also respond immediately to their own sound through acute music listening ability, often coordinating with other musicians around them.

Although there is discussion over whether improvisation skills can be taught, there are some basic steps that allow children a safe, secure context in which to experiment with improvisation. Begin by stressing *play and participation over performance.* This is critical, since most of the self-confidence issues regarding the arts is centered around the idea that children can "get it wrong" or the idea that what they create is less than perfect. In the activities below there are no correct or incorrect musical utterances. All of it is exploratory and meant to develop the child's inner sense of confidence and skill building while playing.

1) Instrumental Improvisation
- Pentatonic Improvisation on Xylophones
  - Remove the "F" and "B" bars to make the instruments pentatonic.
  - Clap a simple 4 beat rhythm, and have students play any notes on the xylophone in that rhythm.
  - After they are confident and familiar with the process, ask them to play the last note together on "C" for example, so they set up a tonal goal for their short improvisation.
  - Increase the length of the rhythms clapped to 8 beats, then to 16 beats. After 8 beats, they can play a "G" which is the V or dominant of the C scale in order to create another goal. Then they can end on "C" on beat 16. This gives the improvisation shape.
- Solos and Groups
  - When they are comfortable with the process above, have a few soloists volunteer to play their measures alone. This can be alternated with whole group/ solo/whole group/solo, to create an improvisatory piece.

2) Body Percussion Improvisation
- Snapping, Clapping, Patsching, Stomping
  - Begin by practicing echo clapping, using many different rhythmic patterns in different meters (e.g. 2/4, 3/4, 4/4, 6/8 in 2, 3, 4, 6, 8, 9, 12, or 16 beat patterns). These become the embodied tools with which students will create their improvisation
  - Have them experiment with these rhythms either just clapping or on their body first using body percussion - clapping, stamping, snapping or patsching) until they become confident in producing different rhythms.
- **Question/Answer.** Another place to start is to provide a question for the group in a 4-beat pattern and then have them respond with their own 4-beat pattern. The question/answer technique is slightly more difficult than echoing in that echoing merely imitates what the leader has done, and answering requires the creation of a *different* rhythm.
- **Question/Answer Advanced.** An even slightly more difficult answer is one that involves a part of the question. For example, in a linguistic question and answer, you might ask: "Where are you going?" The answer usually includes part of the question, with a slight modification of words or word order. For example, "I am going to school." Similarly, a musical answer should also contain part of the question, plus have a sense of closure or finality. For example:

QUESTION: POSSIBLE ANSWERS:

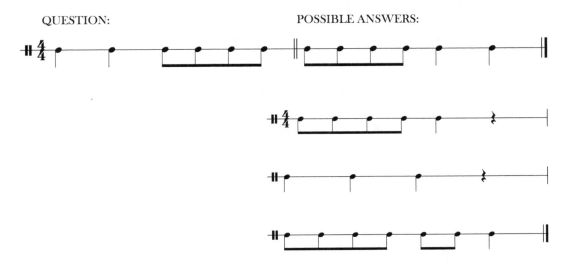

- Closure or finality means that it should sound final, and not end with eighth or sixteenth notes, which imply that there will be a next measure. Ending with quarter notes, half notes, or even quarter notes and a rest gives a sense of finality to the rhythm.

3) Vocal Improvisation

While one might think that vocal improvisation is the easiest type of improv, it is actually very challenging. Below are both vocal and instrumental sample activities from the book *Free to be Musical,* (Higgins, et. al, 2010), which will help guide students to feeling comfortable with improvisation.

Activities from Free to be Musical: Group Improvisation in Music
- Keep breathing
    - Breathe, and concentrate on your breath.
    - Gradually add a sound to the exhaled breath.
    - Get an instrument and figure out how to play it to the exhaled breath—change if you like.
- Be free
    - Start and end in silence.
    - Play with an instrument however you want, not listening to anyone else.
    - After a while, begin to tune in to other people.
- Dig-a-dum
    - Chant dig-a-dum dig-a-dum, over and over.
    - Then add patch, clap, snap, stamp, slap or any other vocalization such as dee, too, bah.
    - Transfer the rhythm to non-pitched percussion instruments.
    - Have each child play the rhythm four times, while the group responds four times. Listen for timbral differences.
    - Transfer to pitched percussion.
    - Expand to have them add in other rhythms while keeping some dig-a-dums.

Children's Compositions using Abstract Notation

Children are natural composers and experiment with sound all around them. Capturing their sounds, however, is difficult to do in regular notation, and children do not have the ability to formally notate something using staff paper and lines. But expressive abilities of music do not have to be limited. Using abstract notation is one way around this. Children can draw simple shapes and textures to express sounds and compositions that they've invented, or can read the work of another child who has written in this type of notation.

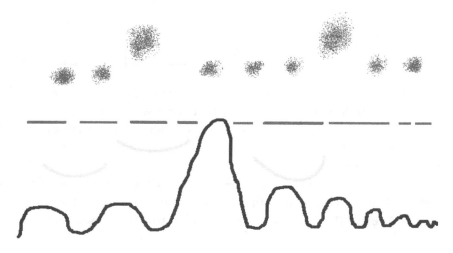

Abstract notation: Example 1

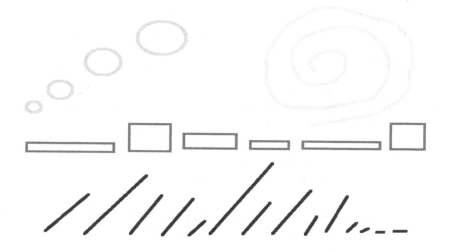

Abstract notation: Example 2

Above are some examples of this type of notation. Swoops, lines, dots, etc., can represent many vocal sounds. Although this is not typical or standard notation, there are very specific musical attributes that can be visually represented such as sound, silence, and duration or the length of the sound. In the first example, the pink lines indicate the duration of a sound and then silence. Other visuals require some advanced decision-making. For example, does the the tall, big, blue bump in the middle of the squiggly line in the first example equal a loud sound (dynamics) or a higher pitch or both? Does a "shorter" or smaller bump equal softer or a lower pitch or both? Exactly what sound does each shape represent? Smooth? Rough? Short? Long? Sharp? Should you use a vowel? Consonant? An onomatopoeic sound? A word? Body percussion? What is the tempo of the piece? How do you read the piece? Left to right or right to left? Top to bottom or bottom to top? In terms of texture, does the first example consist of four separate lines or voices, or should they be performed all together? At what tempo is the piece to be performed? A child can be the conductor of the piece, and set a tempo by slowly moving their finger along the "score" as other children perform their different parts.

After a successful vocalization or body percussion, the next step is to assign instruments to the different lines. A circle might represent a drumbeat, a swoop could be a slide whistle, etc. Still, decisions about crescendos and decrescendos, tempo, and score reading have to be made, but there are endless possibilities for vocalizing and playing these child-centered compositions.

References

Andreasen, N. (2006). *The creative brain: The science of genius.* New York: Plume Reprints.

Berger, A., & Cooper, S. (2003). Musical play: A case study of preschool children and parents. *Journal of Research in Music Education, 51*(2), 151-165.

Bogod, L. (1998). *Learning Styles and Multiple Intelligences.* Retrieved from http://www.ldpride.net/

Burnard, P. (2000). Examining experiential differences between improvisation and composition in children's music-making. *British Journal of Music Education,* 17(3), 227-245.

Campbell, B. (2008). *Handbook of differentiated instruction using the multiple intelligences.* Boston, MA: Pearson, Allyn, & Bacon.

Campbell, P., & Wiggins, T. (Eds.) (2012). *The Oxford handbook of children's musical cultures.* New York, NY: Oxford University Press.

Campbell, P. (1991). The child-song genre: A comparison of songs by and for children. *International Journal of Music Education, 17,* 14-23.

Campbell, P. (2010). *Songs in their heads: Music and its meaning in children's lives.* New York, NY: Oxford University Press.

de Vries, P. (2006). Being there: creating music-making opportunities in a childcare centre. *International Journal of Music Education, 3,* 255-270.

Gardner, H. (1999). *Intelligence reframed: Multiple intelligences for the 21st century.* New York, NY: Basic Books.

Hallam, S. (2006). "Musicality" in *The Child as Musician*, ed. Gary E. McPherson. New York: Oxford University Press, 93-110.

Hallam, S. (2010). "The Power of Music: Its Impact on the Intellectual, Social and Personal Development of Children and Young People. *International Journal of Music Education,* August vol. 28 no. 3, 269-289.

Harwood, E. (1998). Music learning in context: A playground Tale. *Research Studies in Music Education, 11,* 52-60.

Higgins, L., Campbell, P., & McPherson, C. (2010). *Free to be musical: Group improvisation in music.* Latham, MD: Rowman and Littlefield Publishers.

Koutsoupidou, T., & Hargreaves, D. J. (2009). An experimental study of the effects of improvisation on the development of children's creative thinking in music. *Psychology of Music, 37*(3), 251-278.

Marsh, K. (1995). Children's singing games: Composition in the playground? *Research Studies in Music Education, 4,* 2-11.

Marsh, K. & Young, S. (2006). "Musical Play." in *The Child as Musician,* in. Gary E. McPherson. New York: Oxford University Press, 289-310.

Niland, A.. (2009). The power of musical play: The value of play-based, child-centered curriculum in early childhood music education. *General Music Today, 23,* 17-21.

Saracho, O. (2013). An Integrated Play-based Curriculum for Young Children. New York: Routledge

Young, S. (2003). Adults and young children communicating musically. D. J. Hargreaves, et al., (Eds.). *Musical Communication,* New York, NY: Oxford University Press.

Young, S. (2003). *Music with the Under-Fours.* London: Routledge Falmer.

Vocabulary

collaborative musical play: people of gender and culture differences related to one another through music

convergent thinking: following a particular set of logical steps to arrive at one solution, which in some cases is a "correct" solution

divergent thinking: a thought process or method used to generate creative ideas by exploring many possible solutions

educable: capable of being educated or taught

improvisation: an advanced and highly sophisticated technique in which the musician must draw upon all of their previously practiced skills and techniques in order to compose

singing game: an activity based on a song verse, which has actions or movements associated with it

Chapter 11

Music and Inclusion

Chapter Summary. Allowing all children equal access to an art form is more difficult than it sounds. Social pressures, stereotypes, and changing attitudes and perspectives can inhibit inclusion and lead to exclusionary practice. This chapter addresses the issue of several types of musical inclusion, including music and gender, and music for children with autism, ADD/ADHD, learning and physical disabilities.

I. Gender in Music

Most of us never consider whether music is gendered, but any system that is part of a culture, even a musical one, is bound to include any general perceptions and values of the society as a whole.

What is gender? The term **sex** refers to the biological and physiological characteristics that define men and women, while **gender** refers to society's constructed roles, expectations, behaviors, attitudes, and activities that it deems appropriate for men and women. Many of us can remember the first time we became aware of our gender. For some, it was an article of clothing that was too "boyish" or "girlish" to wear, while for others it was noticing certain behaviors such as preferring to play with trucks and cars rather than dolls, and realizing the *societal expectations* that encourage boys to play with trucks and cars. We incorporate gender into all aspects of our daily lives from a very early age onward, and can be socially uncomfortable if we are unsure of someone's gender or have issues coming to understand our own.

Perceptions of the individual based on their gender and race influence all of us in all areas. We contextualize, filter, draw conclusions, and make inferences, in part, based on someone's physical attributes. Many educators have studied the role of gender and how it affects teachers and teaching. For example, individual teachers may prefer one gender to another, but the entire educational system in general, favors girls' learning styles and behaviors over that of boys. Grades are affected in addition to access to certain opportunities and promotion to leader- ship roles. Boys and girls may express different musical interests and abilities with girls showing self-confidence in literacy and music and boys showing confidence in sports and math, but teachers also discuss boys and girls musicality differently (Green, 1993).

Is music gendered? Music is highly gendered in ways that we might not even think about. Societies attribute masculinity to different genres of music, instruments, and what musicians should look like when performing. For example, genres like heavy metal and rock are gendered not only in the fact that male musicians dominate them, but also in that they are perceived as male-oriented in subject matter, with appeal to a male audience. Gender lines are not as straightforward as one might believe, however. In performance, there is a great deal of gender bending or borrowing that can occur. On stage, male musicians may co-opt female gendered attributes as part of a performance, such as Heavy or Hair Metal band members wearing long hair and make-up.

Musical instruments are also "gendered." Our choices as to which instrument to play, in other words, are not entirely our own. Society, friends, and teachers, play a significant role in our music selection process. As a culture, and even as children, we have very particular notions of who should play what instruments, with children as young as three associating certain instruments with gender (Marshall and Shibazaki, 2012). In a 1981 study, Griswold & Chroback found that the harp, flute, and piccolo had high feminine ratings; the trumpet, string bass, and tuba had high masculine ratings.

As Lucy Green mentions above (1993), boys and girls have different musical interests, and teachers discuss musicality differently regarding boys and girls, and are likely to offer differences in opportunity, instrument selection, etc. For example, according to a 2008 study, girls are more likely to sing, while boys are more likely to play instruments such as bass guitar, trombone, and percussion. One interesting exception to boy's dominance of percussion is that, participation in African drumming was far more egalitarian, with an equal number of boys and girls playing (Hallam, 2008, p. 11-13).

Activity 11A

THINK ABOUT IT

You might have an early memory when deciding what instrument to play in the school band or for lessons at home. Why did you decide on which instrument to play? Were you influenced by what instrument other girls or boys or professional musicians were playing? Did your parents or teachers encourage you in one direction or another?

II. Music Therapy and Healing

Throughout this book, we've learned about the many connections that music has on mental and emotional development. Music, is of course, more than entertainment, and affects the body directly through its sound vibrations. Our bodies are made up of many rhythms—the heart, respiratory system, our body's energy, digestive systems etc. These vibrations result in something called **entrainment**, where our bodies try to sync up with the tempo of the music. Music can affect our heartbeat, blood pressure, and pulse rate, and reduce stress, anxiety and even depression.

The fact that the body and mind are so affected by music forms the basis for most music therapy. Music Therapy is defined as "A systematic process of intervention wherein the therapist helps the client to achieve health, using musical experiences and the relationships that develop through them as dynamic forces of change" (Bruscia, 1989, p. 47). "Musical experiences can include singing or vocalizing, playing various percussion and melodic instruments, and listening to music...Music therapists tap into the power of music to arouse emotions that can be used to motivate clients" (Pelliteri, 2000).

Music for Well-being and Learning

Music can be used to create any number of environments for children to flourish cognitively and developmentally. Music creates a general sense of well being, while creating a positive environment in which to learn, create, and function. For example, playing soft classical music, particularly Baroque music (Bach, Vivaldi, etc.) increases attention and the ability to concentrate, allowing the listener to work more productively.

Music also has a direct impact on the heart rate. The heart responds by beating more quickly when listening to faster tempos, and slower when listening to slower tempos. It also responds to dynamics (loud and soft) and to certain pitch frequencies.

Tempo and related activities.

Activity	Music
High energy activities • General stress release, increases alertness and energy • Dancing • Working out • Mood pick-me-up	130 beats per minute • Dance music is usually 120–140 beats per minute • Classical music in a tempo marked *allegro* or *presto* would be appropriate; divertimento
Medium energy activities • Increases productivity and performance • Increases alertness, artistic expression • Good for individual or group project work • Concentrating on a single activity • Homework, project construction, etc.	80–100 beats per minute • Baroque or classical music in a tempo marked *andante*; theme and variations, fantasia, giocoso, intermezzo • Pop or rock music ballads
Lower energy activities • Alters brain waves to promote relaxation • Increases creativity, thinking, problem solving • Calms the body and mind after a high impact activity • Returning from recess or active playtime	60–80 beats per minute • Baroque or classical music in a tempo marked *adagio* or *largo* • Bach, Albinoni, Vivaldi, Mozart • Lullabies, classical or folk (i.e., Brahms lullaby)

In addition to the beats per minute (tempo), the timbre, expression, and volume (dynamics) of a song also have an impact. For example, a loud orchestral piece, even if it has 60 beats per minute, will not aid the body into a calm state as well as a softer, more soothing piece with a few instruments. Low-pitched instruments such as drums impact the body with vibration and rhythm that influence body rhythms and movement, whereas higher-pitched frequencies such as flute and voice demand more attention and focus. Pieces such as Stravinsky's *Rite of Spring* or Orff's *Carmina Burana*, for example, would not be good choices as they are likely to promote agitation and frenetic activity rather than concentration and productivity.

Activity 11B

TRY THIS

Go to a website such as Pandora (www.pandora.com), Stereomood (www.stereomood.com) or Spotify (www.spotify.com). Select different types of music and note down the general beats per minute using a watch or clock. Then take stock of your physical reactions. For example, how do you respond to the *workout* genre on Pandora? Does your heart rate increase? Are you able to concentrate with this type of music in the background? What about the *easy listening* genre?

Compare: Does the Music Therapy selection on the Mood/Relaxed channel on Spotify create the same physical reaction as any of the classical adagio selections suggested above? How about the Mood Booster channel? How does Stereomood compare in terms of changing your mood? Document any physical reactions you might have had.

III. Learning Disabilities, Special Needs Children, and Music

Any group of students has a wide range of abilities, and each child presents a unique challenge in terms of the best way to reach their maximum learning potential. Some students may be gifted or already familiar with the material, while others are challenged simply by the arrangement of the room. Some children, however, require more extensive modifications to the curriculum in order to succeed. Regardless of where you work, you are likely to be in a position where you will encounter students that require additional help. Music can greatly assist these children in a variety of ways, helping and nurturing them in learning and development.

- Special Needs
- Learning Disabilities
- Autism
- ADD or ADHD
- Behavior Problems
- Physical Disabilities
- Hearing Loss
- Visual Loss

The strategies outlined below can be used in any general music work with children, but are particularly helpful techniques aimed at aiding individuals with specific needs. Many of the techniques introduced in this textbook are used in music therapy and to treat Autism

Spectrum Disorders (ASD). Musical activities such as singing, singing/vocalization, instrument play, movement/dance, musical improvisation, songwriting/composition, and listening to music, are types of musical therapy interventions to assess and help individuals practice identified skills.

Assessing Appropriate Songs for Special Needs Children

As with selecting any material for any child, you will need to assess the particular needs of the student, including speech and developmental levels. If the child is pre-verbal or verbally limited, a simple song (limited lyrics, simple phrases) would be more appropriate than something complex.

Musical activities, including singing or playing instruments, can increase the self-esteem level of the child. Pamela Ott suggests asking the following questions when selecting material, keeping in mind that simply doing the activity successfully is one of the most important goals (Ott, 2011):

- Have I chosen an activity that will interest my child?
- Have I modified the activity to the appropriate level to ensure a successful experience?
- Am I prepared to modify the activity even more if it appears to be too difficult for my child?
- Will the music made by my child in this activity be pleasing to him?
- Have I praised my child for attempting the activity?

Often children require a well-structured day in which to work successfully. In addition to integrating music in the day, as discussed in the next chapter as well, music can also help to organize and structure the day for children who have trouble transitioning from activity to activity.

Possible uses for music throughout the day include:

1. Organization
    - **Activity:** lining up, cleaning up
    - **Aesthetic Purpose:** motivation
2. Transitions
    - **Activity:** changing from one activity to another
    - **Aesthetic Purpose:** change of mood, re-focus energy
3. Rituals
    - **Activity:** Greetings/Hello, goodbye, holiday music
    - **Aesthetic Purpose:** Prepare students mentally, provides stability and repetition
4. Interstitial
    - **Activity:** Short break between two subjects or activities
    - **Aesthetic Purpose:** Provide relaxation, moment of expression, and alternate uses for cognitive functioning

Sample Day that includes Music

1. Use music before the school day begins
    - **Ritual:** Set the mood/change the atmosphere in the room using sound
2. Students enter and settle in to the room
    - **Ritual:** "Good Morning," and/or movement activity "Head Shoulders"

3. Morning Work, Attendance, Calendar
    - **Organization:** i.e. "If you're ready for P.E. line on up, line on up."
4. Special (Music, Art, Physical Ed)
    - **Transition:** Focus for Math
5. Math Stations
    - **Organization:** Line up for Lunch
6. Lunch
    - **Transition:** Focus ready for reading
7. Reading/Literacy Stations
    - **Interstitial:** Break song/movement
8. Writing
    - **Interstitial:** Movement/song break
9. Social Studies/Science/Health
    - **Transition:** Movement activity/song
10. Snack/Play time
    - **Organization:** Focus: Line up for Library or Lab
11. Computer Lab or Library
    - **Transition:**
12. Pickup and pack-up
    - **Organization:** "Clean up song"
13. Dismissal
    - **Ritual:** "Goodbye" song

Examples of Hello rhymes and songs might include "Hi There, Hello There." If the body percussion is too complex, simply say the rhyme or clap to the rhyme.

Hi There, Hello There

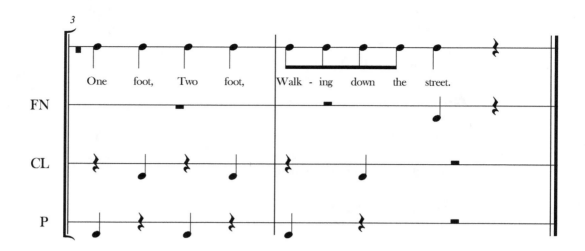

Good Morning

Good mor - ning, good mor - ning, and how do you do? Good

mor - ning, good mor - ning I'm glad to see you. We greet ev - ery

mor - ning with a "How do you do?" So hap - py to see you good

Everybody's Welcome

Eve-ry-bod-y's wel-come yes, yes, wel-come, Eve-ry-bod-y's wel-come, come a-long and go.

Oh glo - ry we're all here now, Oh glo - ry come a-long and go.

The More We Get Together

The   more   we get to - geth - er,   to - geth - er,   to - geth - er,   the

more   we get to - geth - er   the   hap - pi - er   we'll   be.   For

your friends   are   my friends and   my friends   are   your friends. The

more   we get to - geth - er   the   hap - pi - er   we'll   be.

Head and Shoulders (Key of B flat)

Head, should - ers, knees and toes, knees and toes.   Head, should - ers, knees and

toes, knees and toes,_____ Eyes and ears and   mouth   and   nose,

Head, should - ers, knees and   toes, knees and toes.

Strategies and Songs for Enhancing and Encouraging Verbal Skills

For children who are pre-verbal or speech-delayed, substituting nonsense syllables helps them successfully sing a favorite tune. "Doo," "boo," "la," etc., are easily pronounceable and fun for children to articulate.

Other familiar songs to help increase verbal awareness include songs with word substitutions or nonsense syllables such as Sarasponda or Supercalifragilisticexpialidocous. The song B-I-N-G-O is an excellent example in which to practice internalizing the pitch since the singer has to clap the rhythm and silently think the pitch in their head.

B-I-N-G-O

American play party song

Another song with an opportunity for children to insert a rhythm is "I'm a Nut." Although the song does have quite a few words, the refrain is repetitive with only three words, and provides two empty beats for clapping or playing an instrument.

I'm a Nut

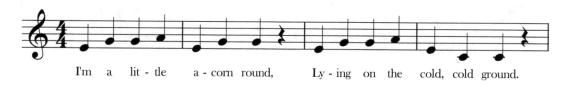

I'm a nut   I'm a nut   I'm a nut,   I'm a nut.

Any song can be adapted to allow the insertion of rhythm simply by substituting a word or phrase with a clap (or instrument). The substituted word or phrase can be part of the rhyme or not. For example, in the silly song "Skidamarink," the phrase "I love you" can be clapped, or even just the "you." Words such as "morning" "afternoon" "moon," etc. are also good candidates for substitution.

Skidamarink

Skid-a-ma-rink a-dink a-dink   skid-a-ma-rink a-doo

I love you,   skid-a-ma-rink a-dink a-dink

skid-a-ma-rink a-doo   I love you,   I love you in the

morn-ing and in the af-ter-noon,   I love you in the

eve-ning and un-der-neath the moon, oh,   skid-a-ma-rink a-

dink a - dink   skid- a-ma- rink a - doo,   I   love   you.

Silly songs and rhymes with interesting onomatopoeic sounds and simple, repetitive words are also highly useful, such as "Galumph Went the Little Green Frog" and "Jelly in a Bowl."

Galumph Went the Little Green Frog One Day

Ga - lumph   went   the   lit - tle green   frog   one   day,   Ga -

lumph   went   the   lit - tle green   frog.   Ga - lumph went the lit - tle green

Jelly in a Bowl

Jel - ly in a bowl,   jel - ly in a bowl,   wib-ble wob-ble wib-ble wob-ble,   jel - ly in a bowl.

The remainder of the chapter contains material from the National Association for Music Educators regarding some tips and general strategies for working with children who have special needs.[1]

Music for Special Needs and Learning Disabilities

Many classrooms today are inclusive, meaning that they will include children who have special needs. Preparing to help these children requires additional thought and strategies.

General Strategies for Students with Special Needs

Avoid sensory overload and be predictable.
- Keep your classroom organized and free from distractions.
- Keep directions simple and direct.
- Establish lesson routines (e.g., beginning and ending songs).

---

[1] Reprinted with permission. Copyright NAfME, 2012, http://www.nafme.org/strategies-for-students-with-special-needs/

Lesson preparation

- Present materials in as many modes as possible to address different learning styles.
- Develop a hands-on, participatory program that emphasizes varied activities like movement, instruments, rhythm, speech, sound exploration, melody, and dance for best effect.

Strategies for students with learning disabilities

Students who have difficulty reading

- Prepare simple visual charts.
- Use color to highlight key concepts (e.g., do=blue, re=red, mi=green).
- Isolate rhythm patterns into small pieces on a large visual.
- Indicate phrases with a change in color.
- Introduce concepts in small chunks.
- Use repetition, but present material in different ways.

Students with visual impairments

- Teach songs by rote and echoing patterns.
- Provide rhythm instruments—such students can learn to play them without problems.
- Assign a movement partner for movement activities.
- Read aloud any information you present visually.
- Get large-print scores when available.
- Give a tour of the room so students can become familiar with where things are.

Students with behavior problems

- Use routine and structure—it can be comforting for these students.
- Remain calm and don't lose your temper.
- Maintain a routine from lesson to lesson (e.g., begin and end with a familiar song).
- Vary the drill by playing or singing with different articulation and dynamics for students who can't maintain focus for long.
- Use props like puppets to give directions in a nonthreatening way.
- Use songs or games that contain directions to help children who struggle to follow verbal directions or who have authority issues.

Students with physical disabilities (e.g., cystic fibrosis, heart trouble, asthma, diabetes, epilepsy)

- Have students sing to help breathing and lung control.
- Adapt Orff instruments by removing bars so that any note played will be correct. Orff instruments fit nicely onto a wheelchair tray.
- Acquire adaptive instruments—adaptive mallets, Velcro straps for hand drums and other percussion instruments, and one-handed recorders are available. Find other adaptive musical instruments with an Internet search.
- Develop activities for listening and responding to recorded music for children who are physically unable to move and/or play an instrument.

Students with higher learning potential

- Offer a variety of activities, such as acceleration (design assignments that allow students to go to differing levels), enrichment (extra lessons), technological instruction (computer programs for composition, research, or theory).

- Find a mentor for a student.
- Offer advanced ability ensembles.

Debrot (2002) says you can address a variety of skill levels in one piece of music: While some children play complex patterns, others can sing or play a simple steady beat. "Every student has a learning style that is unique," says Debrot. "Presenting material aurally, visually, tactilely, and orally will insure that you connect with the varied learning styles for all students. The use of speech, movement, instruments, and singing in each lesson will insure that each child feels some degree of success."

Music and Autism

Music has been found to be successful in working with children who have Autistic Spectrum Disorder. Using music activities and songs helps to greatly increase independent performance and reduce anxiety. Music was found to help reduce the stress of transitions such as the shift from home to school, help children remember step-by-step routines like clean up time, and also increase the community and group inclusion of children with and without disabilities (Kern, 2004).

Iseminger (2009) refers to employing an "Intentional Approach" when dealing with students on the autism spectrum, particularly those with difficulty with transitions. The following examples are helpful in preparing autistic students in advance for transitions.

- To ease a transition from an Autoharp unit to a recorder unit, make an announcement ("Today is the last day for Autoharp because next week we begin playing the recorder."), and put a visual clue on a large calendar (e.g., "Last day for Autoharp" or "Autoharp STOP," "First day for recorders" or "Recorders YES").
- To show a DVD (e.g., The Nutcracker in December), put a picture of the DVD or a TV on the calendar for that date at least a week ahead of time.
- To prepare for a concert dress rehearsal, post a picture of risers or the children standing on risers on that date.
- When the class is finished working on a song, put it in an "All Done" folder to show that the class won't be working on it anymore.
- Write a short, simple picture story for the autistic child to read during the week preceding the major changes.
- Keep the number of changes to a minimum. Following a concert, introduce new songs slowly after reviewing the choir's favorite song from the concert. Finish with a familiar song.

Shore's work (2002) explains the musical benefits for those on the autism spectrum. Music provides an alternative means of communication for nonverbal students, and can also help other verbal students organize their communication. Music can help to improve children's self-esteem in that they can participate and possibly excel in the musical endeavor. Music is also a social and communal activity, and a child with autism can enter into the communal and social interaction of music making.

Success with Autism: Visual Aids and Predictability[2]

Iseminger (2009) notes that two main areas where teachers can help students with autism are in creating appropriate *visual aids* and achieving *predictability*. "Children with special needs are concrete learners, and visual information makes words more concrete.

---

2 Reprinted with Permission from NAfME http://www.nafme.org/success-with-autism-predictability © National Association for Music Education

Pictures of a student sitting in a chair or playing the recorder give clear directions. Those on the autism spectrum are often stronger visual than auditory learners and have a tremendous need for visual information." Also, autistic children act out due to increased anxiety and fear, not from autism itself. As a classroom teacher, taking steps to minimize anxiety will help with managing classroom behavior.

Most teachers use some type of visual cues and supports such as charts, books, musical instruments, and music notation. Making these visuals simple and accessible will greatly help autistic children in the class.

- Use rhythm notation and beat icons to make rhythm a visual event. Point to four quarter notes or four icons while the class pats a steady beat.
- Show a picture of a recorder with correct fingering rather than a fingering chart.
- Clarify lyrics with pictures made from design software (e.g., Boardmaker), or decorate counting songs with pictures of each number and object.
- Post your lesson plan. List song titles to cross out or erase as they're completed. Or make a tab system with pictures and Velcro or magnets. As each song or activity is completed, you or the child can pull off the tab and put it in a folder marked "All done."

Managing Behavior

- To reward positive behavior: For a 30-minute class, prepare a file folder with a Velcro strip with the numbers 1 through 6. At the end of the strip, post a picture of a reward (e.g., favorite book or swing on the playground). For every 5 minutes the child follows directions and stays on task, she earns a star-shaped tab. When she sees all six tabs in place, she knows 30 minutes are done, and she gets her reward.
- To establish negative consequences: Prepare a card with 3 square tabs. At the first verbal warning, remove the first tab; repeat for a second infraction. Removing the last tab means removal from the classroom or other appropriate consequence.

Tips for creating predictability

Physical Structure
- Establish a seating arrangement, and keep it the same all year.
- Assign the student to an appropriate-size chair, carpet square, or a masking tape outline on the floor.
- For a child who can't sit still, assign two chairs across the room from each other. Have her alternate chairs for each activity, providing the movement she craves.
- For a child who refuses to sit in a chair, photograph him sitting in his chair and sitting on a carpet square. Post both photos, and ask him to choose between them when entering music class. He gets a sense of control, yet you prescribe the limits.

Routine Structure
- Keep the structure of your lessons the same from session to session. For example, begin with a fun rhythm activity to get students going, and finish with a quiet relaxing or listening activity to calm them. The exact song or activity may vary, but the basic nature of the activity is the same and predictable.
- Establish your music routine the first day of class as a whole experience. Children with autism will show signs of discomfort or distress because they don't know the routine. If you can overlook and tolerate some obvious distress and complete the lesson, the child will have experienced the entire routine and established it

mentally. On the second day, she'll likely show fewer signs of distress because now she knows what to expect. If a child shows severe aggression, obviously this can't be ignored.

- If a child is unlikely to tolerate an entire first class, introduce him to music class for short periods, starting with the ending routine, or the last 5 minutes of class. After several successful 5-minute sessions, he can come in for the activity preceding the final activity, and so on, until he's in music class for the full period. (This also works for a child already in class who's struggling and feeling overwhelmed.)

"Sometimes you just have to plow through the struggle or upset to establish the routine," says Iseminger. "They are taking it in, despite what it looks like, calming down after one or two class sessions."

Students with ADD or ADHD[3]

Attention Deficit Disorder (ADD) and Attention Deficit Hyperactivity Disorder (ADHD) are two of the most common factors for special needs in today's classrooms. ADD and ADHD are disabilities and fall under the designating category of "Other Health Impairment." This NAfME post addresses both issues and gives guidance to mediate its effects in the classroom.

Many teachers recognize the signs of attention deficit disorder (ADD) and attention deficit hyperactive disorder (ADHD): an inability to maintain attention, impulsive behaviors, and/or motor restlessness. Students can have mild, moderate, or severe symptoms and can be found in both general education and special education classes.

Elise S. Sobol teaches at Rosemary Kennedy School, Wantagh, New York (for students with multiple learning disabilities, including those with autism and developmental difficulties) and is the chairperson of Music for Special Learners of the New York State School Music Association.

Sobol (2008) suggests the following strategies for students with ADD with or without hyperactivity:

- Teach and consistently reinforce social skills.
- Mediate asking questions.
- Define and redefine expectations.
- Assess understanding of content.
- Define and redefine appropriateness and inappropriateness.
- Make connections explicitly clear.
- Take nothing for granted.
- Reinforce positive behavior.
- Define benefits of completing a task.
- Include 21st-century relevance.
- Clearly mark music scores with clues to recall rehearsal information.
- Establish support through creative seating to enhance student security.
- Post your rehearsal plan.
- Repeat realistic expectations each session.
- Choose a repertoire that enhances character development and self-esteem.
- Use lots of rehearsals to embed information into short term memory.

---

[3] Reprinted with permission from NAfME http://nafme.org/tips-for-teaching-students-with-add-or-adhd/ © MENC: The National Association for Music Education (menc.org)

- Be informed if a student takes medication to help regulate impulsive responses. Plan student participation accordingly.
- Follow classroom and performance program structure strictly so students know the sequence "first," "then."

Sobol subscribes to William Glasser's *Choice Theory*: Students will do well if four basic needs are addressed in the educational classroom or performance setting. All students need to feel a sense of:

- **Belonging**—feeling accepted and welcome.
- **Gaining power**—growing in knowledge and skill and gaining self-esteem through successful mastery of an activity via realistic teacher direction.
- **Having fun**—improving health, building positive relationships, and enhancing thinking. Students need to be uplifted and spirited to add to the quality of their successful program.
- **Being free**—making good choices and expressing control over one's life. Students need to be a part of their educational process. Each student gains importance and dignity as he or she participates in teaching and learning to set goals, make plans, choose behaviors, evaluate results, and learn from each experience to do things better.

Teaching Students with Behavior Problems[4]

"Students with behavior disorders are generally unhappy individuals, and they often make everyone around them unhappy as well," says NAfME member Alice-Ann Darrow (2006) "They're generally disliked by their peers, their teachers, their siblings, and often even their parents." They may also be diagnosed with learning disabilities, attention deficit and hyperactivity disorders, depression, and suicidal tendencies.

Darrow recommends some instruction accommodations:

- Seat these students close to the teacher and beside model students.
- Plan learning activities that are motivating and desirable. Students become disruptive when they're not actively engaged.
- Give clear, uncomplicated directions. Students often misbehave when they're confused about what they're supposed to do.
- Use the student's name and look at him or her. Students misbehave more often when they feel anonymous.
- Define expectations for classroom behavior and be consistent in administering consequences.
- Make a desirable activity contingent upon completing a less desirable activity. Keep a list of desirable activities such as listening to CDs or playing music Bingo.
- Think "do" instead of "don't." Make a positive request ("Watch me") rather than a negative one ("Don't bury your head in the music").
- Think "approval" instead of "disapproval." Reinforce a student who's doing what you want rather than admonishing a student who's misbehaving.
- Find opportunities for problem students to behave appropriately and feel good about themselves. Ask them to help move risers or put instruments away so you can reinforce good behavior.

Darrow also uses strategies from *Teaching Discipline* by Madsen and Madsen (1998):

---

[4] Reprinted with permission from NAfME http://www.nafme.org/teaching-students-with-behavior-problems/ © National Association for Music Education (nafme.org)

- Avoid labeling students—they often live up to the label.
- Reserve emotions.
- Choose your battles—prioritize which behaviors are most disruptive and will receive your time and attention.
- Use peers for tutoring or as part of your management strategies. Problem students often respond better to peer approval/disapproval. Peers can redirect students' attention when they're off-task or ignore attention-getting behaviors.
- Analyze problem situations—what are their trigger events, and what consequences extinguish or reinforce the problem behavior?

Adapting Instruction, Expectations, and Attitude

Adapt your expectations of students and your instruction. "Appropriate behaviors have to be shaped—shaped through successive approximations to the desired behavior," says Darrow. "Shaping desired behaviors takes time." When starting, she recommends accepting and reinforcing behaviors that come close to the desired behavior.

Developing more positive attitudes about teaching students with behavior disorders goes a long way to reduce the stress of teaching them.

Music and Students with Physical Disabilities[5]

More students with physical disabilities, orthopedic conditions, and fragile health are participating in school music programs. Elise Sobol, chairperson of Music for Special Learners of the New York State School Music Association, offers some advice:

Assistive Technology

"Technological advances such as the innovative SoundBeam," says Sobol, "allow 100% accessibility to students with even the most severe limitations to experience the joy of making music, exploring sound, creating compositions, and performing expressively."

The British SoundBeam system translates body movement into digitally generated sound and image. This technology is available in the U.S. through SoundTree. Click on "Music Education," then on "Music Therapy."

"Although it may be challenging for teachers to find adaptive instruments to suit the individual needs of their students," Sobol says, "the music market catalog offerings are expanding." See distributors such as West Music, Music Is Elementary, Musician's Friend, among others.

Instructional Strategies

Sobol finds the following helpful:
- Make sure the class content will support students' IEP requirements.
- Build motor skills (through consultation with goals of assigned occupational and physical therapists).
- Enhance vitality by building self-esteem through music.
- Design lessons that build on reduced or limited strength.
- Ensure accessibility to and inside classroom or performance space.

---

[5] Reprinted with permission from NAfME http://www.nafme.org/dont-let-physical-disabilities-stop-students/ © National Association for Music Education (nafme.org)

- Make the environment safe and secure. Organize instruments, props, AV equipment, etc. to permit wheelchair access. Intercom allows calling for help in case of a health alert.
- Always follow school policies for universal precautions and protections against infection.
- If a paraprofessional or teacher aide is not assigned to a specific student, use a buddy system.
- Assess student capability—what a student can do—and adapt musical instruments with materials such as Velcro (e.g. to hold a triangle on the wrist) to enhance student's ability to play. Design, create, and invent for individual and unique situations.

Books to Read Aloud

Sobol has found success with the following:
- *Knockin' on Wood: Starring Peg Leg Bates*, by Lynne Barasch—Inspirational. For building disability awareness and as an educational tool for success in the performing arts.
- *Puppies for Sale* by Dan Clark—About a puppy with a missing hip socket and a boy with a leg brace, it promotes positive character development.
- *What's Wrong with Timmy?* by Maria Shriver—About a child with disabilities and forming new friendships.
- *I Am Potential: Eight Lessons on Living, Loving, and Reaching Your Dreams* by Patrick Henry Hughes and Patrick John Hughes—Born without eyes and malformed limbs, Patrick became a member of the marching band at the University of Louisville.

Music and Students with Hearing Loss[6]

Students who are deaf or hard of hearing can succeed in music class. MENC member Elise Sobol shares some of her instructional strategies.
- First and foremost, follow the student's Individualized Education Program (IEP) for instructional adaptations. If the student has an educational or sign language interpreter, work closely with the interpreter for optimal success.
- Second, face the student so that eyebrow and lip-mouth movements are clear.

The following suggestions may also be helpful:
- Position student near the sound source for best amplification. Being near an acoustic instrument or speakers offers the greatest benefit from the sound. A hands-on experience is best, especially if the student is deaf.
- If the student has an FM amplifier system, make sure to position your microphone so the student can hear you. As newer assistive listening devices develop, be sure to receive training on them.
- Select instruments appropriate to the student's range of resonant hearing with a sustaining quality. Match instruments to students' functional independence and enjoyment.
- Use visual aids. "Give all lessons an auditory/visual/tactile/kinesthetic component to support contextual learning for students of all challenges," Sobol says. "Visual strategies are most significant to students whose hearing is compromised. It's their

---

[6] Reprinted with permission from NAfME http://nafme.org/interest-areas/guitar-education/music-and-students-with-hearing-loss/ © National Association for Music Education (nafme.org)

primary means for receiving information." Written material, music notation, and color-coded charts and diagrams on overhead projectors or SMART Boards enhance teaching and learning.
- Use signing. "Music teachers naturally use gestures to indicate musical meaning in demonstrating dynamics, tempo, entrances/exits, standing up/sitting down, etc.," Sobol says. "Learning basic finger spelling to enhance musical activities with pitch and using sign language to enhance a song performance is very helpful. Sign language is a beautiful way to communicate; all students will benefit."
- Demonstrate the characteristics of the music and support lesson content with movement.
- Use Windows Media Player for recorded music. It dramatizes sound with unique artistic rhythm and design.
- Choose instruments that are held close to the body (e.g., guitar, sitar, violin, viola, cello, and bass are held against the body) so students can feel the resonance of the instrument as well as the sound vibrations. Some percussion or wind instruments fit the bill as well.
- Use a keyboard that lights to sound or touch to make the music visual.

Music and Students with Vision Loss[7]

Visual impairments range from low vision to blindness and can demand a variety of strategies. MENC member Elise Sobol urges educators to work closely with the special education team in their school district including the assigned vision teacher where applicable, and consult the student's Individual Educational Program (IEP) to match any and all accommodations and learning supports.

These supports may include an assistive device such as a cane, technology and transcription software such as a Braille printer to translate text and music, a therapy animal such as a seeing-eye dog, or a teacher aide, depending on the student's educational needs.

Instructional Strategies

Sobol has had success with the following:
- Make the music room accessible and free of floor wires for sound equipment, etc.
- Seat students in the front of the room and away from potential glare.
- Enlarge print per individual student needs. Lighthouse International recommends 16 to 18 point font depending upon typefaces.
- Use contrasting colors; white on black is more readable than black on white.
- Use tactile props in classroom music. Keep them simple and proof them with your fingers, not your eyes. Try different texture materials, rough like sandpaper, raised like playdough and pom-poms, or pipe cleaners—check art supply stores for variety to suit lesson plan.
- Use audio enhancement for visual directions.
- Enhance memory with sequential learning.
- Record parts and lessons on MP3/CD/tape for classroom focus and home practice.
- Keep a consistent classroom set up with good lighting so the student can make a mental map of the classroom. Notify student of and describe any changes made to the classroom.

---

[7] Reprinted with permission for NAfME http://www.nafme.org/strategize-for-students-with-vision-loss/ © National Association for Music Education (nafme.org)

  • Above all create safety in space and place for music learning and fun.

Books to Read Aloud

Sobol recommends reading the following in the classroom:
  • *A Picture Book of Louis Braille* by David Adler—Braille became blind at the age of 4 and learned to play the organ, violin, and cello.
  • *Knots on a Counting Rope* by John Archambault and Bill Martin Jr.—A moving story of a Native American who was born blind and had a special mission.
  • *Helen Keller: Courage in the Dark* by Johanna Hurwitz—The story of her indomitable will and devoted teacher.
  • *I Am Potential: Eight Lessons on Living, Loving, and Reaching Your Dreams* by Patrick Henry Hughes and Patrick John Hughes—Born without eyes and malformed limbs, Patrick became a member of the marching band at the University of Louisville.
  • Biographies of musician role models such as Ray Charles, Stevie Wonder, José Feliciano, and Nobuyuki Tsujii (Gold medal winner, Van Cliburn Competition).

References

Gender

Alden, A. (1998). *What does it all mean? The National Curriculum for Music in a multicultural society.* (Unpublished MA dissertation). London University Institute of Education, London.

Armstrong, V. (2011). *Technology and the gendering of music education.* Aldershot, U.K.: Ashgate.

Davidson, J. and Edgar, R. (2003). Gender and race bias in the judgment of Western art music performance. *Music Education Research, 5*(2), 169-181.

Eccles, J., Wigfield, A., Harold, R., & Blumenfeld, P. (1993). Age and ender differences in children's self- and task perceptions during elementary school. *Child Development, 64*(3), 830-847.

Green, L. (1993). Music, gender and education: A report on some exploratory research. *British Journal of Music Education, 10*(3), 219-253.

Green, L. (1997). *Music Education and Gender.* Cambridge, U.K.: Cambridge University Press.

Green, L. (1999). Research in the sociology of music education: Some introductory concepts. *Music Education Research, 1*(1), 159-70.

Griswold, P., & Chroback, D. (1981). Sex-role associations of music instruments and occupations by gender and major. *Journal of Research in Music Education, 29*(1), 57-62.

Hallam, S. (2004). Sex differences in the factors which predict musical attainment in school aged students. *Bulletin of the Council for Research in Music Education, 161/162,* 107-115.

Hallam, S., Rogers, L. Creech, A. (2008). Gender differences in musical instrument choice. *International Journal of Music Education. 26* (1), 7-19.

Marshall, N., & Shibazaki, K. (2012). Instrument, gender and musical style associations in young children. *Psychology of Music, 40*(4), 494-507.

O'Neill, S. A.,Hargreaves, D. J., & North, A. C. (Eds.) (1997). *The social psychology of music.* New York, NY: Oxford University Press.

Autism

Iseminger, S. (2009). Keys to success with autistic children: Structure, predictability, and consistency are essential for students on the autism spectrum. *Teaching Music, 16*(6), 28.

Kern, P. (2004). "Making friends in music: Including children with autism in an interactive play setting. *Music Therapy Today, 6*(4), 563-595.

Shore, S. M. (2002). The language of music: Working with children on the autism spectrum. *Journal of Education,* 183(2), 97-108.

Hourigan, R. (2009). Teaching music to children with autism: Understandings and perspectives. *Music Educators Journal, 96,* 40-45.

Music Therapy and Healing

Bruscia, K. (1989). *Defining music therapy.* Spring Lake, PA: Spring House Books.

Eagle, C. (1978). *Music psychology index.* Denton, TX: Institute for Therapeutic Research.

Campbell, D., & Doman, A. (2012). *Healing at the speed of sound: How what we hear transforms our brains and our lives.* New York, NY:Plume Reprints.

Campbell, D. (2001). *The Mozart effect: Tapping the power of music to heal the body, strengthen the mind, and unlock the creative spirit.* New York: Quill.

Debrot, R. A. (2002). *Spotlight on making music with special learners: Differentiating Instruction in the Music Classroom.* Lanham, MD: Rowman & Littlefield Education.

Hodges, D. A. (Ed.). (1980). *Handbook of music psychology.* Dubuque, IA: National Association for Music Therapy.

Music for the Classroom and Home. (2020). Advanced Brain Technologies. https://advancedbrain.com/blog/music-for-the-classroom-and-home/

Ott, P. (2011). *Music for special kids.* Philadelphia, PA: Jessica Kingsley Publishers.

Pelliteri, J. (2000). Music therapy in the special education setting. *Journal of Educational and Psychological Consultation, 11*(3/4), 379-91. Retrieved from http://www.soundconnectionsmt.com/docs/Music%20Therapy%20in%20Special%20Education.pdf

Sobol, E. (2008). *An attitude and approach for teaching music to special learners.* Lanham, MD: Rowman and Littlefield.

Hourigan, R. (2008). Teaching strategies for performers with special needs. *Teaching Music* 15(6), 26.

Hourigan, R, and Hourigan, A. (2009). Teaching Music to Children with Autism: Understandings and Perspectives. *Music Educators Journal* 96(1), 40-45.

Behavior Problems

Adamek, M., & Darrow, A. (2005). *Music in Special Education.* Silver Spring, MD: The American Music Therapy Association, Inc.

Darrow, A. (2006). Teaching students with behavior problems. *General Music Today,* Fall 20 (1) 35-37

Madson, C., & Madsen, C. (1998). *Teaching discipline: A positive approach for educational development* (4th ed.). Raleigh, NC: Contemporary Publication Company of Raleigh.

Resources

Khetrapal, N. (2009). Why does music therapy help in autism? *Empirical Musicology Review, 4*(1), 11-18. Retrieved from http://hdl.handle.net/1811/36602

James, R. et al. (2015). Music therapy for individuals with autism spectrum disorder. *Review Journal of Autism and Developmental Disorders* 2, 39–54 https://link.springer.com/article/10.1007%2Fs40489-014-0035-4

Big Picture. (2014). *Music and autism.* http://bigpictureeducation.com/music-and-autism

American Music Therapy Association. (2015). http://www.musictherapy.org/

Vocabulary

Attention Deficit Hyperactivity Disorder (ADHD)/Attention Deficit Disorder (ADD): a psychiatric disorder characterized by significant problems of attention, hyperactivity, and impulsivity not appropriate for a person's age

Autism: a neural development disorder characterized by impaired social interaction and verbal and non-verbal communication. One of three recognized disorders on the *Autism Spectrum,* which includes Asperger Syndrome and Pervasive Developmental Disorder

disability: a disability, resulting from an impairment, is a restriction or lack of ability to perform an activity in the manner or within the range considered normal for a human being (World Health Organization)

entrainment: the patterning of body processes and movements to the rhythm of music

gender: the constructed roles, expectations, behaviors, attitudes, and activities deemed appropriate for men and women

music therapy: a health profession in which music is used within a therapeutic relationship to address physical, emotional, cognitive, and social needs of individuals

sex: biological and physiological characteristics that define men and women

Chapter 12

Music Integration

Chapter Summary: This chapter introduces the reader to processes and vocabulary of music integration, including a general definition of arts integration, and strategies and examples for integrating music with other subject areas.

> Musical training is a more potent instrument than any other, because rhythm and harmony find their way into the inward places of the soul.
>
> *—Plato, Republic, Book III*

Arts Integration, when done correctly, transforms both the art and the subject area into a whole greater than the sum of its parts. In short, Arts Integration can be magical, inspiring learning and setting off a spark in each child. Imagine the difference in a child's learning experience if classroom teachers incorporated the arts into their lesson. From a teaching perspective, artistic experiences help teachers discover their students' enthusiasm through a new medium. They also aid in creating positive and interesting lessons that fully engage the student. For the student, music not only strengthens emotional and cognitive development, but also allows a new outlet of expression, and a new means of learning through listening and making sound. The arts provide a platform through which teachers can tap into a child's creativity and humanity while teaching content material. The arts give students an opportunity to express and explore material in a medium to which they might not otherwise have access.

Incorporating music is beneficial to both teacher and student as it strengthens the bond between them through a (hopefully) mutually satisfying aesthetic experience. Teaching and learning occurs between the art forms and any number of diverse subject areas.

I. What is Arts Integration?

Let's begin with a commonly accepted definition of arts integration from the Kennedy Center's ArtsEdge website along with a checklist to help guide the teacher in the creation of an integrated lesson.

A definition of arts integration

Checklist for an Arts Integrated Lesson

Approach to Teaching
• Are learning principles of Constructivism (actively built, experiential, evolving, collaborative, problem-solving, and reflective) evident in my lesson?
Understanding
• Are the students engaged in constructing and demonstrating understanding as opposed to just memorizing and reciting knowledge?
Art Form
• Are the students constructing and demonstrating their understanding through an art form?
Creative Process
• Are the students engaged in a process of creating something original as opposed to copying or parroting?
• Will the students revise their products?
Connects
• Does the art form connect to another part of the curriculum or a concern/need?
• Is the connection mutually reinforcing?

Evolving Objectives
• Are there objectives in both the art form and another part of the curriculum or a concern/ need?
• Have the objectives evolved since the last time the students engaged with this subject matter?

Defining Levels of Integration

Not all lessons that use the arts can be called "integrated." Some lessons incorporate the arts, but do not incorporate the learning objectives and other criteria that fully integrate them, while others follow a deeper level of integration. Silverstein & Layne (2014) identify 3 categories of Arts Integration:

1. **Arts as Curriculum**—presence of arts teachers in the school teaching art, music, etc. using the state standard goals for their own specific discipline.
2. **Arts-Enhanced Curriculum**—using the arts as a device, strategy or "hook" to engage students or teach something else (i.e. using the alphabet song to teach the alphabet.) No explicit objectives in the art form are articulated. Does not require teacher training in the arts discipline.
3. **Arts-Integrated Curriculum**—Students meet dual-objectives in both the art and the content area. Results in deep understanding about the art form. Teachers require professional development to learn about the arts standards.

There is nothing wrong about any of these three ways of using the arts, and sometimes it is quite appropriate to use one style over another for various curricular or other reasons. Although integration is a worthy goal, it is sometimes not feasible.

Using Music in Arts-As-Curriculum

Most schools still contain music and art teachers, who are valuable assets in providing input regarding art strategies, teaching materials, etc. This is definition of an arts-as-curriculum strategy, where the arts teacher teaches their separate material. Fully integrating the arts requires a time commitment and instructional expertise, but often there isn't the time, resources, or incentive to fully learn or implement the entire process for a lesson. How might you utilize the music teacher in your school to enhance your lesson? What are some ways to work with the specialists to benefit the student's learning experience?

Using Music as Arts-Enhancement

There are many things to be learned from arts-enhancement as well. Using the arts yourself to enhance your lesson provides opportunities for students to experience music during the school day in a non-content related way.

There are ample opportunities for children to experience music in their day, including singing, moving, clapping, or stomping that are not directly related to teaching content area but provide students an alternate form of expression, a chance to re-group and focus, for motivation, learn about proper group and individual expectations and behavior, and to make transitions between subjects and activities. How might you use music to "enhance" a science or language arts lesson? Vocabulary or poetry lesson?

Sample chart for Arts-Enhancement opportunities

1. Organization
   - **Activity:** lining up, cleaning up
   - **Aesthetic Purpose:** motivation
2. Transitions
   - **Activity:** changing from one activity to another
   - **Aesthetic Purpose:** change of mood, re-focus energy
3. Rituals
   - **Activity:** Greetings/Hello, goodbye, holiday music
   - **Aesthetic Purpose:** Prepare students mentally, provides stability and repetition
4. Interstitial
   - **Activity:** Short break between two subjects or activities
   - **Aesthetic Purpose:** Provide relaxation, moment of expression, and alternate uses for cognitive functioning

Sample Day that includes Music

1. 9:10 Use music before the school day begins
   - **Ritual:** Set the mood/change the atmosphere in the room with sound
2. 9:20 Students enter and settle in to the room
   - **Ritual:** "Good Morning," and/or movement activity "Head Shoulders"
3. 9:25 Morning Work, Attendance, Calendar
   - **Organization:** i.e. "If you're ready for _____ clap your hands" (or stomp your feet, etc.)
4. 10:00-10:40 Special (Music, Art, Physical Ed)
   - **Transition:** Focus for Math
5. 10:45 Math Stations
   - **Organization:** Line up for Lunch
6. 11:30 Lunch
   - **Transition:** Focus ready for reading
7. 12:10-12:50 Reading/Literacy Stations
   - **Interstitial:** Break song/movement
8. 12:50-1:30 Writing
   - **Interstitial:** Movement/song break
9. 1:30-2:10 Social Studies/Science/Health
   - **Transition:** Movement activity/song
10. 2:10-2:25 Snack/Play time
    - **Organization:** Focus: Line up for Library or Lab
11. 2:25-3:05 Computer Lab or Library
    - **Transition**
12. 3:10 Pickup and pack-up
    - **Organization:** "Clean up song"
13. 3:15 Dismissal
    - **Ritual:** "Goodbye" song

Song Examples (see Chapter 11 for more examples from this list)
(Substitute any subject such as math, reading, physical education, art, instead of music, and any action instead of "stand on up" or "clap your hands.")

If You're Ready for Music

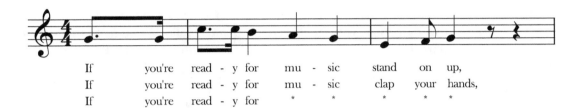

Janet Elder, in her article on "Brain Friendly Music in the Classroom" (n.d.), suggests the following reasons to incorporate music into the classroom:

Reasons for using music in the classroom can be divided into four groups:
1. Music's effect on the physical body and brain
2. Music's effect on the emotional body
3. Music's effect on the physical and learning environment
4. Music's effect on group coherence and intimacy

For example, as mentioned in Chapter 11, music's beats per minute (b.p.m.) or tempo, has a direct impact on the human body.

Elder also goes on to suggest specific songs to use for different classroom situations, such as playing classical music during individual or group work or "Get Up Offa That Thing" by James Brown for stretch breaks. There are many, many different types of songs and places to use them when working with children, and the inclusion of music in the daily routine can improve transitions and the overall mood of a classroom.

Class Times When Music Is Appropriate

Source: adapted from Elder (n.d.) "Using Brain-Friendly Music in the Classroom"

Class Activity	Musical qualities to look for in song selection	Song examples
As students enter class.	Select loose, upbeat, uplifting music, or music that pertains in some way to the course or topic that day. Songs with humor also start the class on the right foot.	"Star Wars," "Summon the Heroes" and other John Williams' Olympic music, "Walk Right In" (Rooftop Singers), "Thanks for Coming" and "Hello, Welcome to the Meeting" ("Laughable Lyrics" CD), and "The More We Get Together" (Raffi).
To welcome students back after a weekend or holiday break		"Hi-Ho, Hi-Ho, It's Off to Work We Go!", "The Flintstones" ("Yabba Dabba Do" TV theme, Aron Apping), "Monday, Monday" (Mamas and Papas), "Reveille" bugle call ("Authentic Sound Effects, Vol. 3").
To comment on the weather.		On a rainy day: • "Raindrops Keep Falling on My Head" (B.J. Thomas), "Here Comes That Rainy Day Feeling Again" (The Fortunes), "Come Clean" (Hilary Duff). For sunny days: • "It's a Beautiful Morning" (The Rascals), "Good Day Sunshine" (The Tremeloes), or "Walking on Sunshine" (Katrina and The Waves).
To get students on their feet.	Students need a change after 15-20 minutes of sitting. Use any of these when you want to have them stand up to stretch, change where they are sitting, or move for some other reason.	"Get on Your Feet" (Gloria Estefan), "Line Up" (Aerosmith), "Stand Up!" (David Lee Roth), "1-2-3-4" (Ataris), "Up!" (Shania Twain), "Get Up Offa That Thing" (James Brown), "Arkansas Traveler" ("Smokey Mountain Hits" CD)
As students are moving into collaborative groups.	Look for songs with themes of friends, help, or general encouragement.	"Help," (Beatles), "We Can Work It Out," (Beatles), "You've Got a Friend" (Carol King), "Lean on Me" (Bill Withers), "Reach Out" (The Four Tops), "I'm into Something Good" (Herman's Hermits), "Call Me" (Blondie), "You Can Make It if You Try" (James Brown).
After a pair-share review *(Students make the immediate connection between these songs and having to recall/review material)*	Select songs with titles or lyrics that include "remember," "memory," etc.	"Thanks for the Memories" (Bob Hope and Shirley Ross), "Always Something There to Remind Me" (Naked Eyes), "Unforgettable" (Peggy Lee)

As low background music when students are working in small groups, in pairs, or individually, or when they are taking a test.	The volume should be low enough that you could speak at a conversational level without raising your voice. The music should act as a filter for unwanted noise and help create a relaxed, mentally alert state. If any student objects to background music, you should not use it. However, if the entire class likes background music, try to play the same baroque music during the test that was used during the original presentation of the material: it acts as an auditory memory cue.	"Water Music Suite" (Handel), "Brandenberg Concertos" (Bach), "Eine Kleine Nachtmusik" (Mozart), and music by Telemann, Vivaldi, or Corelli in a major key. Soft piano or violin concertos with orchestral accompaniments work well.
To use music to create positive stress or add drama		"James Bond Suite" (Henry Rabinowitz and the RCA Orchestra), "Law and Order" (TV theme), "Jeopardy" (TV theme); "Mission Impossible" (TV theme); "Jaws" (movie theme, John Williams), "In the Hall of the Mountain King" (from "Peer Gynt" by Grieg)
To energize students or have them physically move:	Select highly rhythmic music in a major key or any upbeat music or song. Beats per minute should be 70-140.	"Shake It Up" (The Cars), "Fun, Fun, Fun" (Beach Boys), "Bonanza" (TV theme), "Listen to the Music" (Doobie Brothers), "We Got the Beat" (Go-Gos),
To relax or calm students, to use for stretching, or activities such as reflection, journaling, and visualization.	Beats per minute should be 40-60.	"The Lake House" (movie theme; Rachel Portman), "Chariots of Fire" (Vangelis), "The Reivers" (movie theme), "Peaceful, Easy Feeling" (Eagles);
To celebrate successes or to honor students.		"Olympic Fanfare" (John Williams), "In the Zone" (David Banner), "I Just Want to Celebrate" (Rare Earth), "Celebrate" (Three Dog Night), "Celebration" (Kool and the Gang), "We Are the Champions" (Queen).
To end class:	Select upbeat, fun, or funny music; lyrics may pertain to leaving.	"Never Can Say Goodbye" (Gloria Gaynor), "So Long, Farewell" (from "The Sound of Music"), "Who Let the Dogs Out" (Baja Men), "Happy Trails" (Roy Rogers/Dale Evans).
For other purposes. Beginning of class Encouragement, motivation, support: *Funny, and therefore stress-reducing*		

II. Using Music in Arts-Integration

An arts integrated lesson plan will be similar to a regular lesson plan, with the exception that it will have a place for *both* the arts learning objectives as well as the objectives for the content area, and will allow students the opportunity to construct understanding through both disciplines.

Consider that you have to create a lesson plan to celebrate the Martin Luther King, Jr. holiday. It is, of course, nice to add a song somewhere in the lesson, perhaps a song from the Civil Rights Movement. This does not make the lesson integrated, but rather an Arts-Enhanced-Curriculum as discussed above. Integration requires that there be music objectives as well as subject area objectives, and that both subjects are treated equally. Keep in mind that *any lesson can be made into an arts-integrated one,* by simply delving in deeper to the art form itself to find structural details and meaning from which to draw. To make a lesson integrated, it is necessary to include social science or history goals and objectives as well as musical information, goals and objectives. For example, including information about the song that incorporates the music itself (form, timbre, melody, rhythm, etc.), while discussing the genre of civil rights songs itself.

To demonstrate a deeper understanding of the tenets and issues of Civil Rights, social science connections can be made not only to slavery in the previous century, but to the pro-union struggle in the earlier part of the 20th century. Students could demonstrate their understanding of Martin Luther King's leadership and the famous marches of the 60s through song by recreating the march on Washington, DC while singing a civil rights song ("We Shall Not be Moved," "This Little Light of Mine," "We Shall Overcome," etc.) The types of songs used for demonstrations could be analyzed, including their roots in the pro-union movement, gospel and religious music, and/or the use of call and response in the songs, which dates back to slavery and early African-American culture, and particularly how music was used during the protests. A follow-up might focus on blues, jazz and other genres inspired by the music of the Civil Rights movement.

Activity 12A

TRY THIS

Which one of these examples represents Arts as Curriculum, Arts-Enhanced Curriculum, and an Arts-Integrated Curriculum?
- Students sing a song they learned in music class for a school assembly
- Students have to explain how sequential groupings work in math and music
- Students learn the song "50 Nifty United States"

NOW TRY THIS

- Students complete a unit on the lifecycle of a caterpillar. How might this lesson be changed to reflect an Arts-Enhanced lesson? Arts-integration? Arts as Curriculum?
- Create your own examples of the three types of curriculum.

Music Integration with Core Subjects: Vocabulary, Concepts, and Learning Standards

In order to successfully create arts integrated lessons, begin with the state learning standards in the content area in which you are working, then consider the art form you will be using. Explore vocabulary that may help you to work between the two disciplines. Below are two examples of vocabulary lists from Institute for Arts Integration and STEAM, a website dedicated to integration and innovation in teaching.

Activity 12B

TRY THIS

Review the vocabulary lists below. Identify which terms work best for music instruction. Select three of the terms from either list and give an example of how you might use that term to illustrate music concepts in addition to either a math or literacy concept.

Arts Literacy: Common Vocabulary

Source: Susan Riley, Institute for Arts Integration and STEAM

Grade	Shared Vocabulary between Literacy and the Arts
K	Illustrations, illustrator, listen, setting, space, title, beginning, end.
1	Audience, character, collaborate, connections, expression, fluent, phrase, plot, segment, sequence.
2	Analyze, compare, contrast, expression, genre, introduction, point of view, rhythm.
3	Audience, comparative, dialogue, effect, line, mood, narrator, plot, point of view, scene, stanza, theme.
4	Animations, categorize, drama, elements, meter, narration, pose, stage direction, theme, verse.
5	Analyze, compare, conclude, contrast, dialect, dialogue, evaluate, expression, fluent, influence, interpret, mood, multimedia, perspective, perspective, reflection, theme, tone, voice.
6	Bias, convey, elaborate, interpret, multimedia, perceive, point of view.
7	Alternate, analyze, audience, categorize, collaborate, composition, concept, embellish, exposure, format, function, interact, medium, mood, segment, structure, tone, unique.
8	Analyze, bias, characterization, elaborate, evaluate, imagery, point of view, style, symbolism, theme.
9 and 10	Bias, coherence, clarity, comedy, character motivation, diction, dynamic, monologue, mood, plot structure, purpose, soliloquy, theme, tone, tragedy, digital media, quality.
11 and 12	Context, diction, digital media, nuance, perspective, satire, structure, style, subplot, subtle, theme, voice.

Math and the Arts: Common Vocabulary

Source: Susan Riley, Institute for Arts Integration and STEAM

Grade	Shared Vocabulary between Literacy and the Arts
K	Compare, opposite, before, different, similar, object, measure, pattern, curves, slide.
1	Similar, object, symbol, group, pattern, compare, half, describe, side, size, parallel, curves, slide, turn.
2	Form, sequence, pattern, group, interpret, symbol, slide, reflect, turn, measure, three-dimensional, line of symmetry, intersect.
3	Expression, form, product, length, symbol, combinations, weight, angle, symmetry, line, dimensions.
4	Comparison, expression, produce, symmetry, measure, length, interpret, frequency, distance, lines.
5	Patterns, form, expression, variation, inverse, sequence, symbol, product, ratio, part, whole, quarter, half, organize, arrange, scale, line, distance, vertical, diagonal, horizontal, symmetry, transformation.
6	Scale, measure, compose, symbol, expression, grid, collection, interval, simulation, symmetry.
7	Point, area, proportion, analyze, compose, notation, expression, value, range, scale, drawings.
8	Expression, value, notation, frequency, non-linear, rigid, symmetry.
9 and 10	Expression, notation, properties, model, measure, acceleration, scale, direction, structure, value, range, vary, inverse, frequency.
11 and 12	Linear, range, oblique, measure, symmetry, composition, variation, velocity, arc, chord.

III. Generating Ideas for Integrated Lessons

The following grid offers a process for generating integration ideas using music, particularly in making connections across the disciplines. The first row of the grid contains an example of how to generate ideas from a musical concept.

Concept(s)/Grade

Begin by selecting one music concept to work with. In the first column of the grid below, the word "staff" is written. The lesson is to teach the musical staff to 2nd grade students.

Objectives

What are your main objectives for the lesson? What should children be able to do by the end of the lesson that they couldn't do at the beginning? Note: "SWBAT" stands for "Students Will Be Able To."

Activities

What activities could you use to teach the staff? Where would you begin? You might begin by teaching the line and space notes for the treble staff (EGBDF and FACE), and teaching the mnemonics that accompany those note names (i.e. E-Every; G-Good; B-Boy;

D-Deserves; F-Fudge). Even at this point, writing the lines on the board, on a smart board, PPT, or even making lines on the floor with tape can be a visual accompaniment to the lesson, and help students learn through body movement as well as visual learning.

Integration Ideas

How might you integrate this concept using different core subject areas? What higher order thinking skills, or vocabulary? Look at the second grade Vocabulary grid above from Education Closet concerning math and the arts and Music and Literacy and select the most appropriate terms to apply to the lesson:

- (Math and the Arts) Form, Sequence, Pattern, Group
- (Arts Literacy) Analyze, Compare, Contrast

Common Core Learning Standards

Now refer to the earlier chapter in the book to find the appropriate common core learning standards for the lesson.

Idea Generator: Concept, Objectives, Activities, Integration, Standards

Music Concept Grade	Objectives	Activities	Integration (connections, constructivism, creative process, understanding)	Learner/ Common Core Standard
Ex. Concept: Reading the Music Staff Grade: 2nd	SWBAT identify pitches on lines of the treble staff SWBAT analyze the correlation of skipping and sequential regarding the pitches on the treble staff. SWBAT understand correlations across disciplines of math, literacy and music between sequential movement and skipping movement	Review (or teach) the pitches of the treble staff, first using sequential alphabet letters, then using the acronyms EGBDF, and FACE. Create huge lines of treble staff on the floor using masking tape. Mark each line or space with large letters for each note. **Movement:** Have students physically move across the floor staff, first **sequentially** and then **skipping** line to line and space to space, reciting the letters as they go.	**Literacy: Analyze** the letters EGBDF as a mnemonic for "Every Good Boy Deserve Fudge." Brainstorm, having students create their own acronyms for EGBDF and FACE. **Compare** and **contrast** the pitch names on the staff with the letters of the alphabet. Which direction do they go? What are the differences between letters of the alphabet and music pitch names? **Math:** Discuss the **form** of the staff. Is there a **pattern**? What is it? Does it **alternate** (skip)? Is it sequential (all in a row)? **Math, Music and Literacy:** (EGBDF). Have students count **sequentially**. **Sequence** the letter names by saying them in a row (EFGABC). Then create a **pattern** by skipping every other letter of the alphabet (B – D – F or A – C – E). Then correlate with math by switching to numbers. Practice grouping by 2s.	Bodily-Kinesthetic, Visual-spatial/ Creating, Performing, Participating
1. Concept: Rhythm: Eighth and Quarter notes Grade: Kindergarten				
2. Melody: Pitch Grade: 4th				
3. Timbre: Voice Grade: 1st				

Idea Generator (blank): Concepts, Activities, Materials, Integration

Music Concept Grade	Activities	Integration (connections, constructivism, creative process, understanding)	Learner/ Common Core Standard	Objectives
1.				
2.				
3.				

Example Integrating Music, Language Arts and Social Studies: "Goober Peas"

(see also "Erie Canal" Lesson Plan in Chapter 6)

Many older songs offer excellent material for integration. For example, the song "Goober Peas" provides students a very inside look at the life of a Confederate soldier during the Civil War. In this case, both the music and lyrics are highly informative, as is the situation in which the song was sung, lending itself to integration through three areas: music, language arts and social sciences.

Materials:

Timeline: Civil War history timeline including various battles, Sherman's March, etc.

Song: "Goober Peas"

Text: *The Personal Story of Life as a Confederate Soldier, "The Letters of Eli Landers"* http://www.socialstudies.org/sites/default/files/publications/se/6602/660207.html

Goober Peas

Southern U.S. folk song, 1866
Sung by Confederate soldiers during the Civil War

2. When a horse-man passes, the soldiers have a rule
To cry out their loudest, "Mister here's your mule!"
But another custom, enchanting-er than these,
Is wearing out your grinders, eating goober peas. (refrain)

3. Just before the battle, the General hears a row
He says, "The Yanks are coming, I hear their rifles now"
He turns around in wonder and what d'ya think he sees?
The Georgia militia, eating goober peas. (refrain)

4. I think my song has lasted almost long enough
The subject's interesting but the rhymes are mighty tough
I wish the war was over so free from rags and fleas
We'd kiss our wives and sweethearts and gooble goober peas. (refrain)

Integration Process Questions

How might you integrate this song beyond that of "Arts as Enhancement"? What learning principles will you use? How will students be engaged? Demonstrate their understanding? What will be the processes of creation? What connections to other parts of the curriculum can be made? Are the standards present for both the art and the subject? Go through Silverstein & Layne's Arts Integration checklist below to see how to incorporate an integrated level of understanding to the lesson.

Approach to Teaching
- Does the lesson contain learning principles of Constructivism (actively built, experiential, evolving, collaborative, problem-solving, and reflective)?

Understanding
- Are students engaged in constructing and demonstrating understanding knowledge rather than memorizing and reciting?

Art Form
- Are the students constructing and demonstrating their understandings through an art form?

Creative Process
- Are students engaged in a process of creating something original as opposed to copying or parroting?
- Will the students revise their products?

Connects
- Does the art form connect to another part of the curriculum or a concern/need?
- Is the connection mutually reinforcing?

Evolving Objectives
- Are there objectives in both the art form and another part of the curriculum or a concern/need?
- Have the objectives evolved since the last time the students engaged with this subject matter? Have the objectives evolved since the last time the students engaged with this subject matter?Have the objectives evolved since the last time the students engaged with this subject matter? (Silverstein & Layne, 2014).

Analysis: Vocabulary and Concepts

You'll find an abundance of material to integrate and connect after analyzing both the music, lyrical/poetic aspects, and social contexts. The musical forms, phrases, harmonies and the poetic structure reveal a great deal of material apart from the content of the lyrics.

Music	Poetry/Lyrics
• Dotted rhythm • Verse + refrain • 4 phrases per verse • 4 verses in the song	• Long-short long-short (**trochee** stressed-unstressed) • Ballad style • Rhyme scheme (AABB) • Narrative story telling/ballad

Social Studies

Setting: Civil War, soldiers resting on the roadside while waiting for orders for the next confrontation.

Date Written: 1866.

Singers: Popular in the South among Confederate Soldiers (losing the war).

Sentiment: Expresses the living conditions of Confederate soldiers and the public, as the war was lost. Sherman's troops laid waste to much of Georgia, cutting off food supplies.

Song Vocabulary

Students may not be familiar with these terms:

Goober Peas—another name for boiled peanuts. Eaten by Confederate soldiers during the war when rail lines were cut off, making food and rations scarce.

Messmate—a person/friend in a military camp with which one regularly takes meals.

Grinders—teeth.

Row—an argument or fight (rhymes with "cow").

Georgia Militia—a militia organized under the British that fought the Union during the Civil War. They fought in Sherman's devastating "March to the Sea" and in the last battle of the Civil War at the Battle of Columbus on the Georgia-Alabama border.

Yanks—Refers to "Yankees" or Union soldiers of the North.

Rags and fleas—Tattered clothing and poor health conditions.

Activities:

Sing the song "Goober Peas;" Read some of the letters of Eli Landers.

Questions to think about (Historical perspectives of soldiers)
• What conditions did the soldier's have to endure?

- What was happening towards the end of the Civil War?
- How do you think they felt during this time? (i.e., anxiousness, anticipation, weariness while waiting by the road).
- Overall, what do the lyrics express on behalf of the Confederate soldiers?
- What does the reference to the *Georgia Militia* mean in terms of the fighting?

Ideas for Integration

- **Constructivism:** Analyze the music, text, and history (timeline). **Reflect** what it would be like to be a soldier in the Confederacy during the beginning, middle, and end of the Civil War. **Problem Solve** as to how to obtain food after the railroad lines were cut off, strategize as to earlier successes during the war.
- **Student Engagement:** (historical perspectives). **Experience:** learn and sing the song. Divide into groups and read Eli Landers letters from different years comparing changes in attitude for a confederate soldier over time from the beginning of the war to the end of the war.
- **Art Form: Analyze** by comparing Eli Landers' letters to the lyrics of the song. What are the differences in historical facts? Sentiment? In terms of the song itself, explore the meaning of the music itself apart from the lyrics—sing the melody of the song on a neutral syllable. What does the melody remind you of? What kind of emotion do you hear in the melody, rhythm and phrasing? Does it seem to complement the lyrics or oppose them? Why might this be the case?
- **Creative Process:** Work collaboratively to create further verses of the song or write "letters home" that will express the feelings of soldiers facing defeat. Read the letters from home along with singing the new verses of the song.
- **Objectives** (See below)

What Learning Standards or Objectives can you incorporate for this lesson for each of the following?

1. Language Arts/Social Studies
   a. Language Arts 3: Use knowledge of language and its conventions when speaking, reading, or listening.
   b. Writing 3: Write narratives to develop real or imagined experiences or events using effective technique, descriptive details, and clear event sequences.
   c. Reading 2: Determine a theme of a story, drama, or poem from details in the text; summarize the text.
2. Music National Standards
   a. 1: Singing, alone and with others, a varied repertoire of music.
   b. 6: Listening to, analyzing, and describing music.
   c. 8: Understanding relationships between music, the other arts, and disciplines outside the arts.

Additional Songs for Integrating History/Social Studies

(see also "Erie Canal" Lesson Plan in Chapter 6)

Other examples include songs that are informative and contain a long narrative or historical information for students. For example, the song "Christofo Columbo" chronicles much of the famed voyage including detailed geographic references in a fun and light song.

Christofo Columbo (Christopher Columbus)

Ring Lardner, 1911

I'll sing to you a-bout a man whose name you'll find in hist'-ry, He

solved a prob-lem long and deep which long had been a myst'-ry Na-vi-ga-tors young and old gave

way to him quite fit-ly, His name it was Co-lum-bus and he came from sun-ny It'-ly. He

knew the earth was round ho! That land it could be found, ho! That

ge-o-graph-ic hard and hoa-ry, na-vi-ga-tor gy-ra-to-ry Chris-to-pho Co-lum-bo.

To the Kings and Queens of Europe, Columbus told his theory,
They simply thought him crazy, and asked him this here query,
How could the earth stand up if round, it surely would suspend,
For answer, C'lumbus took an egg and stood it on its end.
Refrain
In Fourteen Hundred and Ninety-two, 'twas then Columbus started,
From Pales on the coast of Spain to the westward he departed,
His object was to find a route, a short one to East India,
Columbus wore no whiskers, and the wind it blew quite windy.
Refrain
When Sixty days away from land, upon the broad Atlantic,
The sailors they went on a strike which nearly caused a panic,
They all demanded eggs to eat for each man in the crew,
Columbus had no eggs aboard, but he made the ship lay too.
Refrain
The hungry crew impatient grew, and beef-steak they demanded,
Equal to the emergency, Columbus then commanded

That ev'ry sailor who proves true, and his duty never shirks,
Can have a juicy porterhouse, "I'll get it from the bulwarks."
Refrain
Not satisfied with steak and eggs, the crew they yelled for chicken,
Columbus seemed at a loss for once, and the plot it seemed to thicken,
The men threatened to jump overboard, Columbus blocked their pathway,
And cried: "If chicken you must have, I'll get it from the hatchway."
Refrain
The sailors now so long from home with fear became imbued,
On the twelfth day of October their fears were all subdued,
For after Ninety days at sea, they discovered America's shores,
And quickly made a landing on the Isle of Salvador.
Refrain

When Johnny Comes Marching Home Again

Patrick Gilmore, 1863
American Civil War song

Johnny Has Gone for a Soldier

Traditional English folk song popular during the Revolutionary War

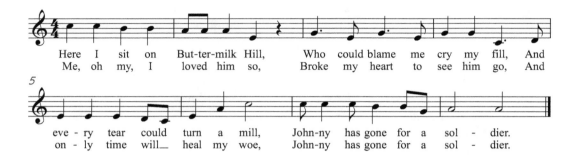

Here I sit on But-ter-milk Hill, Who could blame me cry my fill, And
Me, oh my, I loved him so, Broke my heart to see him go, And

eve-ry tear could turn a mill, John-ny has gone for a sol - dier.
on-ly time will_ heal my woe, John-ny has gone for a sol - dier.

IV. Music and Literacy/Language Arts

Of all of the content area relationships with music, language arts and music have one of the closest bonds. This bond is rooted within the inseparable relationship between lyrics and music that has existed for thousands of years. People in across countless cultures have chanted or sung poetry for all types of human rituals, ceremonies and for entertainment. When we listen to a song, a musical phrase usually accompanies a phrase of lyrics; a verse or refrain emerges from a short poem. For centuries, ballads, and epics were all sung, as were Biblical chants and Vedic hymns. Long stories and epic tales used music to draw in the audience and to help the reciter's memorization.

In addition, there is an intrinsic relationship in the discrimination of phonemic sounds and musical sounds for children learning to read. Language and music are intertwined to the point where there is evidence of a connection in the brain between phonemic sound discrimination and musical sound discrimination. In a 1993 study, for example, Lamb and Gregory examined the correlation between phonemic and musical sound discrimination for children reading in their first year of school, and discovered that a child's ability to discriminate musical sounds is directly related to reading performance, primarily due to their awareness of changes in pitch.

This close relationship allows for multiple avenues for integration. The use of music to build characters through sound expression; create tension in the narrative; highlight important moments in the plot, and so forth, are examples of the high compatibility between words and music.

Creating a "Sound Carpet"

Since music and language have such a close relationship, one of the easiest ways to begin is to combine the two. Creating a **sound carpet** entails taking a story and adding sound effects, **leitmotifs**, instruments, vocal sounds, body percussion, and actors and/or a narrator, in order to bring literature to life. The goal of a leitmotif is to help the listener identify the main characters and give each a very short musical pattern, so that every time their name is mentioned, someone plays that pattern. Also, sound effects can be added to enhance the action or bring a fuller meaning or experience. For example, if the story introduces a chiming bell, hit a bell or, for more advanced or older students, play a bell peal on the glockenspiel. Folk tales and fairy tales from around the world are excellent sources for this type of activity

Characters and Leitmotifs

To create a *sound carpet*, begin by making a list of the main characters in the story. For example, the story *The Princess and the Frog* has three main characters—the King, Princess and Frog. Sample leitmotifs might look like this:

King: (temple blocks and bass xylophone) ♩₀♩♩

Princess: (glissando on glockenspiels)

Frog: scrape guiro; hit hand drums ♩♩♩ (say "ribbit!")

Help students create a short phrase or *leitmotif* for each of the main characters—think of *Star Wars*' Darth Vader theme as an example. Every time the name is introduced in the story, their leitmotif should be played. To help the creative process, you might give students a short, simple rhythm to work with to create the motif. Then play the leitmotif on an instrument that helps describe that character. The King's leitmotif, for example, might be 4 quarter notes played on a trumpet sound on a keyboard, or using an interval of a 5th on any instrument to sound regal and stately.

Sound effects

Next identify locations in the story where sound effects can be used. A running stream could be a glissando on a xylophone; thunder can be played with drums; footsteps with a woodblock, etc.

Body Percussion and Vocals

Then add body percussion (clapping, stomping) or vocal sounds (moans for wind, yells and whoops) to increase the creativity and excitement level in the story.

Introduction and Finale

Add a short song whose lyrics are based on the story, to be sung and played by everyone at the opening and closing of the story.

Finally, assign a narrator, speaking or acting parts, and along with your instruments and sound effects, you have a complete performance that incorporates music composition and creativity along with language arts and theater.

References (Integration)

Appel, M. (2006). Arts Integration across the Curriculum. *Leadership*, Nov/Dec., 14-17.

Burnaford, G., Aprill, A., & Weiss, C. (Eds.). (2001). *Renaissance in the classroom: Arts integration and meaningful Learning*. Mahwah, NJ: Lawrence Erlbaum and Associates.

Elder, J. (n.d.) Brain-friendly music in the classroom. https://www.yumpu.com/en/document/read/14989401/using-brain-friendly-music-in-the-classroom

Goldbert, M,. & Bossenmeyer, M. (1998). Shifting the role of arts in education. *Principal*. 77, 56-58.

Gullatt, D. (2008). Enhancing student learning through arts integration: implications for the profession. *The High School Journal, 85*,12-24.

Ingram, D., & Riedel, E. (2003). *What does arts integration do for students?* (CAREI Research Reports). Minneapolis, MN: Center for Applied Research and Educational Improvemen*t*. Retrieved from the University of Minnesota Digital Conservancy, http://purl.umn.edu/144121

Ingram, D., & Meath, M. (2007). *Arts for academic achievement: A compilation of evaluation findings from 2004-2006*. Minneapolis, MN: Center for Applied Research and Educational Improvement. Retrieved from the University of Minnesota Digital Conservancy, http://purl.umn.edu/143647

Jenson, E. (2002). Teach the arts for reasons beyond the research. *The Education Digest, 67*(6), 47-53.

Koutsoupidou, T., & D. J. , Hargreaves. (2009). An experimental study of the effects of improvisation on the development of children's creative thinking in music. *Psychology of Music, 3*, 251.

Luftig, R. (2000). An investigation of an arts infusion program on creative thinking, academic achievement, affective functioning, and arts appreciation of children at three grade levels. *Studies in Art Educatio,*: 208-227.

Mishook, J., & Kornhaber, M. (2006). Arts integration in an era of Accountability. *Arts Education Policy Review, 107*(4), 3-10.

Moore, D. (2013). Make art not the servant. Retrieved from http://educationcloset. com/2013/02/27/make-not-art-the-servant/.

Rabkin, N., & Redmons, R. (2006). The arts make a difference. *Educational Leadership, 63*(5), 60-64.

Riley, S. (2012). *Shake the sketch: An arts integration workbook*. Westminster, MD: Author.

Ruppert, S. (2006). *Critical evidence—How the arts benefit student achievement*. National Assembly of State Arts Agencies. Retrieved from http://www.nasaa-arts.org/ Research/Key-Topics/Arts-Education/critical-evidence.pdf.

Silverstein, L. & Layne, S. (2014). "What is Arts Integration?" *ArtsEdge.Kennedy-Center. org*. http://artsedge.kennedy-center.org/educators/how-to/arts-integration/ what-is-arts-integration

References (Music and Literacy)

Butzlaff, R. (2000). Can music be used to teach reading? *Journal of Aesthetic Education,* 167-178.

Cardany, A. (2013). Nursery rhymes in music and language literacy. *General Music Today, 26*(2), 30-36.

Carger, C. (2004). Art and literacy with bilingual children. *Language Arts, 4,* 283-292.

Darrow, A. A. (2008). Music and Literacy. *General Music Today, 21*(2), 32-34.

Fisher, D., McDonald, N, & Strickland, J. (2001). Early literacy development: A sound practice. *General Music Today, 14*(3), 15-20.

Lamb, S., & Gregory, A. (1993). The relationship between music and reading in beginning readers. *Educational Psychology: An International Journal of Experimental Educational Psychology, 13*(1), 9-27.

Snyder, S. (1994). Language, movement, and music—Process connections. *General Music Today, 7*(3).

Vocabulary

arts integration: an approach to teaching in which students construct and demonstrate understanding through an art form. Students engage in a creative process, which connects an art form and another subject area and meets evolving objectives in both

leitmotif: a recurrent theme throughout a musical or literary composition, associated with a particular person, idea, or situation

sound carpet: extensive and liberal use of music, sound effects, and character leitmotifs in the performance of a narrative or story

trochee: in poetry, a trochee refers to a syllable pattern of stressed-unstressed, or long-short

Chapter 13

Musical Multiculturalism and Diversity

Chapter Summary: As part of 21st century teaching and common core state standards, it is important to "teach to reach"—in other words, organizing your materials and presentation to reach as many children as possible in as many possible ways. We've discussed many ways of teaching in this book, and this section concerns teaching multicultural material and teaching to culturally diverse learners. This chapter will look at the history of multiculturalism and diversity education, the field of ethnomusicology, and strategies for teaching using multicultural music aesthetics. It also includes case studies from several different culture areas.

Music, as a diverse human practice, is central to the constitution of cultural and individual identities.

—David Elliot, *Music Matters*

I. Multicultural/Diversity Education

A Brief History of Multiculturalism in the U.S.

The United States has always been a multicultural nation. Throughout its history, however, the country's majority population has struggled with how to accept different cultures and cultural perspectives of different minority populations. For centuries, tensions and debates revolve around the less dominant group (**subaltern**) vying for equality within the dominant culture. Should immigrant groups keep their culture (language, food, dress, customs), an idea known as **pluralism**, or try to blend in with the culture of the dominant group, an idea referred to as **assimilation** or metaphorically as the **melting pot**? These ideas and debates developed from waves of immigration into the U.S., when African slaves in the 1700s and an influx of European immigrants in the 1800s who were brought in to work as laborers, began to threaten the dominant Anglo-Saxon, Protestant population.

Immigrants were encouraged to **acculturate** as quickly as they could—meaning that they must learn a new language, giving up traditions, customs, heritage, etc., in order to blend and **assimilate** into the general population.

Some groups, however, had a very difficult time "melting," particularly people of color. The concepts of **multiculturalism** or **cultural pluralism** developed partially to create a climate which encouraged understanding the differences between cultural groups. Gold (1977) offers a reason for this when he writes: "…multiculturalism equates with the respect shown the varied cultures and ethnic groups which have built the United States and which continue today to contribute to its richness and diversity" (p. 18).

With its roots in ethnic and racial groups in the U.S., the idea of multiculturalism is now paired with the concept of diversity, in which all types of groups and individual identities are included (i.e., gender, religion, age, physical attributes, ability). This inclusive nature has broadened the scope, and contributes towards a greater pedagogical understanding.

Why teach Multiculturally?

There are many reasons for the inclusion of diversity in education, not the least of which is a mandated curriculum in many school districts. This aside, however, there are pressing 21st century learning issues that demand multicultural teaching material. Rapidly changing populations in the U.S. will dramatically alter the demographics for the remainder of the century. Hispanic Americans, Asian Americans, African Americans, and Americans of mixed ethnicity will become the majority in the near future.

Source: Natalie Sarrazin

Three ethnically mixed seven-year-old boys: Hispanic-American, African-German, Indian-American.

Thinking in multiple dimensions will not only be an asset, but indispensable. Luckily, the ubiquitous nature of music and arts as an expressive form found in all cultures, allows for extensive exchanges of ideas from all corners of the globe.

Rationale for Teaching Multiculturally

Teaching Multiculturally Is…

Inclusive: It provides an opportunity for expression on behalf of many different groups that might otherwise not be represented.
- Consider the children in your classroom. If you have a heterogeneous class make up of many different ethnicities, abilities, races, providing activities validates who

they are as people, and sends a message that their voices are valued. If you have a **homogeneous** class, exposing them to ideas and beliefs of others only helps to expand their worldview in a 21st century classroom.

    Pedagogically Sound: Including multiple perspectives and views on material not only enriches the curriculum content, but also provides radically different frameworks and paradigms to students on content.

- For example we may be familiar with the concept of a "beat" from a Western perspective, but when exposed to the idea of a beat from Java's gamelan music, we might develop a new appreciation of what a beat is, what it can do, and how it can be understood.

Teaching Multiculturally also...

    Raises Awareness: Promotes awareness of self and others, fosters respect, tolerance and understanding.

    Is Integrative: Provides excellent opportunities for integration as a natural entry or pivot point to other subject areas such as social studies, history, literature, language, and all of the arts.

Drawbacks

    Most teachers, however, feel that they are not familiar enough with any material out of their comfort zone, and this is understandable. Also, there are time constraints, scheduling issues, materials and resources, and perhaps curricular or administrative support. Most teachers are also concerned regarding which cultures to include, and if they include too many, that they will be covering the content very superficially.

    To be successful teaching multiculturally, it is important to:
- Familiarize yourself with the material/culture in advance.
- Teach indigenous concepts instead of Western ones.
- Use pedagogies that are indigenous or a close approximation to them.

II. Ethnomusicology and Music Teaching

    To address some of the drawbacks and difficulties in teaching music from another culture, I'd like to turn to the field of ethnomusicology. The field of ethnomusicology is well positioned to contribute toward multicultural and diversity education, and, after a brief description of ethnomusicology, its tenets will be applied towards an examination of them. Recently, scholars such as Patricia Shehan Campbell, Therese Volk, and David Elliott have begun blending the disciplines of ethnomusicology and music education, bringing some of the field research and holistic view from ethnomusicology into the pedagogical practice of music education.

    Ethnomusicology is the study of music as culture. Ethnomusicologists:
- Study *all* the world's music.
- Study music within a total musical system, including songs, musical instruments and music production, as well as the people and culture that the music represents.
- Compare what is typical of a culture as well as what is personal, idiosyncratic, and exceptional.

Ethnomusicology, at its foundation, examines the relationship between music and culture. Ethnomusicologist Alan Merriam developed a "tripartite model" through which to understand the complex interactions between concept, behavior, and sound.

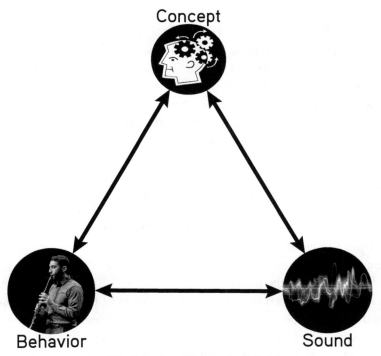

The Merriam Tripartite Model

Three components: Sound, Concept, and Behavior

We've discussed the idea of sound earlier in the book (i.e., timbre, melody, harmony, rhythm), and most of us can listen and recognize the elements of music to various degrees. We tend to think less, however, about the **concepts** or ideas that our culture has about sound and music. Ethnomusicologist Jeff Todd Titon states that we perform music in two ways. First, we perform the music itself (i.e., on instruments, by singing), and second, we perform the *ideas* associated with music. What does this mean? Growing up in a culture means that we have undergone a process called **enculturation**—meaning that we are familiar with the practices, rules, taboos, patterns, and beliefs about our culture's ideas about music without having to actively learn them. If you look back at the brief quiz in the first chapter, you will find that you know things about music just having experienced and listened in your everyday life. As an ethnomusicologist or researcher for your classroom, however, it is important to be able to articulate the culture's beliefs about music by observing people's behavior and thoughts about music.

> ## Activity 13A
>
> ### TRY THIS
>
> One way to objectively view your own culture is to step back and imagine that you are an immigrant or an alien, perhaps, and are viewing the culture for the very first time. What might you observe about music in this culture? What do people believe about certain genres of music? Are certain types of music good? Harmful? What about musicians in general? Do we value them? Is it considered positive or negative to be a professional musician? When should certain types of music be played? When should you listen to certain types of music?

The third concept from Merriam's model concerns our **behavior** as performers, audience members, listeners, etc. When do we perform music? How do we do it? What particular movements, gestures, and instruments do we use? Who performs? Who is allowed to perform certain music? Who is prohibited or "discouraged" from performing? Think about a type of music and its gender or racial makeup. Certainly, there are few genres of music that are performed equally across the board.

What this type of analysis does is to help us understand the **cultural values** associated with music, and what is important about sound and the concepts and behaviors associated with it. What is considered beautiful about a type of sound, instrument or voice? What a culture values, is an insight into that culture's **aesthetics**. Let's take a genre of music and find its cultural value and musical aesthetics. One example to consider might be opera. We might begin with a broad question as to whether opera is important and how it fits in with our culture.

Sound: In terms of opera's **musical aesthetics,** (i.e. what is considered beautiful or pleasing), opera requires a well-trained, loud, and large voice with heavy vibrato. It takes years of practice to perfect this sound, uncountable hours of lessons, training, coaching. Singers, do not, for example, learn opera in their garages or simply by listening to recordings. Opera singers do not use microphones or any type of amplification technology. They are required to project their voice without assistance, which requires immense physical support. They sing arias, recitatives, choruses supported by an orchestra. The most popular repertoire they sing is mostly European, written in the 18th and 19th centuries.

Behavior: Singers on stage are expected to act in a certain way. They raise their arms in a gesture that amplifies our perception when singing high notes, they don't jump around or dance when singing, smash their guitars on the ground, bite the heads off bats or set things on fire. Since opera is part of our Western Cultural heritage, there are institutions (conservatories, performance venues, etc.,) developed for those interested in this type of training and who have the requisite talent. Audiences who attend operas are usually able to afford the price of a ticket and are of an educational level and demographic cohort that supports, understands, and appreciates the form.

Concepts: As a genre, we believe opera to be a classical form, complicated, and with a long tradition and heritage rooted in the European classical tradition. Although we might not listen to it regularly or even at all, we all hold it in very high esteem, and an important part of a highly cultured society. Alternatively, we may not offer any national financial support.

Activity 13B

TRY THIS

Think of a style or genre of music (i.e., classical, rap, rock, punk, heavy metal, country). Now go through the aesthetics of that genre according to Merriam's Tripartite Model. What are the musical aesthetics of that music? What is culturally valued? Not valued?

III. Aesthetics and Multiculturalism

Our journey through Merriam's model explores values and aesthetics, allows a deeper understanding of how to incorporate multicultural music into lessons. The process begins with discovering the musical aesthetics and particular values of the culture or sub-culture you're working with. This might mean working with broad categories of Chinese, Indian or West African music, or narrow sub-cultures such as hip-hop music, Motown sound from the 1960s, or even the sound of an individual singer.

Regardless of what material you are trying to incorporate, thoroughly understanding the aesthetics and values will be highly beneficial to preserving the **integrity** and **authenticity** of both the music and culture. To do this requires preparation of research and practice.

Begin by selecting one culture area in which you are interested. Conduct research by reading about and exploring available teaching materials on that culture. Depending on your resources, you might want to actually acquire further knowledge and skills such as attending professional development activities or workshops, webinars, courses, or even contact people in your area that might be familiar with that culture. Starting with your own classroom is an excellent first step. There are always parents willing to come in and share traditions!

Teaching the music or arts of that culture is the next step. Fortunately, there are ways in which to use pedagogies that you already know in order to teach the material, without compromising its integrity or authenticity. The approach is to step back and ask questions to find commonalities in both cultures from which to work.

- How do children learn in this (new) culture (**enculturation**, pedagogies)?
- What musical aesthetics (**sound**) are found in this (new) culture's music?
- What music does this (new) culture value (concepts, beliefs)?
- What **behaviors** are associated with this music?

Transmission

Most cultures around the world use aural-oral transmission process to teach many things, but especially music. Direct interaction with the *sound* is crucial, and notation cannot replace this experience. Children learn from each other by listening and joining in, learn by listening to recordings, or learn aurally from adults. In some cultures like India, even the classical music is transmitted aurally, with almost no notated music at all.

Aural transmission also enhances brain function since memorization is essential, along with mental mapping of melodies and rhythms. In the aural transmission process, modeling is a key factor. Since there is no restriction tying the singer to a "fixed" notation, children are free to just imitate or to explore, improvise and play with the sound.

Case Study 1: West Africa

For example, traditional music learning in West Africa takes place aurally. Let's explore ways to utilize familiar pedagogies to approximate the core cultural values associated with music in West African culture. Note that the rhyme itself is *not* from West Africa, but it is the *process* of aural transmission itself that is one of the main goals of the lesson. This works well an opening lesson that 1) engages students using a familiar rhyme, 2) utilizes a culturally-based teaching process, and 3) transmits the cultural values of improvisation or "showing off," musical play, communal music making, and musical flexibility, among other musical aesthetics.

Music pedagogy of West Africa compared to the U.S.

	W. Africa	**U.S./Western**
Pedagogies	• Aural • Call and Response • Imitation • Story-songs with morals • Mnemonic Drum Language	• Aural and Written • Call and Response • Imitation • Songs (can have stories) • Rhythmic Speech
Musical Aesthetics	• Complex Rhythms Polyrhythms • Complex Melodies Polyphony • Nasal vocal quality • Movement/dance • Complex Body Percussion/ Clapping	• Simple Rhythms Duple/ Triple Meter • Simple melodies, unison or two-part harmony • Chest based vocal quality • Action songs • Simple Body Percussion/ Clapping

Values/Beliefs	• Everyone capable of music making and dancing • Dance and music are highly integrated • Musical and rhythmic improvisation highly valued • Linguistic flexibility highly valued	• Beliefs about talent inhibit participation • Dance and music less integrated • Musical and rhythmic imitation highly valued • Linguistic imitation highly valued
Behaviors	• Music making highly communal • High confidence level performing in front of others • Posturing and "showmanship" highly valued	• Music making more individualized • Some hesitancy performing in front of others • More reserved behavior common

While this list may be daunting, it is helpful in order to visualize the components necessary for a successful lesson—one that uses familiar pedagogies, materials, and processes between the two cultures. There is enough pedagogical overlap between the two to not only make a lesson work, but to contain a reasonable level of authenticity in its quest to successfully convey the intended musical and cultural material and values.

Revisit the pedagogies introduced in Chapter 4, Dalcroze, Kodály and Orff, to find excellent sources and approaches for teaching both Western and world musics. Dalcroze offers natural movement of the body, dance/movement and music; Kodály offers melodic and rhythmic sequencing; and Orff-Schulwerk offers a variety of aural singing and rhythmic body percussion techniques, including story-songs and literature, along with layers of percussion. This particular case study on West African music relies solely on aural learning, which means that a rote method is applicable to the music learning. In West Africa, rhythm is complex and highly valued, and involves communal/group participation, improvisation, and movement. West African music also integrates literature, movement, body percussion, rhyme, and music, so the Orff approach is probably the most applicable teaching method. Let's take a simple playground rhyme as our material to teach West African musical and cultural values. (Note: This is but one variation of this particular rhyme.)

My mother, your mother live across the way.

Every night they have a fight and this is what they say:

'Icka backa soda cracker, icka backa boo.

Icka backa soda cracker, out goes you!'

Rhythm: the rhyme is very simple with 8 beats in each line.

X	X	X	X	X	X	X	X
My	mother	your	mother	live a-	cross the	way	(r)
X	X	X	X	X	X	X	X
Every	night they	have a	fight and	this is	what they	say:	(r)

My Mother Your Mother

Learn the rhyme first using rote learning (call and response or echo). Then have the students clap on each beat. Repeat until the rhyme becomes embodied, and flows freely. Next, drop the "Icka Backa" section, and recite only the "my mother" section, while maintaining the steady beat clap throughout. Have everyone think the "Icka Backa" words in their head in order to remember the length of that section.

The rhyme itself implies that there is an inherent dialogue between the two mothers. This is perfect for implementing one of the essential elements of West African dance and music, where people take turns "showing their stuff" in a playfully confrontational way.

Form a circle. Communal learning lends itself to performing in a circle, and indeed most game songs are performed in a circle. Clap and say the rhyme several times. Choose two "mothers" to step out into the middle of the circle to face off against each other *musically* (no fighting or yelling)!

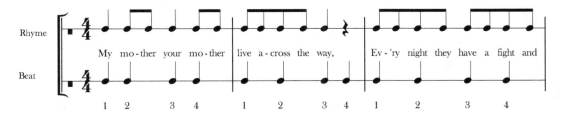

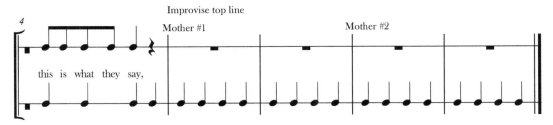

Each "mother" takes 8 beats to improvise using body percussion. Mother 1 "talks" for 8 beats, and Mother 2 then responds also taking 8 beats. Take turns around the circle alternating the rhyme with two new "mothers" in the center battling it out through rhythm, movement, and improvisation.

Improvisation

Improvisation, contrary to what many people think, does not involve "making it up on the spot." Instead, improvisation can be taught to some degree in that it requires a set of tools and prior experiences from which to draw. Think of improvisation as "quickly assembling" shorter rhythm or pitch patterns that you've already mastered.

To prepare for the improvisation part of this rhyme, use rhythm cards for several weeks prior. Have the students clap the various rhythms using a variety of strategies, (call and response, game playing, even note reading, etc.) so that they are able to internalize the sounds and patterns. Then slowly build up from shorter 4-beat improvisations to 8-beat ones. This will reduce the anxiety of having to perform an 8-beat improvisation in front of the group.

Polyrhythm

Although improvisation is very important in many parts of Africa, so are complex rhythms called **polyrhythms**, which consist of two contrasting rhythms played together. The simplest and most basic polyrhythms are: two against three or three against four. To best illustrate a polyrhythm, the following system, known as the T.U.B.S. or Tiny Unit Box System, was developed as a way for participants to visualize the inner workings of a polyrhythm. Even though there are shaded areas that look like they represent musical "measures," polyrhythms are referred to as additive rhythms (e.g. 2 + 3 + 2 + 3) rather than divisive (beats in a measure). Simple polyrhythms usually appear in eight or 12-beat groups.

Example 1: Two against Three

3-beat rhythm	X		X		X		X		X		X		X		X		X		X		X		X	
2-beat rhythm	X			X			X			X			X			X			X			X		

Example 2: Three against Four

4-beat rhythm	X			X			X			X			X			X			X			X		
3-beat rhythm	X				X				X				X				X				X			

Try clapping the above examples. For the Two against Three rhythm, divide the class into two groups and assign the Two-beat rhythm line to one half and the Three-beat rhythm line to the other half. Switch the groups. After everyone becomes comfortable with the rhythm, create smaller groups of people on each line, and eventually assign the rhythm to just two people. Some students may even be able to play a three-beat on one leg and a two-beat on the other. Then try the same process with the Four against Three rhythm.

Children's clapping games and rock passing games provide very simple but accessible examples of polyrhythmic learning. Students can learn to feel, hear, and perform the multi-part music from a very early age, and become progressively more advanced as they grow.

Multi-modal complexity is very much part of many children's game songs from Zimbabwe. The Zimbabwean game song "Sorida" contains a melody accompanied by body percussion and hand clapping in pairs of partners.

Sorida

Traditional Zimbabwe Children's Song
Done with partners facing each other.
R L Clap indicates a paddy-cake style of clapping across to your partner.

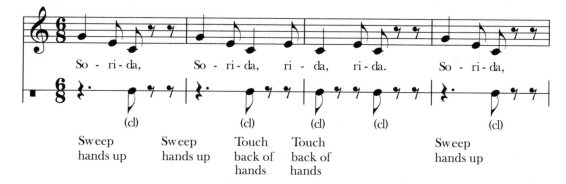

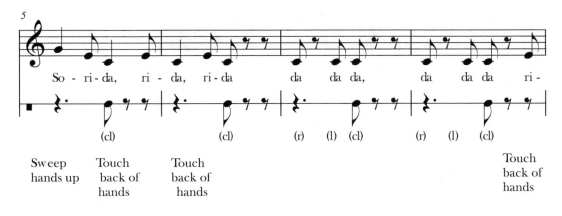

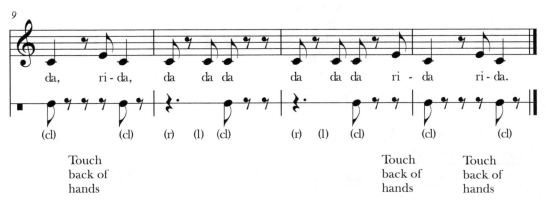

Another example of a rock-passing game from Ghana in West Africa is "Obwisana." In this game, all children sit closely in a circle, each with a small rock in front of them. Rock passing games such as "Obwisana" start out very simply, but the rocks can be tapped in more complex polyrhythms after the children master the easier rhythms. These games, like all children's songs and games, carry great meaning. The lyrics mean "the rock crushed my hand, grandma," and is meant to assure the child that there are always people to take care of them in their lives, either in their family or village. The rock-passing accompaniment reflects the idea of a tight-knit community and cooperation, for if even one child fails to pass their rock on the beat to the next child, the entire song cannot continue.

Obiswana

Children's rock passing game from Ghana

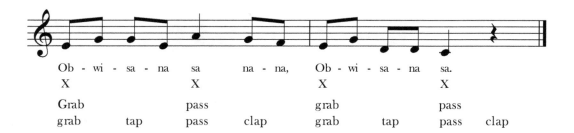

Ob -	wi -	sa -	na	sa	na - na,	Ob -	wi - sa - na sa.
X			X			X	X
Grab			pass			grab	pass
grab	tap		pass		clap	grab	tap pass clap

Case Study 2: India

In comparison with African music, Indian music is much less familiar for most Westerners, and therefore a little more difficult to teach. The basic components of India's classical music, for example, differ from Western music's five basic elements (Sound, Melody, Harmony, Rhythm, and Form), in that India does not utilize harmony in its classical genres.

However, harmony is present in India's popular music, such as Bollywood's film music. Indian classical forms more than make up for an absence of harmony with highly complex and intricate melodies and rhythms.

Western Classical Music Aesthetics compared to Indian Classical Music Aesthetics.

Indian Classical Music Aesthetics	Western Classical Music Aesthetics

• Improvised:
    • The performer *is* the composer.
	• Performer and composer separate:
	    • Pieces composed by a composer separate from the performer, sometimes by hundreds of years.

• Contains NO Harmony:
    • Melodies and rhythm complex and independent
	• Melodies tied to harmonic progressions:
	    • Music Based on Harmony.

• Is not done in groups, but with individual performers:
    • Soloist.
    • Drummer.
    • Drone.
	• Group performers (orchestra, choral).

• Contains lots of ornamentation.	• Little ornamentation.
• Expression— begins slow and soft, gradually becomes louder and faster.	• Quick and frequent changes of expression—Dramatic dynamics, tempo changes.
• Similar to Western Symphonies, these *raga* performances can last up to 1 hour.	

Classical Indian musical aesthetics require only three major components in an ensemble: a drone, a solo instrumentalist or vocalist, and a drum.

LISTEN DRONE

Melodies are based on **raga**, which is a set of pitches similar to what we think of as a scale, but with many more non-musical characteristics. Like a scale, a *raga* contains a certain set of pitches or notes. Some notes are flat, others sharp, etc. There is also often a mood associated with a *raga*, such as a time of day the song should be sung, or a season of the year like monsoon season, hot season, or winter. A *raga* might also be associated with a particular deity. The pitches of the scale have their own syllables called **sargam**—which is very similar to our solfege system. Just like the term *solfege* which is made up of the syllables "sol" and "fa," *sargam* is comprised of the syllables sa re and ga, the first three pitches of the Indian scale.

Sa   Re   Ga   Ma   Pa   Dha   Ni   Sa

Indian music has roots that are thousands of years old. There is cultural meaning in every aspect of Indian music. For example, each syllable of the *sargam* (solfege) is based on the sound of an animal.

Indian (Sargam)	Western (Solfege)
SA'	DO'
NI (elephant)	TI
DHA (horse)	LA
PA (cuckoo/nightingale)	SOL
MA (dove/heron)	FA
GA (goat)	MI
RE (bull/skylark)	RE
SA (peacock)	DO

Animals are very prevalent in India, particularly in the rural areas where you can hear the cries of peacocks, the whinnying of goats, and even the occasional cry of an elephant. These are familiar sounds to many children growing up in India.

Singers in training spent a lot of time learning to improvise with these syllables. Here are a few typical warm ups for the voice.

- SS, RR, GG, MM, PP, DD, NN, S'S'
- SRG, RGM, GMP, MPD, PDN, DNS'
- SRSRG, RGRGM, GMGMP, MPMPD, PDPDN, DNDNS'
- SRGSRGM, RGMRGMP, GMPGMPD, MPDMPDN, PDNPDNS'

In India, there really isn't any notation at all since music is improvised, but in the 19th century, musicians developed a system for notation that is used to teach beginners. Here is an example of what that notation would look like for singing the song *Frere Jacques*. Dashes equal rests, and the slur underneath two notes is equal to two eighth notes.

C Major mode, 4/4 time, medium tempo

S R G S	S R G S	G M P -	G M P -
Fre-re Jac-ques	Fre-re Jac-ques	Dor-mez vous,	Dor-mez vous?
1	2	3	4

P D P M G S	P D P M G S	S P S -	S P S -
Son-nez les ma-ti-nes,	Son-nez les ma-ti-nes,	Din din don,	Din din don
1	2	3	4

Below is a song in one of the *raga* called *Raga Bhupali*. This *raga* is meant to be sung in the evening, and has a mood of devotion. It is a pentatonic *raga*, which means that only 5 pitches are used, Sa, Re, Ga, Pa and Dha.

Melody

Song in *Raga Bhupali*

		S'S'D P	**G R S** R
G - P G	D P G -	**G P D S'**	R' S' D P
S' P D P	**G R S** -	**S' S' D P**	**G R S** R
G - P G	**D P G** -		

Raga-s are made up of short characteristic patterns that often show up in compositions. The bold letters indicate patterns that are commonly found in many Bhupali songs.

Rhythm

Rhythm or **tala** in Indian music is very complex. Instead of having short measures of groups of 2s or 3s, there are long cycles of many beats.

Tala: A rhythmic cycle containing a fixed number of beats (e.g. 16, 14, 12, 10, 8, 7, or 6).

Indian musicians use the rhythm syllables of *dha*, *dhin*, etc. to learn rhythms on their drums (such as *tabla*). The second line of the table below indicates the vocal syllables for this particular 16-beat cycle. The third line of the cycle contains an X and numbers 2, 0, and 3, which are also guides to counting the cycle. Musicians say the rhythm syllables and then clap on the X, 2 and 3. The 0, however, is called an empty beat. On 0, the musician waves their hand instead of clapping. Try saying the rhythm syllables and clapping on the 1st, 5th, and 13th beats, and waving on the 9th beat of the cycle.

Tintal Rhythm Cycle (tala)
16-beat cycle, (4+4+4+4)

1 Dha X	2 Dhin	3 Dhin	4 Dha	5 Dha 2	6 Dhin	7 Dhin	8 Dha
9 Dha 0	10 Tin	11 Tin	12 Ta	13 Ta 3	14 Dhin	15 Dhin	16 Dha

X = Sam, the first beat and most important moment in music.

Activity 13C

TRY THIS

The 16-beat *tala teentala*, is used in all of the above song examples, from Frere Jacques to the song in Raga Bhupali. Try singing the songs given above while clapping (on beats X, 2, and 3) and waving (on beat 0).

Children's Music in India

Since many rural children in India do not have access to televisions, computers, or other electronic forms of entertainment, children play lots of games and learn many songs from each other in their local vernacular or regional language. Indian films, however, are all musicals, and contain five to six songs each. Children and even adults are exposed to and learn many, many of these popular film songs.

Source: Natalie Sarrazin

Children playing on a roof in a Bihar village, 2009.

Many parents restrict media viewing, for families with access, limiting the number of films they see as well as the hours spent watching television, listening to radio, and playing video games. Computer gaming and television watching is curtailed by these parents to one hour per day in exchange for study time.

Source: Natalie Sarrazin

High School Music Class, New Delhi, India, 2009.

Below is a children's game song called "Okaa Bokaa Teen Tarokaa" from Bihar, India. This rhyme and song is a good example of a children's game song, which has many, many parts to it. The lyrics contain many references to animals, foods, perfumed oils, etc. There is also mention of a king and a princess, referring to a time when India was comprised of many feudal states ruled by kings.

Okaa, Bokaa

Children's rhyme game from Bihar, India
Translation N. Sarrazin

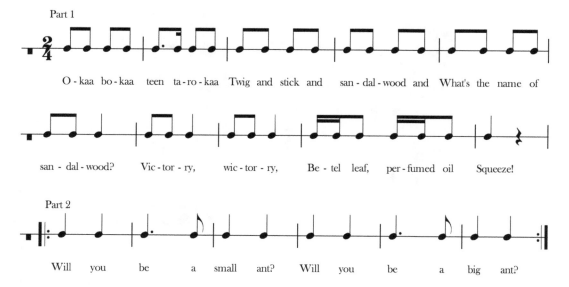

Everyone is seated in a circle very close together for this game song. The actions for this rhyme are indicative of life and culture in India, and include motions that are both familiar and unfamiliar to children's game songs in the U.S. For example, the beginning of the rhyme consists of an elimination game similar to "eenie, meenie, miney, mo" but pinching the back of the hand in the next section is rarely found in children's game songs. Grabbing ones earlobes in India is a sign of contrition for one's actions. It indicates that you are sorry and would like forgiveness.

Okā Bokā Tīn Tarokā

Children's rhyme game from Bihar, India
Translation N. Sarrazin, A. Dwivedi

Hindi

Part 1
Okā bokā tīn tarokā
Lauā lāthī chandan kāthī
Chandanā ke nām kā
Ijayī bijayī
Panawā phūlelawa puchūk

Part 2
Chiuntā leba ki chiuntī

Part 3
Atkan chatkan dahī chatākan
Ban phūle banaila
Sawan mē karailā
Neuri gailī chorī
Dhar kān mamorī

Part 4 (chant)
Chiuntā ho chiuntā
Maamā ke gagariyā kāhe phora lā
ho chiuntā

Part 5
Lātā lāti chal bariyāti

Part 6
Tār kāte tarkul kāte kāte re ban
khājā
Hāthi upar ghanta bāje chamak
chale re raja
Rājā ke dulari beti khub bajāwe
bājā
Int māro jhint māro chhup

English

Part 1
Okā bokā tīn tarokā (three goats)
Twig and stick and sandalwood
and
What is the name of sandalwood?
Victory, wictory
Betel leaf, perfumed oil, squeeze

Part 2
Will you be a small ant? Will you
be a big ant?

Part 3
Pitter patter, splitter splatter
Wildflowers bloom in the jungle
Bitter gourds grow in the
monsoon
Someone's mongoose was stolen
Hold the ear and twist!

Part 4 (chant)
Ant, silly ant,
Why did you break uncle's vase?
O ant, silly ant

Part 5
Kick and kick and then go to
Baryaati

Part 6
Cut the palm tree, cut the palm
grove, cut the palm fruit open
Atop the elephant the bell rings
and the King arrives in splendor.
The lovely daughter of the King
beautifully beats the drum.
Hit it, hit it, hit it, chop it off!

Game Directions

Part 1
Children sit in a circle and place
both hands in front—palms down,
fingertips touching the floor (like
a spider). The leader taps the back
of each hand to the beat. On the
word "squeeze" (*puchūk*) the hand
is flattened. Leader continues
until all hands are flat.

Part 2
Leader pinches the back of each
flattened hand and lifts them into
a pile in the middle of the circle.

Part 3
Leader places hand on top of the
pile and alternates slapping her
hand palm up and palm down to
the beat.

Part 4 (chant)
Each child grabs the earlobes
of the child next to them in the
circle and sways to the beat.

Part 5
Chaos! Children kick their feet
rapidly in the middle of the circle
touching soles with the others.

Part 6
Children create a tower of fists
in the middle, with the thumb
extended up, each child grabbing
the upturned thumb of the child's
hand beneath. The leader makes
a sawing motion to cut down this
fist tower, "chopping" off a hand
or two from the top when they
say "hit it, chop it!"

Activity 13D

TRY THIS

How does this game song compare to other game songs you are familiar with? Does
it remind you of other games? What are some of the lyrics in the song that tell you
about different cultural elements in India? Which movements are different from
those found in Western children's songs? Which are similar?

Case Study 3: Japan

Japanese Aesthetics

Japanese music can also be challenging, since its aesthetics are very different from those found in Western music. If we think back on the elements of Western music (sound, melody, rhythm, harmony, form), we see that almost all Western rhythm emphasizes a continuous, steady pulse or beat. Western music is very melodically and harmonically oriented, with a continuous rhythmic pulse. We need to grasp a melody and a drum beat or steady pulse in order to *make sense* of what we are hearing.

In traditional Japanese music such as *gagaku* or *shakuhachi* however, a steady beat is non-existent, and the emphasis is overwhelmingly on timbre, which is part of sound. Stringed instruments such as the *biwa* are used sparingly to play a fixed harmony or chord that marks time rather than plays a melody, and the short sound patterns from an instrument such as a single small drum or gong, might be front and center. How are we supposed to listen to this music? Japanese music relies on subtle changes and exploration of timbre rather than continuous sound. It takes a great deal of listening and understanding to be able to listen to and appreciate this music.

In Japan, key cultural, musical and artistic aesthetics include:

- Ritual
    - Process over product
- Nature
    - Reference to, reproducing, or connecting with (i.e. Shakuhachi made of bamboo)
- Simplicity
    - Minimal sound, maximum effect
- Space/silence
- Form and the destruction of form
    - Idea of impermanence
- Variation
    - Multiple perspectives

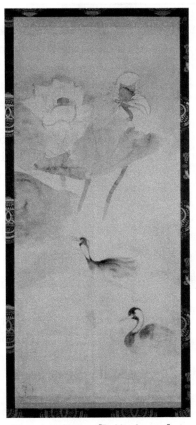

Tawaraya Sōtatsu [Public domain], via Wikimedia

17th Century Japanese Painting, "Waterfowls in Lotus Pond"

Traditional Japanese art such as that pictured above, uses the same aesthetics. Notice all of the white space in the painting, and its minimalist nature. In the music, this white space is represented by silence. The same goes for Japanese flower arranging *ikebana*, where a single flower in a simple vase succinctly expresses the nature of Japanese aesthetics and worldview.

Japanese musical aesthetics are difficult to apply in the classroom. The first thing that children will want to do is play a steady beat on the drum and create a melody. This is so ingrained, that it is almost impossible to unlearn this Western cultural norm.

Classroom equivalents of traditional Japanese instruments.

Category	Traditional Japanese Instruments	Classroom Equivalent
Wind	Hichiriki (type of oboe) Ryūteki (transverse flute) Shō (mouth organ) Shakuhachi (bamboo flute)	Duck call Recorder Harmonica Pan pipe
String	Biwa (4 stringed lute) Koto (13 stringed zither)	Guitar Autoharp
Percussion	Shoko (small gong struck with 2 horn beaters) Kakko (small, hourglass-shaped drum struck with 2 wooden sticks) Tsuri-daiko (drum on a stand with painted head played with padded stick) Shakubyoski (clapper made from pair of flat wooden sticks)	Gong Hand drum Djembe Woodblock

However, approaching Japanese music from the perspective of timbre and silence, and to use visuals such as the classical paintings above to represent the simplicity of the music can help.

- Begin by passing out various percussion instruments, and even pitched instruments such as an autoharp, glockenspiel, or xylophone.
  - Have students create as many different timbres as possible on their instrument, and as many "cool sounds" as possible. Remember, the autoharp should just play one chord with a lot of space in between strumming.
  - Practice simple rhythmic patterns (ti-ti-ta, ta ta, ti-ti ti-ti) on the instruments.

- Hitting the small drum or gong, for example, is not a matter of creating a steady beat, but of bringing subtle changes in timbre to the composition. This concept can be taught using an object like a bouncy ball. Take a bouncy ball, and drop it on the floor once. At first, it hits with a loud thwack. Each successive bounce, becomes both fainter and faster. Imitating this sound on a small gong or drumhead will approximate the type of play with timbre that is required.
- Then work to put the group together. Remember, only one or two sounds should be played at a time, with a lots of silence in between, no harmony or melody or steady pulse should emerge. Silence, called *ma*, is very important in Japanese music. If you look at the classical nature painting above, you will see a lot of "white space." This white space in art is equivalent to silence in music.

- Instruments should be played slowly, thoughtfully, and deliberately, not rushed and with a lot of stylized movement (dramatic but slow sweeps of the arm, positioning of drumsticks or mallets far in advance of striking, attentive and very alert and still musicians when not playing).

After some practice with this, it will be easy to plan an integrated multicultural lesson using something like *kamishibai*, or Japanese story cards. Having children play Orff instruments and classroom instruments as sound effects using the aesthetics above, would add greatly to the stories, as would composing an original song for the stories.

Japanese Kamishaibai (Japanese Story Cards)

The information below comes from an MENC article and interview with Dorothy Kittaka about Kamishibai, the multicultural, literacy-oriented Japanese story cards. The material introduces Japan to children, and provide a lesson rich in culture, literacy, and music. Click here for Kittaka's complete lesson plan.

Reprinted with Permission from NAfME. Kamishibai: Emotional Hook for Learning. Posted on June 10, 2009, Linda C. Brown © MENC: The National Association for Music Education (menc.org)

"Kamishibai is a delightful way of introducing literature, culture, and the arts" to children, says MENC member Dorothy Kittaka. This traditional Japanese form of storytelling will draw students in while they make connections with music, the visual arts, language arts, history, culture, and character education.

What is Kamishibai?

Kamishibai ("paper theatre") is picture storytelling that uses painted cards to illustrate a story that's written on the back of the cards. The traditional stories teach life lessons and emphasize traits such as:
- Integrity
- Caring
- Common Sense
- Initiative
- Perseverance
- Organization
- Flexibility
- Problem Solving
- Responsibility
- Cooperation
- Patience
- Friendship
- Curiosity
- Courage
- Resourcefulness
- Sense of humor

Original Kamishibai stories are written in dialog form, so the storyteller becomes an animated actor voicing different characters, making a compelling drama.

How to use Kamishibai:
- Select a story and read it to the class using the story cards. (For example, the "One Inch Boy" teaches that no matter what size you are, you can still achieve and be brave and honorable. Good for grades K–2.)

- Have students use percussion instruments, tuned xylophones, and body percussion to add sound effects as you read the story again with the story cards.
- Have students compose songs to go with the Kamishibai story as a class, in groups, or individually.
- Have students create poems and haiku as a class to reflect the story line. This works with even very young children.
- Tell the story again with story cards and musical accompaniment. Record it for listening and critiquing.
- Older grades can write their own stories, illustrate them, and compose songs for them.

For more information and lesson plans on Kamishibai by Dorothy Kittaka, go to http://www.kamishibai.com/index.html

Multicultural Music: Finding Sources, Making Plans

Reprinted with Permission from NAfME. "Multicultural Music: Finding Sources, Making Plans." Posted on Wednesday, November 19, 2008, Linda C. Brown © MENC: The National Association for Music Education (menc. org) National Association for Music Education webpage.

"Part of my teaching philosophy is to introduce students to other cultures and help them discover a bigger world," says MENC member Linda White.

In searching out sources of multicultural music, White suggests:

- Read books about other cultures (not just music-related books).
- Attend concerts with musicians and music from other places.
- Take classes that teach music and games from other countries.
- Invite parents or others in the community from other countries to school—for classroom visits or assemblies.
- Attend sessions on multicultural music at MENC, Orff, and Kodály conferences, and consult with the clinicians.

Recommended Resources

- MENC and Orff magazine articles
- Japanese Kamishibai (a form of storytelling)–great for introducing Japanese stories and incorporating Japanese songs. (See Kamishibai Story Theater)
- Mary Goetze and Jay Fern's Global Voices in Song DVDs–full of dances, songs, games, and background about various cultures.

Evaluating Multicultural Teaching Material

As a professional working with children, you will be constantly searching for new material to bring to your students such as songs, games, activities, lesson plans, etc. But how do you judge these materials? What is their value? In terms of musical material, it is important to assess the sonic aspects as well as the written. Is there a download or recording involved? What is the quality of that recording? What is the content included? How relevant or valuable is that content?

In terms of any teaching material, it is important to look and listen for quality content. However, if we are not familiar with the culture from which the recordings or material came, our job is more difficult. How do you assess an unfamiliar sound? Below is a rubric for evaluating multicultural music material including the content of the text, notation, and any recording.

Multicultural Material Evaluation Rubric

Summary	Describe the book's content. What is included? What is its presentation? Layout? Format? Sections?	Provides a general overview of the book itself.
Author	What evidence do you see in the book of their experience and knowledge?	While it might seem like someone from the culture itself might have a more "authentic" perspective, this does not necessarily mean they do. Look for time spent researching in the culture, teaching, advanced degrees, field specialty (i.e., ethnomusicologist).
	Is there a secondary author? What is their role?	Many times the primary author does not have enough insider knowledge of the language, and has to rely on someone with that knowledge to help with song lyrics and other cultural attributes.
Notation	Does the book contain printed notation? If so, what type of notation is used?	Mostly, books used in the U.S. will use standard 5-line staff notation. However, many cultures have their own forms of notation such India, Indonesia, and China, etc. Are any of these types of notation used in the text?
	Are the songs arranged in any way?	A song arrangement typically means adding voices such as making a choral arrangement or adding instruments to the melody such as a piano accompaniment or Orff accompaniment.
	Is the arrangement typical for the culture or not? Do they include any indigenous instruments?	Many cultures have their own styles of arrangement, but adding piano chords or vocal harmony particularly for Asian music, is not typical.
Lyrics	Do the songs have lyrics in English? The original language? Both? Is a pronunciation guide included? Are the meanings of specific words explained?	Often, books will include a *transliteration* of how to pronounce the lyrics as well as a *translation*. Some will even write the lyrics in the script of the original language.

Movement/ Dance	Are dance, game, or movement instructions included? If so, are they clearly written with photographs, diagrams, and illustrations? Are the movements indigenous or Westernized?	Similarly, you would prefer if the movements included along with the song were indigenous to the song itself and not merely added on as movement unassociated with the culture.
	Do any of the movements have symbolic or cultural meaning? Which?	
Recordings	Are there recordings included with the book? (tape, CD or online downloads or mp3s)? Who recorded the songs and who is singing on the recordings? (i.e., people from within the culture or outside? children, adults?) Which instruments or arrangements are used (i.e., is it only synthesizer or piano or are authentic instruments used? Is harmony added?)	The most authentic recordings are those made in the field itself, of course, but it is also informative to have singers from that culture in the studio creating a professional recording. In some older recordings, the singing would be re-recorded by a Western chorus, which took away from the experience of hearing the song. Also, to save money, a synthesizer would be used to accompany the recordings rather than authentic instruments.
Context	How much written cultural context is included in the book in general or for each song?	Books vary widely on their inclusion of cultural information, but some type of description adds tremendously to the value of the book and to the understanding required to evaluate and learn the material.
	How much of the original song's function and meaning is included?	Knowing the original function of the song is an additional way of digging deeper into the culture. Knowing how a song works in the lives of children is greatly beneficial.
	Do the notes offer a description of the culture, values, customs, historical, geographic, and economic issues that may add to an understanding of the music?	Having even some general details including maps, pictures, photos, quotes, and individual stories, and historical information helps.
Conclusion	Would you recommend/use this book, why or why not?	After reflecting on all aspects of your evaluation, would you use this book in your classroom or recommend it to others to use, why or why not?

References

Adzenyah, A., Maraire, D., & Tucker, J. (1996). *Let your voice be heard! Songs from Ghana and Zimbabwe*. Danbury, CT: World Music Press.

Boyer-Alexander, R. (2002). *Celebrating African-American history through plantation songs and folklore*. Milwaukee, WI: Hal Leonard.

Brumfield, S. (2006). *Hot peas and barley-o: Children's songs and games from Scotland*. Milwaukee, WI: Hal Leonard.

Buenker, J., & Ratner, L. (2005). *Multiculturalism in the United States: A comparative guide to acculturation and ethnicity*. Westport, CT: Greenwood Press.

Campbell, P., McCullough-Brabson, E., & Tucker, J. (1994). *Roots and branches: A legacy of multicultural music for children*. Danbury, CT: World Music Press.

Campbell, P., & Frega, A. (2001). *Songs of Latin America: From the field to the classroom*. Van Nuys, CA: Alfred Music.

Elliott, D. (1995). *Music matters: A new philosophy of music education*. Oxford: Oxford University Press.

Gold, M., Grant, C., and Rivlin, H. N. (Eds.). (1977). *In praise of diversity: A resource book for multicultural education*. Washington, DC: Teacher Corps. Retrieved from http://books.google.com/books/about/In_Praise_of_Diversity.html?id=5LU0AAAAMAAJ

Kiester, G. (2005). *India: Games children sing: 16 children's songs and rhymes*. Van Nuys, CA: Alfred Publishers.

Knapp, D. (2011). The inclusive world of music: Students with disabilities and multiculturalism. *General Music Today, 25(1), 41-44.*

National Association for Music Education. (2009). *Kamishibai: Emotional hook for learning*. Retrieved from http://nafme.org/kamishibai-emotional-hook-for-learning/

Sarrazin, N. (2008). *Indian music for the classroom*. Lanham, MD: MENC, Rowman and Littlefield.

Sarrazin, N. (2006). India's music: Popular film songs in the classroom. *Music Educators Journal 93(1)*, 26–32.

Sarrazin, N. (2006). Multicultural music in the classroom: Teaching burden or good musicianship? *Asia Pacific Journal of Arts Education 3 (2)*.

Sarrazin, N. (1995). Exploring aesthetics: Focus on Native Americans. *Music Educators Journal 4*, 33–36.

Volk, T. (2004). *Music, education and multiculturalism: Foundations and principles*. Oxford: Oxford University Press.

India Resources

References
- *The Raga guide: Survey of 74 Hindustani raga-s [CD].* (1999). Ganarew, England: Nimbus Records.
- Kiester, G. (2006). *Games children sing—India.* Van Nuys, CA: Alfred Publishing.
- Sarrazin, N. (2006). India's music: Popular film songs in the classroom. *Music Educators Journal, 93*(1), 26–32.
- Sarrazin, N. (2008). *Indian music for the classroom.* Lanham, MD: MENC, and Rowman Littlefield.

Children's Literature
- Arnett, R., & Turakhia, S. (2003). *Finder's keepers.* Columbus, GA: Atman Press.
- Somaiah, R., & Somaiah, R. (2006). *Indian children's favourite stories.* Rutland, VT: Tuttle Publishing.

Internet
- *The Music of India.* David Courtney's encyclopedic website. Everything from classical to film to folk. Excellent resource: www.chandrakantha.com
- *Music India Online.* Many musical genres (classical, folk, film)! mio.to/#/
- Downloadable: Tanpura Drones. http://www.ocf.berkeley.edu/~mrahaim/
- Kennedy Center ArtsEdge's "The Music of India: An Exploration of Indian Music". https://www.kennedy-center.org/education/resources-for-educators/classroom-resources/media-and-interactives/media/international/music-of-india/
- Introducing India. https://www.pbs.org/thestoryofindia/teachers/lessons/

Vocabulary

acculturate: learning a new language, giving up traditional customs, heritage, etc., in order to blend, melt, and assimilate

assimilation: explains the process of cultural and psychological change that results following meeting between cultures. The effects of acculturation can be seen at multiple levels in both interacting cultures. At the group level, acculturation often results in changes to culture, customs, food, clothing, language, and social institutions. At the individual level, differences in the way individuals acculturate have been shown to be associated not just with changes in daily behavior, but with numerous measures of psychological and physical well-being. Acculturation can be thought of as second-culture learning

authenticity: how closely a performance of a piece of music conforms to the author's intention; how closely a work of art conforms to an artistic tradition; how much the work possesses original or inherent authority, how much sincerity, genuineness of expression, and moral passion the artist or performer puts into the work

behavior: how we act as performers, audience members, listeners, etc.

cultural assimilation: the process by which a subaltern group's native language and culture are lost under pressure to assimilate to those of a dominant cultural group

cultural mosaic: refers to the mix of languages, cultures, and ethnic groups that co-exist in society; intended to champion an ideal of multiculturalism as opposed to other systems like the melting pot, which is often used to describe the U.S.' supposed ideal of assimilation

cultural pluralism: when smaller groups within a larger society maintain their unique cultural identities, and their values and practices are accepted by the wider culture provided they are consistent with the laws and values of the wider society

enculturation: the process whereby the established culture teaches an individual the accepted norms and values of the culture or society where the individual lives; learning your first culture

ethnicity: a socially defined category based on common culture or nationality; can include a common ancestry, dress, religion, dialect, etc.; reinforced through common characteristics, which set the group apart from other groups

homogeneous: the same or similar in nature

melting pot: metaphor for a heterogeneous society becoming more homogeneous, the different elements "melting together" into a harmonious whole with a common culture. It is particularly used to describe the assimilation of immigrants to the U.S. the melting-together metaphor was in use by the 1780s

multiculturalism: the action, process, or practice of including several cultures

multiethnic society: one with members belonging to more than one ethnic group, in contrast to societies that are ethnically homogeneous

musical aesthetics: what is considered beautiful or pleasing to listeners as a result of the music

polyrhythm: two or more contrasting rhythms such as groups of two played against groups of three

subaltern: lower in position or rank, a secondary group. Often this means a lack of access to political and financial power

Western culture: a heritage of social norms, ethical values, traditional customs, belief systems, specific artifacts, and technologies that have some origin or association with Europe; applies to countries whose history is strongly marked by European immigration, such as the Americas and Australasia as well as Europe

Printed in the USA
CPSIA information can be obtained
at www.ICGtesting.com
LVHW081606260124
769959LV00006B/863